Contents

There's Always a Reason

Preparation

Map of Britain

The journey Begins

There's Always a Reason

'Namaste' - Welcome, Hello, Good day, is a traditional Nepalese greeting. Wherever we went in the mountains, everyone welcomed us with clasped palms and a bowed head. Whatever they were doing or carrying, this welcoming ritual accompanied by the word 'Namaste' seemed to be a compulsory action but came from the heart and not from some unwritten rule they were obliged to perform. We soon adapted ourselves and greeted everyone we saw in the same way. For us this was a novelty to begin with but we soon began to realise that this was a greeting of pure friendship without any hostility. Compared to us from the 'civilised west' they had nothing, yet everything. For too many westerners, 'everything' is just a collection of material possessions. Too many people think that success is to be able to buy as much as you can. Real friendship towards strangers has become dominated by an unfortunate air of suspicion. In the West it seems as though we're all guilty until proven innocent, whereas in the Himalaya everyone is innocent and suspecting someone of being guilty first is an unusual event.

In February 2005, along with a few friends, I attended a talk and slide show given by world famous mountaineer Doug Scott. He laid out some brochures, one of which I took home. Being a secondary school teacher within three years of retirement, who over the last thirty seven years had led thousands of children on expeditions into the British hills, I thought what an opportunity it would be to take a group trekking in the Himalaya. Not only would this give a group of children the experience of a lifetime but would make me focus on something very special to finish my forty year teaching career rather than just gradually fade away into the fog of old age.

I discussed my plan with my colleagues who had been prominent members of 'The Mountaineering Club' over the years and asked them if they would be willing to be part of the trek. Overwhelmingly they agreed so I approached the head teacher for permission. I was well prepared to answer any questions he threw at me about the dangers and responsibility of such an adventure. I approached his door, which was always open unless he had a visitor. It was open and I gave a feeble knock so as not to disturb him too much.

"Hi Dave, what can I do for you?"

He had this real gift to make you feel at ease but without taking away the fact that he was in charge.

"I would like to take a group to the Himalayas!"

Without any hesitation or questions he answered,

"Yes, that's fine. No problem!"

I was lost for words. Perhaps he had prior knowledge and had already thought about it.

"How many and when?"

"About fifty students and staff in two years time."

"Ok!"

I thought that perhaps he'd been too engrossed in his work to fully realise what had just been discussed, so I left quickly feeling elated yet thoroughly bewildered because organising adventures with such responsibility is supposed to generate a multitude of questions beginning with 'What if...?' designed to discourage you from wanting to give young people the experiences they need. These questions would come from powers higher up which is viewed upon by teachers as a bid to absolve the administrators of all responsibility if anything goes wrong.

Without hesitation I contacted Community Action Nepal (CAN), set up by Doug Scott to raise money to build schools, health posts and shelters for the Sherpas in the Himalaya.

A meeting was set up with Doug, myself and two colleagues. A date for the trek was set and a route planned which would incorporate visiting two schools at Ghunsa and Lapcha, several monasteries and a climb to see Everest at dawn.

The wheels were now set in motion to choose a team of up to fifty people and raise lots of money to help fund the expedition. We set up a PowerPoint display with a talk shown to all pupils in Years 7, 8 and 9. Years 10 and 11 would have left school by the time the expedition took place. The talk outlined all the excitement that would be encountered but also included all the disadvantages that would be experienced during the 18 days away. Toilets would be just a hole in the ground; no showers or baths; daytime temperatures of almost 20°C could plummet to -20°C in seconds as the sun fell behind the mountains; camping out in the wilds of the Himalaya; trekking at over 2500 metres where the air is thin and a diet totally different to that of most Westerners without the usual fast food alternative. All applicants must also be willing to train and prepare for over a year and would need to raise the £1500 cost per person themselves rather than rely on handouts from over generous family members. We were overwhelmed that over three hundred children applied. After two weeks deliberation, forty one children were selected along with five staff and a local doctor. After many car boot sales, auctions and sponsored walks, over seventy thousand pounds was raised. The team had to gel. Everyone had to get involved with fundraising and training. For six months before the expedition in February 2007, an army physical training instructor offered his services twice a week at Catterick Army Camp. These sessions were designed to build up our strength and stamina for trekking in the rarefied air above two and a half thousand metres.

After two years of preparation we were finally on our ten hour flight to Kathmandu. A couple of days were spent sightseeing then we finally took a small twin engine plane to land on the tiny gravel airstrip at Phaplu, a hundred miles away, high up in the spectacular Himalayan mountains.

We met our team of Sherpas for the first time. Unbelievably for forty seven of us there were sixty five porters, twenty one kitchen helpers, sixteen Sherpas, two cooks and our sirdar named Tej.

Tej was brought up in the Ghunsa region and had helped to bring education, health posts and clean drinking water to the area. He was very well respected and along with many of the Sherpas had been involved with many high mountain and Everest expeditions. One of our Sherpas had proudly climbed Everest twice, the first time when he was only sixteen. We all hero worshipped them and they would do anything for us to make our adventure as comfortable as they could. We all felt confident that we were in very good hands.

A six hour trek on our first day took us up to Ghunsa School, perched on a mountain ridge at just under three thousand metres. When we arrived our tents were being set up on the muddy but dry playground. The children had already gone home for the day. We looked around the bare buildings. Through the windows we saw empty walls where posters and displays of children's work were rare. The toilets comprised of a small brick cubical perched over a sheer drop, with a bucket of water for washing personal parts. The drain holes in the toilets were not designed to take copious amounts of toilet paper and with nearly fifty pampered trekkers stuffing toilet paper down they quickly became blocked. A stick aided by several buckets of water brought from the only tap a hundred metres away soon had the problem under control. Dotted around on the adjacent hill sides were lonely buildings. Whilst we had passed through some small villages on our way here there were no villages within two hours of the school.

There was no light pollution here nor any electricity and the night sky revealed a billion vivid stars. We were enthralled by the clarity of the air and its pureness. Shortly after settling down for the night just after half eight, which was to be the norm, a fox or a dog somewhere up the valley started to howl. This set off another then another until within ten minutes the surrounding valleys echoed with the sound of what must have been a hundred animals. The noise was quite deafening and unnerving. As we settled down to sleep in our tents the Sherpas kept a watchful eye across the campsite.

Next morning we left the tents and trekked up to Lapcha School, about two and a half hours away and five hundred metres higher than Ghunsa. There was soft snow lying around. The school playground was four inches deep in a mixture of squelchy mud and slush. The place was buzzing with children and their parents. Many local people had come out to see us, some having walked for miles. Our students had brought gifts ranging from balloons to recorders. Many of the children had not experienced the joy of playing with balloons before.

Our porters had carried up stoves and food to give us a meal served in the classrooms. The children of Lapcha got nothing to eat for lunch. We were given a display of song and dance by some of the older pupils. Four of our girls put on a ballet display in their boots to the music of the school's only instrument, a drum, and to the singing of *Resham Fi Ri Ri*, a traditional Himalayan folk song. The interaction between the two different cultures happened spontaneously without any prompting or rehearsal which proved to be a very emotional experience for us all. As we left we were adorned with prayer scarves and felt very important.

The next morning we sat around the long breakfast table as usual while our tents were dismantled. The playground at Ghunsa was back to being a playground from its temporary campsite status. We watched as benches were brought out of the classrooms and laid out along the two sides of the yard. The hillsides became alive with children. They came from lower down the valley, higher up the mountain and from valleys several miles away. Their hunger for education meant that some of the children had walked for over two hours to come to school.

Education is not compulsory in the Himalayas and all schools in this area are set up by charities. Ghunsa and Lapcha schools were set up and built by CAN. Parents pay the equivalent of

£7.50 a year for their child's education but many can't afford even that. The majority of children at Lapcha didn't have any uniform but here at Ghunsa most wore a blue shirt with grey trousers or skirt. Girls also wore white leggings to cover their legs. The uniform also cost £7.50.

After enjoying playing with our balloons and other small gifts, the children were lined up at one end of the rectangular playground in their class groups to show us their daily keep fit routine. Our students sat down one side, parents down the other side and our staff sat at the other end along with their staff.

We were given the most outstanding display of friendship. Displays of song and dance, speeches and a prayer scarf for everyone personally given to each of us by everyone of their pupils.

The maths teacher told me that if only he had a text book it would be easier for him to teach. He taught everything out of his head.

The children at both schools had to leave school at fourteen and then that was the end of their education unless there was room for them at the nearest upper secondary school over four hours walk away. This really wasn't feasible so for these children, education came to an end after learning only the basics. They needed an upper secondary school to be built at Ghunsa which would serve both Ghunsa and Lapcha schools.

Back home in England, our school was to be refurbished, many text books would have to be thrown out along with furniture and practical equipment. We enquired with CAN if this unwanted equipment could be transported to these schools. There were many problems including the cost of transporting heavy cargo which is so huge that CAN was unable to afford it. Even if it were possible to transport equipment to the Himalayan region, then everything would have to be carried by donkey train or manually from the airstrip as there are no roads. The only way to get books from Britain to the schools is to actually bring them with you in your rucksack.

On our return from the adventure, everyone submitted their own story for a book that was published by the school to raise some funds and let people know about our experience. The expedition had certainly had an impact on many of our students as well as the staff.

Here are a few extracts from that book:

- *'At Lapcha School the children were crowding round the doors of the classrooms where we were eating our lunch trying to see us because they had never seen so many white people before, and when we came out they were so welcoming and were playing with us and talking with us as though they were our friends. They made us Nepalese tea and gave us a prayer scarf each and blessed us when we left.*

- *The children became overjoyed and this passed on to us. All this happiness was created by the smallest and simplest of things, something that we in England would completely disregard. A balloon.*

- *We were invited into the home of one of the schoolteachers from Ghunsa School. He was so pleased to introduce us to his wife and two small children beautiful and beaming. We were invited to sit in the main room of the house; it only contained a few possessions – a wind up radio and a photograph of his dead brother. That was it!*

- *It was awful to see how some people lived here in Kathmandu, but very eye-opening. People drinking and bathing out of drains, washing hanging everywhere and lots and lots of cows, walking the streets freely! The amount of litter that was piled up everywhere was so disgusting. I knew that I was sharing the same thoughts as everyone else when I realised how lucky I was!*

- *I will always remember one thing the headmaster of Ghunsa said to us it was 'I would love the children of my school to become children like you'. I felt weird inside when he said this it made me feel special.*

- *We left Lapcha School. It was heartbreaking leaving them and we walked in silence until we heard children's voices following us back along the path. They had been let out of school early and were walking home. A group of girls walked with us and somehow managed to grab our hands so we gave them the bobbles in our hair and in our bags. They put them on their wrists. After about an hour they left us and disappeared into some small clay houses. We trudged back to camp and tucked into our sleeping bags ready to meet the children of Ghunsa School in the morning.*

- *The joy on the children's faces as we showed them the gifts was heartbreaking.*

- *As we walked we realised how far the children were walking with us. For many it seemed to be hours before we said goodbye, admittedly this was at our much slower pace, but some of these children must walk miles to school over rough, winding, hilly tracks. Yet they appear smartly dressed and on time! Compare this to England and the difference is stark!*

- *At that moment it put everything in perspective for me, I realised that not only do we take objects and things for granted we take our life for granted. They have so little but they always keep laughing and smiling, they don't miss what they haven't got. They cherish everything which is by far more important than the latest pair of shoes or designer t-shirt. I can't say that I'll not buy new clothes or get my hair done once in a while but I can say that I won't see them as being important any more.*

- *I noticed the teachers. They were huddled in one corner protecting themselves from the ungrateful Himalayan weather, with bigger smiles on their faces than the children. Those teachers would have died for those children, and the children would have died for their teachers. If only we had the same principles in England.*

- *I have never experienced half the emotions I felt on this trip, but being on the expedition opened my eyes.*

Every one of us wanted to help in some way, so after a lot of discussion over the remainder of our trek we decided to raise money to build an upper secondary school at Ghunsa. There was land here where a couple of extra rooms could be built and children over fourteen from Lapcha could also attend. However, a new upper secondary school would mean extra teachers if any were available and they would need paying. The wage for an upper secondary school teacher is less than £1000 per year so our guarantee was to build the school and fund two teachers for five years. The school would cost £8000 and the two teachers £10000 for five years. Our target on returning home would be to raise £18000 within a couple of years.

By the time I retired, £12000 was raised from various fundraising events and £5000 was raised from direct debits. Many who went on the expedition signed direct debits for £5 a month over five years. This gave us a grand total of £17000. Since I was the one who had made the commitment to organise raising £18000 then it was up to me to make every effort to find the extra £1000.

Preparation

Just like most folk in the UK and around the world I can ride a bike. I'm not a member of any cycling club nor have I ever taken part in any cycling event.

For years I've been envious of cyclists fully laden and independently touring wherever they wish. It's been my dream to cycle from Land's End to John o'Groats with everything I needed attached to the bike. Like most people I never had the opportunity due to work and family commitments.

So on looking forward to retirement I made it my target (thought targets would be a thing of
the past) for the first year after retirement, to cycle from Land's End to John o'Groats and at the same time raise the extra £1000 needed for Ghunsa school. Unfortunately I told just about everyone so there was no escaping this challenge.

At my retirement 'Do' I was presented with a '2008 King of the Mountains' Tour de France shirt, a fluorescent vest adorned with caricatures of myself and a great deal of cycling paraphernalia – I was now committed. There would be no way that I could get out of cycling LEJOG!

Why is it that whenever anyone, most likely the man of the house, retires, the jobs around the house seem to multiply in direct proportion to the number of free hours available? I was so determined to fully prepare and train for this mammoth task that I managed to intersperse my training and preparation with the DIY jobs and housework.

My intention was to use Sustrans routes wherever possible and camp – being mostly self sufficient apart from hopefully a bar meal early evening and the use of many tea shops on the way.

Like the majority of casual cyclists the thought of sharing the road with forty tonnes of steel, white van man and Lewis Hamilton 'wannabees' does not have a 'wow' factor.

Many of the Sustrans routes are on canal towpaths, forest tracks, old railway routes, bridleways and quiet country roads. Through towns they generally stick to cycle paths and traffic calmed roads. I needed a bike that was light and could cope with the different surfaces. It also had to be strong enough to carry all my gear and tackle hills up to my meagre standard of fitness. I discussed the matter with friends and colleagues who cycled. I trawled through adverts on the internet and looked at bike specifications everywhere. Gradually, the bike most suitable for my requirements began to take shape. I needed wheels and tyres that could withstand rough surfaces but would also be at home on tarmac. I needed a frame that was light but strong enough to carry heavy loads and be ridden over stones, mud and gravel. It would have to have a wide selection of gears to both help me up hills and eat up the miles on the level. Good brakes to stop me quickly in case of emergencies. Plus comfort and lots of attachment points for water bottles and all the other cycling equipment that I was given upon retirement. At the end of September I collected my Specialized Tricross and couldn't wait to take it for a spin.

The furthest I'd ever ridden in a day was about fifty miles but that was some years ago so any advantage that that had given me had long since disappeared. The furthest I'd ridden recently was about fourteen miles. From that ride I suffered from jelly legs and an agonising sore backside. But the feeling of pain is quickly forgotten about and I was determined to see how I felt after a fifty mile ride on an off road Sustrans Route.

I carefully loaded my new pride and joy into the back of the car and headed off for Whitby. From here I would follow National Cycle Network Route 1 to Scarborough then return by the same route – a total distance of about fifty miles.

First I needed to find a parking place and toured around all the car parks mentioned in the guide book. It's certainly not cheap to park in Whitby. Parking at the recommended car park cost me £5 for the estimated five hours that I would take to cycle to Scarborough and back. Being retired now I thought hard about this and did a quick calculation. If I went out training twice a week and parked in car parks with similar charges then I would be spending several hundred pounds in car parking charges before the actual LEJOG. I could be close on being bankrupt in a year. I would pay the £5 this time but in future would investigate routes where parking was free or perhaps no more than a couple of pounds for the whole day.

With my attention now back to cycling, I thought, 'It's an old railway track so it'll be almost horizontal'. I joined the railway track about a mile uphill from the car park and very quickly attained a comfortable rhythm. From Whitby it ascended gently to Ravenscar then over the next fifteen miles or so to Scarborough it was a dream. The surface was just about all rough apart from the last couple of miles into Scarborough which was smooth tarmac. I met a more experienced cyclist of similar age and we cycled most of the way together. He had a mountain bike and I was curious to compare the differences between the bikes. It felt easy when cycling up the long steady inclines to keep pace with him but on the level his bike was no match for the larger wheels, lightness and higher gearing of my bike. I knew that I'd bought the right bike.

This was a good test for me and my bike. My companion left me on the outskirts of Scarborough and cycled to the sea front. Realising that I had a return trip of about twenty five miles and backside soreness was now beginning to override all thoughts of comfort it was time for me to return. For fifteen miles the track went up! It had seemed level on the way to Scarborough but was in fact downhill. That was why I thought it so easy. The pedalling was relentless, never a break to freewheel, just up, up, up. I read on an information board that this section of railway used to be the steepest and longest incline in England with its 1 in 30 gradient from Scarborough to Ravenscar.

When I eventually arrived back at the car my legs were quite unable to support my body and my backside thought it had been sitting on the tow bar of a dump truck for the past five hours. A full week later any pressure on the bony parts of my rear still resulted in an agonising squirm and painful shuffle to attain a comfortable position at the dining table.

Perhaps a slower build up to fitness would be more appropriate in future so over the next few months up until February I cycled twenty to forty mile routes and gradually increased the weight in my pannier bags.

I began to carefully consider the equipment I would need to take and what clothes I should wear. There was no way I was going to wear those tight cycling shorts – not so bad cycling but they would also need to be worn for having bar meals and shopping! Needless to say the padded bits to cushion the bony parts do stick out and look something like a baby's 'paddy pad' nappy! So having had the experience of a few long training rides I experimented with wearing several pairs of 'Kalvin Kleins' (which I seemed to continually get for Christmas but had hardly ever worn because they can be so uncomfortable in embarrassing places and required a secretive flick to maintain comfort) at the same time under a pair of longish shorts in fine weather and under a pair of thick Ron Hill leggings when it was cold. This worked well protecting the bony parts but the masses of layers and buttons to undo were frustratingly inconvenient in times of need!! It was a bit like trying to line up the punched holes in several sheets of paper to fit into a ring binder when the holes have all been punched in the wrong place. I made sure that I was never desperate. So I did a little more surfing the net and now I am the proud owner of a pair of Madison M-Tec 40 Baggy Cycling Shorts with removable 'paddy pad' so the shorts can be worn for more sociable occasions and the inner can be rinsed out at night to remove any remnants of strain!

Cycling long distances can also incur numb hands which wasn't a problem in the winter because I was wearing thick gloves. However as soon as it became warm and I dispensed with the gloves, my hands became numb. I therefore needed to invest in a pair of fingerless cycling gloves. The prices ranged from about £5 to £50 (How much??) So using the 'retirement' poverty excuse I bought a cheap pair with black leather palms and mesh backs which fastened around the wrist with Velcro. They did stop the numbness but I emerged from each ride with black hands and it took me about five minutes to detach the gloves from my hands. I then bought a cheap pair of red cycling gloves but the padded parts to stop the numbness flattened down after only a couple of rides thus rendering their function useless. I finally ended up with the expensive pair. I chose red and white to match the 'King of the Mountains' shirt that I had been presented with by work colleagues and the cycle helmet that my wife instructed me to buy and wear.

As April approached, with only two months to go and longer daylight hours, it was time to do my longest training ride.

Up with the larks and straight into the shower to freshen up for a long day ahead I noticed an alien lump protruding from my groin. Not the usual lump that men possess but a sort of bulge in the left side of my lower abdomen. 'It's another bloody hernia – that's the third one since 2001!' It wasn't giving me any discomfort so I thought it best not to mention it to anyone otherwise I would be berated from all sides until I was persuaded to postpone the challenge. I put it at the back of my mind but needed to be careful not to lift anything too heavy or do anything too strenuous. My immediate concern was today's adventure.

The longest stage I would encounter during LEJOG would be eighty four miles so I planned a route of similar distance. About four miles into the route I suffered my fourth puncture in the rear tyre. This time I'd bought a 'slime tube'. The theory being that if it punctures, the slime seals the hole. So after digging around in search of the tube in my pannier bags the punctured one was removed and the new 'slime tube' inserted. Using a hand pump is really difficult to get the required pressure into the tyres. Blisters appeared on the inside of my middle finger and I had mixed thoughts about continuing or returning home and watching TV. I chastised myself for being a wimp!

With the wheel replaced and everything packed away I set off again. Bump, bump, bump.....the tyre had come off the rim - "Bugger!" I uncontrollably shouted out. I let the tyre down, pressed it back into place and pumped it up again.

It was a cold morning and my nose started to run uncontrollably so out came the handkerchief to give it a good blow which ended up unintentionally spraying the inside of my glasses. Luck wasn't on my side. I felt like a Mr Bean clone.

With the tyre now re-inflated I set off along Route 1 towards Stockton. Shortly after cycling round the edge of a field I joined an old railway track and became aware of the smell of burning. On turning a corner there was a burnt out Ford Escort nose down in a ditch, still smouldering from its fate a few hours earlier. Two weeks later in the same place there was a burnt out mini but the Escort had been removed.

After another session re-fitting the tyre, this time properly, I headed for Northallerton. Several hours later and riding through many rural picture post card villages I ended up at Cod Beck Reservoir near Osmotherley on The Yorkshire Moors. This beautiful moorland village is the usual start of the infamous Lyke Wake Walk, 42 miles of sheer hell and boredom walking across the widest part of the bleak moors to Ravenscar on the coast in under 24 hours. Allegedly the walk gets its name from the carrying of coffins from Ravenscar to Mount Grace Priory near Osmotherley. There is a Lyke Wake Club of which I am a member, having been so silly as to have completed the walk seven times. I am the proud owner of a tie printed with coffins, seven coffin shaped lapel badges and a large pot mug with a coffin sculpted onto it.

It was downhill all the way from here towards Middlesbrough and home.

Unfortunately a new flyover which was being constructed near my exit from Middlesbrough meant that Route 1 was blocked off – it took me nearly an hour to escape from Middlesbrough avoiding the main intersection to join the cycle path that would eventually get me home. I've got to admit, after 85 miles the paddy pad shorts worked wonders along with the gel gloves. It's just the stiff neck and the hernia to tackle now!

I'd experienced some of the problems that I might encounter on LEJOG, so I needed to think about how I could minimise them. Puncture resistant tyres with slime tubes would certainly help.

Over the last few months spent preparing I'd thought a lot about what equipment to take. I got many ideas from books written by people who had cycled long distances unaided. I thought about the personal items I would need and what I wouldn't need, I asked myself what I could do without? What are the essentials? How many do I take? Where do I draw the line?

If I stuck to the advice given in several books then I would need to carry a spare bike plus spares for that and spares for the spares that might fail.

I decided to put a weight limit on what I would take then I could work to that. Throughout my training I took essentials for a day ride in the pannier bags and weighed them. They weighed about seven kilos in total. They included waterproofs, tools, food and water for the day, spare inner tube (which turned out to be an essential five times), wallet and camera. Because the bulk of my training was done in winter I was wearing more than I would be wearing on the actual challenge but I was always warm enough so I knew that if I took the same items on LEJOG I could stay warm enough no matter what the weather.

I made a limit of twelve kilos and desperately tried to stick to it. Everything was weighed to the nearest gram, nothing was omitted. Unfortunately, even when I cut down on many items, changed some things for lighter ones my final weight was over eighteen kilos. Apart from what I was wearing. (*See Table 1*).

For the actual LEJOG, one of my friends, Julian, expressed an interest in joining me at Carlisle and then cycling with me to Glasgow. In preparation we arranged a seventy mile ride on Sustrans routes.

We cycled along Route 14, Three Rivers Cycleway, to Durham then to Consett. We then joined Route 7, C2C, to Sunderland then on Route 1 back home.

Along Route 7 near Washington three people and a dog off the lead were walking towards us. The sort of dog that looks a bit like a Pit Bull Terrier but thankfully turned out to be a Staffordshire Bull Terrier. Anyway, they're both mean looking dogs and don't look a bit like the sort you'd want to cuddle or throw sticks for. They seem to be more fashioned to retrieving legs.

As we approached the group they moved to the side to allow us through but the dog was slow in responding so the 'macho male in the group', the other two were female, kicked the dog, and shouted "F'in' move"! There was none of this namby pamby 'Here boy......kiss kiss! Come here and I'll give you a treat' rubbish.

I passed the group first, followed by Julian. A further thirty yards on, I was rapidly overtaken by Julian shouting "DOG AFTER US!"

Julian was just a blur as I felt the hot breath from the growling dog's jaws homing in on my right heel. Fortunately as the dog had been conditioned to respond to foul language the macho male was forced into controlling his dog.

"Come 'ere ya f---in' bast'd," loud enough to attract every illegitimate dog within a mile radius. It retreated just before getting a taste of my right heel. Later I noticed a wisp of dog saliva dripping from my shoe.

I caught Julian up about a hundred yards ahead, who stated with a chuckled comment,

"You can't be sure about dogs!"

About two miles from home in torrential rain I encountered my fifth puncture, this time in the front tyre. Those puncture resistant tyres and slime tubes are now a must!

June 2nd was rapidly approaching so I needed to be prepared well before this as my wife and I along with our daughter and her three children were planning a trip to Callander in Scotland for a week.

We returned on Saturday 30th May and went straight off to see some of our friends and their children perform in the local dance school's biannual show then on Sunday 31st it was my wife's 60th birthday party. That only gave me one day, 1st June, to finalise my preparation. I had to prepare everything before our holiday in Scotland.

I found a clear space on the floor, laid everything out and ticked off each item on my sheet as I packed it. I needed to categorise everything and put them in accessible pockets in my pannier bags. It was essential that I knew where everything was. All of the tools went into a little frame bag under the front of the saddle. Valuables went into the easily detachable handlebar bag. First aid kit and washing kit fitted snugly into small pockets in the pannier bags and larger items such as sleeping bag and spare dry clothes went wrapped in a poly bag inside one of the pannier bags. Waterproofs were made easily accessible in the top compartment of one of the pannier bags. Maps, stove and spare food were also wrapped in a waterproof bag and stored inside the other pannier bag. I would use the bag with the spare dry clothes as a pillow.

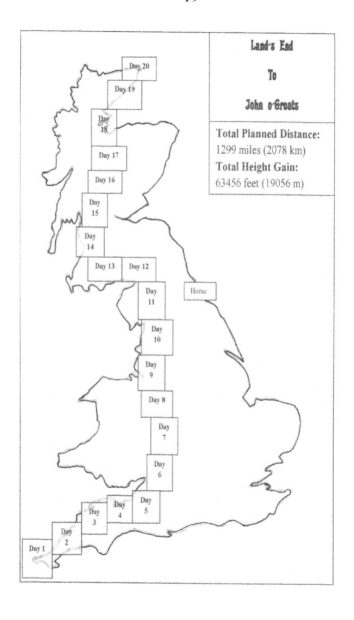

Land's End

To

John o'Groats

Total Planned Distance:
1299 miles (2078 km)
Total Height Gain:
63456 feet (19056 m)

Day 20
Day 19
Day 18
Day 17
Day 16
Day 15
Day 14
Day 13
Day 12
Day 11
Home
Day 10
Day 9
Day 8
Day 7
Day 6
Day 5
Day 4
Day 3
Day 2
Day 1

The Journey Begins

It's finally Tuesday 2nd June and I am awoken at 4am by my 'cock a doodle do' alarm clock which was a bargain buy at the local filling station for £3.99 if purchased at the same time as spending about fifty quid on petrol. I needed to cycle fifteen miles to Darlington station to catch the 07.14 train to Plymouth.

After saying 'Goodbye' to my wife, who was still in the land of nod and only too pleased to see the back of me and get some peace, I headed off at five for Darlington, fully laden with two pannier bags at the back and my tent and Karimat strapped across them. My more valuable items were in the handlebar bag.

I was finally off on my three week adventure. I cycled off the drive, wobbled a bit then bumped into the curb and fell shoulder first onto next door's lawn.

Whilst training I carried up to about 12 to 15kg on the pannier but now, I was fully laden with 20kg. The bike felt unstable and the back end wobbled. At least that was my excuse for falling off before I'd cycled 5 metres. It took me a few miles to get used to it. The big problem with the weight was not so much the cycling but picking the bike up and resting it against something like a post or fence, as with all the weight at the back it tended to have a mind of its own and fall with an almighty crash. Grabbing it when halfway to the ground only resulted in a fully splayed out fall across the back wheel and pannier bags if it fell away from you or a good thump in the tender unmentionables if it fell towards you. Unless the bike and its weight were vertical it was practically impossible to stop it from falling. This was a potentially embarrassing predicament I must bear in mind!

The journey to Darlington station was easy – virtually no hills, no traffic, no wind and clear skies. I covered the fifteen miles in about an hour and a quarter and was waiting for my train for a good hour. I made doubly sure that I was on the right platform, found a vacant seat, made sure the bike was securely propped up and settled down to await my train. The paper shop wasn't even open although there were a few people waiting for early trains to far away towns and cities. Most people were men in suits. Years ago they would have held brown brief cases full of paper and files. Nowadays they hold bigger brief cases except they're black, full of paper and files and laptops. At half six the paper shop opened so I bought a couple of daily papers to help pass away the eleven hour journey ahead.

Not having travelled by train for years, anxiety crept in and I had this fear of being on the wrong platform or getting on the wrong train or even missing it or not being able to find the right carriage for my bike.

My cycle ticket had printed on it *Coach F* and the lady in the ticket office had re-assured me that bikes go to the back of the train.

Firmly settled on the platform seat, with my bike parked next to me proudly advertising '*Land's End to John o' Groats*' printed on the pristine virgin pannier bag rain covers, I watched as a middle aged couple approached me pushing bicycles and wearing cycle helmets. They looked at me and asked.

"You look as though you know what you're doing – which part of the train do the bikes go on?" I felt like a fully fledged professional waiting to travel to an exotic country to partake in an international cycling event.

This being my first time for years taking a bike onto a train I remembered what the lady in the ticket office had told me. With total confidence and without hesitation I told them that bikes go to the back of the train probably in Coach F. They wished me luck on my forthcoming venture and headed off towards the rear of their train now arriving at Platform 1accompanied by squealing brakes and diesel fumes.

After a couple of minutes my attention was taken by two figures with bikes frantically running down the platform towards the front of the train.

How was I to know that there may be occasions when Coach F is at the front of the train and Coach A at the back? I would bear this in mind when my train arrived and also made a special mental note that the carriage letters are displayed to the left of the doors and are quite large. I pretended not to notice their plight.

I browsed through one of the newspapers while I continued to wait and became totally oblivious to my train's arrival not five metres in front of me. I stuffed the papers under the bungee securing my tent, grabbed the bike and wheeled it towards the rear of the train and Coach F. Bugger....they've done it again and put the coaches on back to front. The letters this time are tiny and are displayed on the doors. Why can't they be consistent?

Sure enough Coach A was at the rear but I started to panic a bit when I ran down the platform dragging my bike with me in exactly the same way as the couple I'd so ashamedly misinformed to find there were only five coaches. My ticket read Coach F for bikes and F is the sixth letter of the alphabet.....confusion was now dominant!

To my relief Coach E was missing and Coach F was the last. They do like to put the wind up novice travellers!

All of the doors to the other coaches were open but the door to Coach F was closed...How do I get in? Everyone's on the train, the guard's looking along the platform. There's no handle to open the door! How are you supposed to open a door without a handle? The last time that I was on a train they had handles to open the door and windows that opened by pulling on a leather strap. After months of preparation I had visions of being left on the platform without a hope in hell of getting to Plymouth today, or within weeks as I had to book my ticket weeks in advance. Perhaps the doors are controlled by the guard – do they still have guards I thought? They must because I've just seen one looking along the platform. I saw a button, marked 'PRESS' which had a circular lit up ring around it. I pressed it and to my great relief the door opened. My front wheel almost lifted itself onto the train but the back of the bike had as usual a mind of its own. This had to be almost forced onto the train using strength I thought I didn't possess. I must remember the hernia! There was another bike hanging up on a butcher's hook inside a small compartment through another set of doors, so this must be the right place.

I parked my bike, removed the handlebar bag and retired to my seat through another door with a button. I just got through when the door closed quickly behind me.

About ten minutes into the journey the 'Controller who was not fat', appeared through the door and with authority said,

"You can't park your bike there! – You need to remove the pannier bags and hang it by the front wheel on the hook - Health and Safety Regulations!"

There were four hooks altogether, one was taken by the muddy mountain bike and the other three were empty. This method of parking your bike on a moving train didn't do the bike's front wheel any good. The bike also swung about and kept banging on the side of the carriage. The controller disappeared and came back with a wad of toilet tissue to put between my wheel and the butcher's hook. These high tech gadgets never fail to amaze me. They've come up with an innovative yet destructive idea to squeeze as many bikes into as small a space as possible and yet have to use toilet paper to avoid damaging the bike!

At last I was now settled in my seat for the nine hour journey to Plymouth in Coach F which as well as using the broom cupboard to store bikes is also designated as the quiet coach. No mobile phones, conversation or personal stereos and believe it or not it was very quiet. Looking down the coach I could only see dropped heads. The coach was full of business people either engrossed in work on their laptops, no doubt to help secure a deal in some office at their destination, or asleep. The Cross Country train called at York, Leeds, Derby, Birmingham and Bristol and finally terminated at Plymouth.

Getting out of bed several hours before normal tends to disrupt what normally happens at about half seven in the morning. The body is unwilling to cooperate when normal habits are tampered with.

It was around ten when I ventured to the loo, nearly three hours after my normal routine habit. Train loos have also changed dramatically since I was last on a train. They are now all electric. Having passed the initial test on *'How to open train doors;'* I pressed the *'open'* button and the door slid open very slowly emitting a gentle 'pssst' sound, like someone trying to attract your attention in the middle of a very important meeting – good job I wasn't really desperate. Inside there was an array of buttons. I looked for the *'close'* button and pressed it. It took the door about a minute to close. I've now passed the second test – *'How to close train doors!'* Thankfully there wasn't a queue!

It was through good fortune that no-one else needed to use the loo just after I went in and the door had closed otherwise I would have been fully exposed having only noticed the *'lock'* button after a good five minutes. I will need to re-sit the third test. Perhaps that's why the door opens slowly!

Last year when on holiday in New Zealand there was a similar toilet in the middle of a high street in a town we passed through. I was using the loo when to my horror and immediate panic the door opened by itself to leave me sitting there gazing through the open doorway down the full length of the high street with my trousers around my ankles and bog roll in hand. I was powerless to do anything about it and had to abort my mission instantly. The closed door must have been timed to open after five minutes.

As I lingered in a similar position on the train I asked myself.

'What if there's a time limit on this door?' I didn't linger any longer and would have to wait for my bowels to send a message of desperation: 'Desperate measures required – GO NOW!' Plymouth continued to draw a little closer.

The doors between carriages also had a button to press. But whilst the loo doors were slow to close, these doors only stayed open for about ten seconds then closed quickly as I experienced on my way in. A frail old lady made her way down the narrow aisle as the train approached her station. She was pushing a small case on wheels in front of her and holding a large shopping bag behind her. The aisle was not wide enough for her to carry the bag by her side.

When she came to the door she was just able to press the button with her trolley hand. The door opened. She managed to wangle her case through the doorway and get herself through when the door closed leaving her hand and shopping bag trapped on the other side of the door. She was now in an extremely awkward situation, not being able to reach the button on either side of the door. The train had now stopped at her station. Wanting to exhibit my aspirations to be a Good Samaritan, I was just about to spring to her aid when the door reopened as it had detected a hand with shopping bag attached jammed in it!

The train finally approached Plymouth after a long nine hour journey. The train to Penzance was due to leave only six minutes after my train arrived so in order to be well prepared I made my way to my bike. After all the fuss and regulations churned out by the 'Controller who was not fat', my bike was the only one hanging up and half a dozen bikes were wedged into the tiny gap at all angles which should have been left clear due to Health and Safety Regulations.

My bike was swinging around but I couldn't get anywhere near it because of the other bikes. Before I could get to my bike the others needed to be moved but there was only room to move one of them at a time. Others cyclists came to help but that meant they were taking up the space that I was going to move one of the other bikes to. This situation reminded me of one of those little tile puzzles of a mixed up Edinburgh Castle where you move one tile at a time to end up with the correct picture. The correct picture for me was to get my bike off the hook, stand it up and fasten the bags and tent on. Somehow I managed to lift the bike off the hook and find a space created after a fellow cyclist moved his bike.

This task of clipping the pannier bags onto the pannier and fastening the tent and karimat on is awkward enough when there's lots of room and the bike is resting against something, but in a confined space when having to hold the bike up, dodge other people retrieving their bikes, trying to balance and hold on due to the side to side movement and sudden lurches of the train was not easy. I was also carrying two newspapers, a carrier bag containing sandwiches and two satsumas, plus my handlebar bag containing my valuables.

I put the carrier bag and newspapers on the floor and managed to clip the handlebar bag onto the bike. I picked up one of the pannier bags with my right hand and managed to clip it onto the pannier holding the bike with my left hand, when I noticed two satsumas rolling around the floor to my left, yes they were mine. Fortunately the sandwiches were still in a sandwich bag. Since I was holding my bike up with my left hand I reached under my left arm with my right to retrieve the satsumas which inevitably kept rolling away. Due to the extra weight now on the bike it fell on top of me. I managed to retrieve the satsumas and sandwiches, return them to the carrier bag, lift my bike up and tie the carrier bag to the handlebars. I'd also scattered a couple of bikes behind me with my backside when I bent down. The newspapers I tucked under my left arm. I managed to pick up the other pannier bag and clip it to the other side of the pannier. The tent came next. I placed it across the pannier and reached down for the Karimat, the tent fell off and in my haste to catch it; the newspapers fell from under my arm and were strewn over the floor. The bike fell again. This time of course it was much heavier and took more effort to stand upright. By this time everyone had retrieved their bikes and had disembarked. I just had the tent and karimat to fasten on the pannier. This I managed to do. I picked up the newspapers and stuffed them under the bungees which held fast the tent and karimat.

I was finally off the train and in the queue for the Penzance train which was waiting about ten metres from where I left the train from Darlington holding my heavy bike as it would not stand against anything.

I felt a tap on the shoulder and a voice from behind said. "Is that your helmet on the train mate?"

I checked my head – Bloody Hell, I'd left my new helmet on the other train. I needed to get it. As my bike wouldn't stand of its own accord I just laid it down and made haste to the bike store on the other train. Thankfully I retrieved my helmet, returned to my bike and boarded the train for Penzance – what a panic! Welcome back Mr Bean!

I parked my bike where instructed by the guard, this time it was basically anywhere. So much for Health and Safety Regulations! I sat facing it when I noticed that in my blind panic at journey's end on the other train, I'd put the pannier bags on sideways. The train was quite full so I pretended not to notice but surreptitiously looked round to see if anyone was attempting to read my '*Land's End to John o'Groats'* advert printed on the rain covers with their head resting on one of their shoulders.

The train passed through and stopped at every town on its route including Dawlish with its palm trees and black swans. I remembered spending a family holiday in Dawlish in 1973, the year Sunderland won the FA Cup. This very well used line was built in 1859 primarily to transport minerals and artefacts out of Cornwall but became a well used link for tourists wishing to experience the mild climate of this region. Victorian tourists would have been drawn to this peninsular to discover for themselves the hidden coves and smugglers' inns portrayed in many novels and light operas of the time. Perhaps today's tourists are drawn here to discover the same things but for different reasons. Nothing seems to have changed.

I had by now read every single page in the two newspapers which I bought in Darlington, including the adverts. I had a book in my pannier bag but didn't want to read it in case I finished it before I started the bike ride. I spotted blue Route 3 signs, which is the route I would mainly follow all the way to Bristol, on the minor roads beside stations. The excitement began to build as the train approached my destination.

The train pulled in to Penzance at four o'clock which was the end of the line, and I immediately tried to find Route 3 which progresses along the promenade. I couldn't wait to get started. I looked around for tell tale signs, blue route markers and cyclists. I spotted two fluorescent jackets wearing brightly coloured cycle helmets gliding along through the conglomeration of cars and people in the car park and in next to no time I was following them along Route 3 hopefully towards Land's End.

Over the previous months I'd programmed the whole route to John o'Groats into my 'Best ever Christmas Present' and everything fitted. The route on my Satmap GPS followed the blue signs. I overflowed with confidence until I came to a dead end for cyclists along the promenade with only steps down to the beach for an exit. I stopped and took in the views for a while so that anybody watching me might think my detour was deliberate and hopefully had not thought me incompetent for cycling into a dead end. I turned round and quickly spotted where I'd gone wrong and was again following the blue Route 3 markers. Smugness began to creep in again until I came to a junction and the signs pointed left but the route on my GPS distinctly pointed straight ahead. This was the first big decision I would have to make? Which one do I take?

Perhaps I've programmed the route incorrectly or it's been changed since I put the programme in. I decided to follow the signs; having little confidence in my competence as a navigator they were most likely to be correct.

Off I went following the signs directing me to a little village called Mousehole, pronounced *Mowzel*. A narrow lane took me down a steep hill then along a promenade which followed the contours around a headland before reaching the charming village.

Mousehole probably gets its name from a huge cave nearby shaped like a mouse hole. Like most quaint little villages, there are many tales associated with its past. Dolly Penteath, reputedly the last person to speak Cornish as her native tongue died here over two hundred years ago and also each year just before Christmas, the villagers commemorate the suffering felt by villagers of the past by cooking an enormous fish pie which is shared by the residents of Mousehole and people from the surrounding villages. This is called 'Tom Bawcock's Eve'. I had visions of a huge circular pie with a hundred people sitting around it eagerly tucking into the pie crust before they could sample the delights of the filling. But how big was the oven?

The village is undoubtedly steeped in legend and history and riding through its narrow streets I could feel the history all around. My attention was taken by the tiny shops with matching tiny doorways peculiar to the majority of ordinary buildings erected in the 17th and 18th Centuries. The jumble of narrow streets would have made promising escape routes for fugitives from the press gangs. I needed to keep a close eye out for the blue Route 3 signs as they guided me through this maze of narrow streets. Then as though I'd been hit with a sledge hammer a hill of vertical proportions I'd never met on any of my training rides formed a barrier directly ahead. It was then that I realised my mistake.

There are two routes out of Penzance. The main one goes down through Mousehole then up an unbelievably steep hill to get out while the alternative route follows an arc around the escarpment above Mousehole. When I programmed the route I'd chosen the alternative route avoiding the steep hills into and out of Mousehole. I made a mental note to follow the route I'd programmed into my GPS in future because if I'd chosen a different route then it would have been for a good reason. The route out of Mousehole was my first walk uphill.

The Sustrans route to Land's End from Penzance involves many country lanes with a lot of very steep hills. Normally I would have cycled the ten miles from Penzance to Land's End in under an hour; this route took me nearly an hour and a half. I realised that I would have to cycle back along the route in the morning which was something I would need to seriously think about.

I eventually reached the campsite, which had very good reviews on their website, to find the office closed. There was a note on the door informing new arrivals to find a pitch, camp then pay in the morning when the office opened at 9am. I thought, 'That's ok, I'll be gone by 7am – might get a free night'. I was setting my tent up, along with two more late arrivals when a lady turned up in a car. She said that owing to the fact the office was closed the fee would only be £13 and not £15 as there wouldn't be any showers and she couldn't get a key for us.

I fumbled around for the money and only had £10 and £20 notes. She took £10 and said, seeing as there aren't any showers, that'll do! It appears that her fee formula is based on an *'I'll take whatever I can get'* basis! Fortunately the toilets and washbasins were open for business.

I was relying on the camp shop for milk and a meal at their restaurant. All closed. Fortunately there was a pub up the road called *First and Last* where I managed to get a meal and found a general dealers shop a little further along the road where I managed to get my milk. At nine o'clock I crawled into my tent and for the first time snuggled up in my new light weight down sleeping bag. It all starts tomorrow!

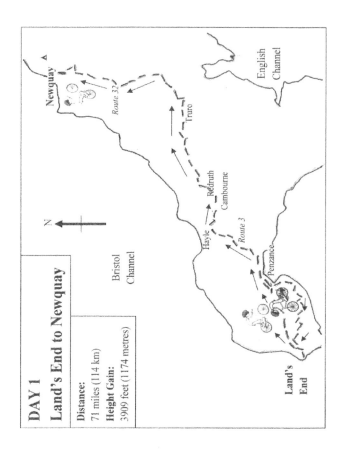

DAY 1

Land's End to Newquay

Distance:
71 miles (114 km)
Height Gain:
3909 feet (1174 metres)

Bristol
Channel

N

Newquay

Route 32

Truro

Redruth
Cambourne

Hayle

Route 3

Penzance

English
Channel

Land's
End

Day 1 – Hills, Hills and more Bloody Hills

I'd set my alarm for six but I suppose the combination of turning in early and the excitement of starting my adventure saw me wake up twenty minutes earlier. The outer tent was running with condensation both inside and out although the inside of the inner tent was only damp. During training I'd intended to spend a couple of nights cycling and camping to improve on my equipment and iron out any unforeseen problems, but never got round to it.

What I needed to do was to adopt a routine to save as much time in the mornings as possible.

1. Wake up.
2. Get dressed.
3. Pack sleeping bag, dry clothes and everything else that wouldn't be needed for breakfast.
4. Light stove and boil water for coffee.
5. Go to loo and have a wash.
6. Water will be boiled on return (depending on how far away the loo is) and make coffee.
7. Pour cereal, always fruit and fibre in my case, into bowl along with milk.
8. Have breakfast.
9. Go back to the loo now that the internal workings have had a chance to establish themselves.
10. Take mug and pan (which doubles as the cereal bowl) and spoon to wash.
11. Clean teeth.
12. On returning to the tent pack both pannier bags and fasten on bike.
13. Take tent down and fasten along with Karimat across pannier bags.
14. Check around to ensure that nothing is left behind.
15. Set off on the next stage.

That was what I did on the first morning and it seemed to work well so that's the routine I intended to adopt.

I was ready to leave at quarter to seven, said goodbye to some fellow campers who were just emerging from their tents, gave them about half a pint of milk I had left and was finally on my way to start at Land's End which was about a mile down the road.

It was warm that morning and it was definitely going to be a hot day.

Land's End was totally deserted. Closed gates, red and white striped tape across openings to stop early birds from stealing a free glimpse of Land's End and not a soul in sight made the whole place feel like a scene from a science fiction film. If it had been misty there would also have been a touch of eeriness about it.

De-commissioned rescue craft were on display. A life boat and a helicopter reminded me of our visit to Universal Studios in California, perched at 'action' angles on their plinths. A mock up of a stone circle trying to convey some druid mystique into the area just didn't look authentic. It was far too neat. The buildings looked false and totally out of character in this wild place. The only other time I had been to Land's End it was free for everyone to roam around and enjoy one of the most famous parts of Britain's heritage and coastline. Unfortunately there is now a fee to visit this unique place and I was unable to visit Dr Johnson's Head or Dr Syntax's Head, the latter of which is the true most westerly point in England; possibly named after the 19th Century fictional traveller of the same name. The most westerly point on the British mainland, by 22 miles, being Corrachadh Mor, Ardnamurchan, in Scotland which I wouldn't be visiting.

Tourists have visited Land's End for generations. Since the 19th Century they would arrive by wagonette, a wagon with seats, to the First and Last Inn, where I had sampled the culinary delights on the previous evening with possibly the same menu as in the 19th Century. The inn is traditionally owned by the same owners of Land's End and incidentally John o'Groats. Thankfully they are unable to impose a charge for End to Enders. You can imagine some greedy entrepreneur devising a medal or some sort of trophy for End to Enders. Anyone up for the Challenge would need to sign in at one end for a fee, complete the Challenge and then sign in at the other end. For an extra fee each successful attempt would probably be awarded with a tatty plastic plaque to hang on a wall or a cheap alloy medal to hang around your neck.

I was looking for 'The Sign' so proudly displayed as the iconic emblem on many pictures of Land's End. I couldn't see it anywhere so reckoned that it must be hidden somewhere behind the iron curtain erected to keep out early birds or late comers who might be trying to avoid paying to stand in a place of natural beauty.

It was now nearly seven and the first bus arrived to await its departure time. The driver wandered about smoking a fag until his leaving time of 06:59 on the dot approached. I took a few photographs and set off for Penzance. About half a mile up the road I saw about half a dozen people impatiently waiting at the bus stop. I thought about remarking that the driver was shortening his life by six minutes and he would be along shortly, but resisted and nodded good morning towards them instead. There wasn't any traffic around and there was no way I was going to cycle on those roller coaster roads back to Penzance so I took the A30. My new plan was to turn off after cycling ten miles or so which would bring me on to the promenade at Penzance.

The journey should take me about forty five minutes. The roads were quiet for the first half hour and the hills were gentle. Then, it was as though the door of a wasps nest had been opened, traffic started to buzz all around, mainly from behind. The road got narrow in places so traffic sometimes had to wait behind me for a gap to overtake. I felt uneasy and was looking forward to my turning. At about ten to eight I spotted a sign for Penzance pointing right and down a hill. Even if that's not the correct one, I thought, I'm taking it just to get off this death trap. I turned right and sped straight downhill onto the promenade at Penzance. It was amazing how the change in environment made me feel so good. It was warm and sunny which made it understandable why Penzance enjoys one of the warmest climates in Britain. I was now away from the busy road and had a good five level miles ahead of me. Everyone I passed said hello, joggers, cyclists and dog walkers. St Michael's Mount stood out proudly in the bay ahead. That was my pointer to turn left away from the south coast and head towards Hayle on the north coast.

St Michael's Mount has been at the heart of many sieges throughout History and was where the first beacon was lit to warn of the advancing Spanish Armada in 1588. Its harbour was used by cargo ships exporting precious tin from the many mines in Cornwall. Today St Michael's Mount is a major tourist attraction.

Because I'd had my breakfast so early, it had been well over three hours since I'd eaten. The shops were starting to open at Hayle and for the very first time in my life I bought a single banana. Eleven pence it cost. I apologised to the shop owner.

The route now took me to Cambourne then Redruth possibly getting its name from the red colour of the stream that ran through the town discoloured by iron oxide from nearby tin mines. Many of the buildings attached to the mines have now been refurbished as memorials to Cornwall's industrial past. I passed an area which could have doubled as part of a Lunar or more appropriately Martian landscape.

Perhaps they were old slag heaps from the mines which were gradually being removed. The whole area was entirely without vegetation, only dirty coloured rocks, mud and dust. There were two small lakes full of an evil looking red and orange coloured liquid. Probably water but not the sort you would want to drink or bathe in. The shore was tinged with orange and red, discoloured by impure iron or tin in the ore that they mined years ago. This blemish on Cornwall's countryside must have been in excess of two miles long and as much as half a mile wide. The Sustrans cycle route went directly through the middle.

I began to wonder if I'd followed the correct track and felt a little uneasy until I saw another cyclist and a National Cycle Network (NCN) Millennium post. The vegetation gradually returned and I was at last out of this hideous environment.

As I approached Truro which is the most southerly city in Britain and the only city in Cornwall, the route started to get steeper. Truro probably gets its name from the meeting of three rivers, 'Tru' meaning three. All streets and roads seemed to drop down towards the rivers. There didn't appear to be any horizontal streets apart from alongside the rivers. Long hills, short hills but all steep. The problem I faced was that since I'd found my way to one of the rivers all of the routes now went up. I was getting hungry again but was reluctant to go down into the town to find a tea shop because I'd have to cycle back up afterwards no matter which way I went.

I left Truro heading north up a very steep hill. In order to save battery life in my GPS I had it set for the screen to go off after three minutes so tended to memorise the immediate route ahead. I remembered that I needed to turn left somewhere up the hill near the railway track so kept a keen eye open for a sign. There were three left turns up the hill making it difficult to decipher which left turn I had to take. I had now left Route 3 so would need to keep a sharp eye out for Route 32 signs. I passed the first and second turns without any visible signs so turned left at the third. A dead end sign informed me that it was a dead end for traffic but that is not always the case for cyclists. I risked the third turn only to find that after a mile it was indeed a dead end not only for traffic but also for pedestrians and cyclists. The road was taking me in the right direction and was parallel to the correct route but on the wrong side of the railway. I returned to the hill and descended to the first turn. This looked more promising but on inspecting my GPS found it was gradually leading me in the wrong direction. After half a mile I returned and climbed the hill again to take the second turn and my last option. Thankfully it was the correct way after I spotted the Route32 sign well hidden under some foliage. I had wasted thirty minutes and a gallon of sweat.

This being my first stage, I had nothing to compare my progress to. It was a very hot day and I needed to get to Newquay between mid and late afternoon. My GPS informed me that I would reach Newquay by about 3pm, not including stops or unplanned detours.

The hills really did start to increase both in quantity and quality (steepness) which meant I was now pushing the bike as much as I was pedalling it. The average temperature was due to be 27°C but it must have been 30°+ in some places today. I found myself using any excuse for a rest.

Making sure you have enough water can be a problem even if you are willing to spend a fortune on bottled water. I managed to get my bottle refilled by knocking on the door of a nursery school I passed. Following the sound of many locks and bolts being undone to protect the children from any untrustworthy strangers walking in through the door, the lady who answered smiled, took my bottle and filled it with cool refreshing water. I was hoping to pass someone out in their garden to ask but never saw anyone.

On my way up yet another hill, which mustn't have been all that steep because I was actually pedalling up it, I spotted a seat overlooking the valley below. This was a good place for a rest and fuel intake. An old lady passed and asked about my ride. We chatted for a while and she took my blog site card – perhaps she'll donate!

A man came past with his dog and again took interest in my venture.

The hills seemed to rise relentlessly. I was struggling to maintain my strength up hills that I would have bounced up during training. A cyclist friend had given me a handful of sachets with energy giving gel to take in times of need. I had only ever used a free sample many years ago, taken during the Great North Run about three miles from the finish. It had been designed to give a quick boost of energy. At that time the gel was in its infancy and tasted foul. It was sickly and quite unpalatable. My friend said that the gels had dramatically improved and came in different flavours with easy to open and use sachets. I decided before I started that I would only use them in times of desperation. On Day One of my journey that time had already come! I took out a sachet, tore the top off and squeezed the sticky sickly slimy gel into my mouth. It found all the nooks and crannies including the hole created by a filling that I'd lost chewing on a hard bit of Fruit & Fibre this morning. The strawberry flavoured substance slithered under my tongue and filled the gaps between my cheeks and gums. It slid down my throat like a globule of oil oozing slowly down a plughole then suddenly disappeared leaving no evidence that it had ever been there. I waited in vain for the rapid boost of energy I'd expected but continued to struggle and grunt up the hills.

At last I had sight of the sea having attained a position high up above the North Cornish coast. There was a fresher atmosphere and it was good to feel the cooler air. I was on the final stretch down to Newquay. The cool gave way to warmth again as I descended, I felt myself starting to shiver and my throat became extremely dry. My tongue constantly stuck to the roof of my mouth and I was unable to generate any saliva to remedy the uncomfortable feeling. I was becoming dehydrated. Even though I was only within five miles of Newquay I knew that I must stop at the first opportunity and buy a drink or replenish my water bottle somewhere but there were no shops or people working in their gardens where I might be able to scrounge a drink. Fortunately the road to the campsite was downhill and I was happy to free wheel practically all the way to the enquiry office. As I booked into the campsite I felt weak and forced myself not to double over with the stomach cramps that were now attacking me with ever diminishing intervals. I felt sick which was either due to the lack of fluid or the sickly energy gel I had taken about an hour ago.

I booked in at about 3 o'clock, quickly found a site, filled my water bottle and drank, put the stove on for a mug of tea and erected my tent while the water boiled. As well as a full litre of water I drank two mugs of tea, curled up on the grass next to my tent to ease the stomach cramps and slept for about an hour.

To add to the misery of stomach cramps I was also suffering from chaffed cheeks on my backside. Not the usual sore backside which can reputably be corrected or eased by a ripe banana accurately positioned down the back of your shorts, but the sort which rubs the skin away. The only answer is a good application of Vaseline which I decided to administer after a shower and again before turning in for the night.

I'd never been to Newquay before so after my enforced nap, I wandered down to the town about a mile away, John Wayne style. Fortunately the stomach cramps had passed. It was bustling with youngsters in their late teens, probably having just finished their A Level exams, it was too soon for any of them to have completed their GCSE's as those exams were still ongoing. However some may consider a day surfing is far more important than a day suffering - behind a desk! I couldn't imagine that so many teenagers lived in Newquay which I'd understood to be predominantly inhabited by the older and even retired generation. I learnt since that the town is a magnet for students after completing their exams to descend on its holiday apartments in their hundreds if not thousands. The beach was alive with surfers and sun bathers. Every bit of sand the size of a beach towel appeared to have been taken. I watched at a distance from the cliff top. The town was full of arcades, fast food outlets and surfing shops. I eventually found a Tesco Express to replenish my larder with sandwiches, biscuits and milk. The supermarket was buzzing with scantily clad students eager to replenish their own larders with ready meals and cans of lager. The shop assistants must have been fed up asking every one of them for their identity as proof of age before pushing their copious amounts of alcohol past the bar code reader. I wasn't asked for any identity. Probably because I didn't have any alcohol or if I did have any, the grey hair and bald head might have had something to do with it!

At the end of the nineteenth century, Newquay was famous for its pilchards and its fishing port. Then over the course of the twentieth century developed into a tourist resort for families and the older generation but now, with the macho image surrounding surfing, the town is attracting teenage students by the thousand.

The receptionist at the campsite had recommended a pub about half a mile up the road, so after my quick look at Newquay, I walked to the pub. Before I went I drank half the litre of milk I had bought.

This was to be my second of hopefully many bar meals during the venture. The problem was I couldn't face a big meal and when it came, chicken and mushroom pie with potatoes and vegetables, I struggled to eat it. I knew that I had to eat as much as possible to give me enough energy for the next day. Being dehydrated had certainly taken its toll on my body. My throat and mouth were still dry even after everything I'd drunk since arriving at the campsite and a further two pints of bitter with my bar meal. I must never fall into this trap again!

I was soon tucked up in my sleeping bag again, reading the book I'd brought – *'Shadows on The Wasteland'* by Mike Stroud which tells his version about himself and Ranulph Fiennes crossing Antarctica unsupported. It makes my effort cycling from Land's End to John o'Groats sound a bit feeble! As I dozed off I thought about an itinerary for the end of the day to ensure that I was always fully prepared. Now that I had one full day under my belt I was more qualified to foresee any problems that might occur.

- At the last shop before the campsite buy a litre of milk, sandwiches for next day's lunch in case a tea shop can't be found, packet of biscuits or cake and fruit plus anything that needs replenishing like breakfast cereal.
- Erect the tent on a suitable spot.
- Unload the bike and put it under the flysheet.
- Have a shower and wash socks each night then 'paddy pad' shorts and 'King of the Mountains' top every 3rd or 4th night in the shower.
- Top up the small shampoo bottle with soap out of a dispenser in the toilets.
- Boil some water for a cuppa.
- Write up log book.
- Go for a bar meal or cook a meal.
- Clean teeth and turn in after applying Vaseline to backside even if it is not sore.

I added another point to my morning list. Drink any remaining milk and don't give it away.

I dozed off well before nine o'clock.

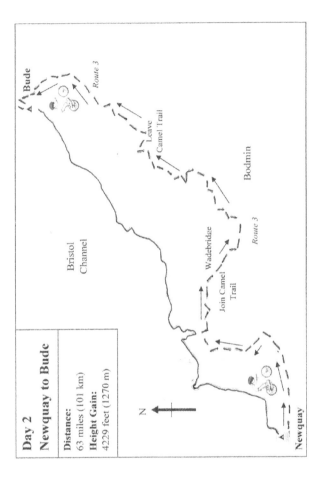

Day 2
Newquay to Bude

Distance:
63 miles (101 km)
Height Gain:
4229 feet (1270 m)

Bude

Route 3

Leave
Camel Trail

Bodmin

Bristol
Channel

Wadebridge

Route 3

Join Camel
Trail

N

Newquay

Day 2 – Riding The Camel

That list I made for a quick getaway in the morning. Well I changed No 1 from *Wake up* to *Lie awake dozing for five or ten minutes then decide whether or not to get up.*

If you were thinking that it wouldn't be as easy to get up on Day 2 as it was on Day 1 then you were right. However, once out of my sleeping bag and a face wash in cold water I was raring to go again. All the dehydration and stomach cramps had gone and I felt alive once again. I left before seven to follow Route 32. Before the route ventures into the countryside it winds its way through the town, partly on a busy road, so I joined the traffic flow as normal. I came to a roundabout and at this point on the Sustrans map there is a caution note which reads – *Take care crossing A3058.* Perhaps whoever produced the map encountered the same selfish female, driving, yes you've guessed it, a big old red Volvo Estate. I was circling the roundabout turning right and according to the rules of the road have the right of way when the aforementioned driver and vehicle approached the roundabout from my left.

I could read her mind through her eyes, she was that close. She was probably a thoroughly decent law abiding member of the community but behind the wheel of her ancient Volvo Estate she turned into an aggressive evil psychopath. She became the Mr Hyde of drivers. She hesitated at the white line but then realised that she was preparing to stop only for a bike which she could easily dominate and not a twenty ton truck which would crush her and her car if she moved; although that might be debatable when in competition with a Volvo Estate.

'*Damn it a cyclist, now I'll have to stop!*'

I concentrated on the movement of her car and looked straight at her. Her face changed from a look of surrender and courtesy to one of aggression and meanness. She turned her head away from me pretending that she hadn't noticed me, leaned back in her seat to assist ramming her foot to the floor and accelerated. There was no way she would surrender to a bike.

She pulled out in front of me and missed my front wheel by less than two metres. I had to brake to avoid being crumpled under her car. I regained my balance and looked up to see the back end of her uncared-for red estate rattle down the road. I imagined her sitting behind the steering wheel cackling like a witch having very nearly injured yet another cyclist. No doubt less than half a mile ahead with her tired old Volvo, she'll be holding back a line of angry, frustrated drivers as she continues on her journey at thirty five miles an hour in a sixty limit.

The route continued down and down which felt great but I knew that sooner or later that meant up and up with probably another couple more ups thrown in. I was walking before I'd ridden five miles. This procedure was repeated many times all the way to Padstow, twenty miles further along Route 32. This was the start of The Camel Trail, the route of an old railway which runs traffic free for over twenty miles and it is level. This is one of the most popular cycle routes in the country.

The relaxing feeling knowing that a long level ride lay ahead was unsurpassable. I stopped at the first seat and soaked up the tranquil atmosphere. I'd cycled almost twenty five miles in two hours, it wasn't yet 9am. There wasn't a cloud in the sky and it was beginning to get hot. There were a few joggers, cyclists and dog walkers around but generally the Trail was quite deserted.

After a quarter of an hour rest, I headed off along this longed for Camel Trail which has spectacular views across the Camel estuary. The tide was out so it was mainly all sand. Pleasure boats and fishing boats lay on their sides as though they were resting after a hard day (or night) at work. Something didn't feel quite right; everything seemed slightly blurred, especially when I looked at my GPS.

Being of that age when the use of reading glasses is essential, I had made enquiries about cycling sunglasses which would allow me to read my GPS while also viewing the surrounding countryside in focus. The only pair I could buy without spending a fortune was a pair of bifocals clipped onto the inside of a pair of cycling sunglasses. Although I could see ahead perfectly well and the map on my GPS was in focus, I could barely read it because the sunglasses were too dark. There were no lighter pairs available on the market with clipped in bifocals so I needed to adapt.

I already had a pair of yellow tinted cycling sunglasses which are fantastic. They brighten everything up on dull days and dull the brightness on sunny days. I needed to make my own bifocals. After experimenting with all sorts of combinations I eventually bought a pair of very narrow reading glasses from a charity shop for £2.95. I later spotted some in another shop for 50p.

After a half hour wrestle trying to prise the lenses out of their frames without too much damage I managed to stick them with

Bluetack to the bottom of my yellow tinted sunglasses. They were perfect. I didn't want to use glue as it might have damaged or marked the sunglasses if I got the lenses in the wrong place.

On leaving my resting place on the Camel Trail I dropped my sunglasses and unfortunately one of the Bluetacked reading lenses fell off and I hadn't noticed. I was only on my second stage of a twenty stage ride and every time I needed to read my GPS I now had to close my right eye and tilt my head slightly to focus on the detail. This action could be construed as a flirtatious wink so I must be careful not to use my GPS if anyone, male or female, is cycling towards me.

A few miles along the Camel Trail lies Wadebridge and thinking about my dehydrated body and stomach cramps from yesterday, decided to stop at the first tea shop for a mug of tea and a toasted sandwich. They went down a treat.

About six miles further on, the trail bypasses Bodmin. A notice board advertising bar meals in a pub next to the trail seemed to be the victim of a menu saboteur. The landlord of the pub showed his frustration and anger by posting this notice which read:

There would usually

be menus displayed here

but unfortunately there is

some moron about

who keeps ripping them down

and taking them away.

Normal service will be resumed

when this cretin grows up

and gets a life.

After a good one and a half hours almost flying along the Camel Trail I arrived at a small car park and picnic area to be confronted by an enormous metal salmon perched on an iron rod to display it in a 'jumping out of the water' pose. The actual salmon had no significance to its name of 'The St. Tudy Salmon' but was one of a collection of giant animal sculptures on a route called 'The Giant's Way' which coincides with the Camel Trail at this point. This particular sculpture was built and erected by the pupils of St Tudy School belonging to the tranquil village of St Tudy named after a fifteen hundred year old saint.

The Camel Trail came to an end at nearby Poley's Bridge and after the long level ride my legs were transposed into a reluctant jelly which refused to tackle any gradient short of a mole hill. I had unfortunately rejoined the unappealing big dipper challenge of the country lanes. What was Route 32 now continued as Route 3 and it went up very steeply. A young couple just out for the day on mountain bikes cycling in front of me also ground to a sudden halt and were probably sharing the experience of the infusion of jelly into their leg muscles. They were slightly ahead of me when I noticed that they had split up, she turned off left and he continued ahead following the same route as me. I was walking within two hundred yards. He continued cycling and disappeared around a bend – he wasn't carrying any load, that's my excuse. At the top of the hill I reached the outskirts of a pretty village called St Breward which had outstanding views towards the sea. The female half of the young couple was waiting at some crossroads as large as life and certainly not out of breath.

I was puzzled – 'How come she was there before me, and where was her friend? He was nowhere to be seen.

She asked me if I'd seen him to which I replied that I hadn't!

I asked her, "How did you get here before me?" to which she replied, "I came round the easy way!" I felt like showing a pet lip but instead left her standing alone to wait for her friend.

The road ascended steeply for about two miles to eventually gain the top of the moor and continued for miles without any significant hills. The road became too wide and official looking, surfaced in concrete and not the usual potholed tarmac, with 'Keep Out' signs neatly standing every hundred metres or so, to be part of a normal moorland road. It turned out to be part of an old World War II airfield which is still used for light aircraft.

I met a couple touring Cornwall; both bikes were fully laden with astronomic sized pannier bags but no tent. They were using

B&Bs for their accommodation, carrying only their clothes. I would wager that of the four bags they had in total and judging by my meagre wardrobe that his belongings would barely fill half a bag and hers the rest! They were intrigued by my Satmap GPS. He thought that one would make a good Christmas present for himself from her. They had also attempted LEJOG last March but on reaching the Lake District were beaten by snow storms. That must have been so demoralising knowing you were half way and had to give in but they were resilient and looked forward to trying it again. They were off in the same direction as me so to avoid cycling with them I waited and enjoyed some refreshment.

Within a couple of hours I entered Bude, avoiding the very steep coastal route. This time sticking to my planned route and not being dominated by the signed route. The campsite was easy to find commanding superb views over Bude and towards the hills to the east which I would be tackling tomorrow. Fortunately camped next to me were an elderly couple in a motor home, plugged into the electricity. They kindly charged my batteries.

Tonight's bar meal was magnificent. Because I'd managed to keep myself hydrated, eaten more than yesterday and had plenty of rests, I was ravenous. Two pints of the local brew and lasagne with sauté potatoes was just the tonic I needed to give me strength for tomorrow's stage. Thoughts of the hills I could see from the campsite teased me with their strength sapping inclines.

With copious amounts of Vaseline the sore cheeks have healed a little and should be back to normal in a few days. My mind drifted back several years when sitting on a bicycle seat would have given me the satisfaction of thinking I was in heaven. Unfortunately at that time I didn't think about the comfort and satisfaction that a bicycle seat could have brought. I had previously had the misfortune to have suffered from piles. 'Piles' has developed into a term which not only sounds painful but brings uncontrollable laughter to the sadistic trait in friends and colleagues. The term haemorrhoid brings similar laughter but conjures up too many hideous visions without the humour. Many people suffer from piles which are usually brought on by a poor diet which induces straining. Mine were incurred by a mixture of both. Not enough fibre, fruit and vegetables, and too much straining by reading the newspaper on the loo. I was told by my GP that piles are varicose veins in the rectum which can be cured with cream if they are small or by a small operation if they are large.

I suppose they affect different people in different ways. They gave me no pain when walking, running or partaking in any activity as long as I was moving about. Sitting down gave partial relief but full relief could be obtained if the seat had its centre raised to support the affected region. A bicycle seat would have been ideal.

However, standing still for more than a few minutes became sheer agony and at the height of my affliction I had to attend two weddings on the same day. During the two church ceremonies singing hymns through gritted teeth only rewarded me with a dig in the ribs from my better half. I'd tried the cream which was having no effect so the only answer was the small operation.

I was given an appointment at the local hospital and couldn't wait to have this pain obliterated from my life. The consultant, who I shall refer to as 'B', the word which refers to an illegitimate offspring, for the next few paragraphs, explained the procedure. Without any anaesthetic, local or otherwise, 'B' pumped air into my bowel to expand it in order to insert a large tube through which he could use a special instrument to 'Band the Piles'! This is a term 'B' was familiar with and informed me that the same method is used by farmers to dock lambs tales. Eventually they fall off.

I lay on my right side, raised my left leg in the air and 'B' started the procedure. The tube felt a little uncomfortable. 'B' then quite nonchalantly remarked,

"You might feel a sharp pain!"

I was strong and courageous; I could withstand anything he threw at me.

Then there was a loud snap followed by the most excruciating pain I have ever felt. This was the proverbial red hot poker. I shouted out in silence!

"YOU BASTARD!"

The pain didn't diminish, it just got worse.

'B' told me that the discomfort I felt from the air he'd pumped into my bowel would disperse, the piles would fall off in a few days and the excruciating pain would eventually go with the help of some painkillers he prescribed. 'B' left the room to practice his sadism on another unwary patient.

The nurse must have felt sorry for me due to the agonised look I had on my face accompanied by bulging eyes. She told me that a hot bath would relieve the pain and gave me a letter to hand in at reception. I waddled out of the room and along the corridor to wait in the reception queue.

I stood in the queue at reception; eyes bulging and teeth gritted with not only a red hot pain in my backside but a pain in my gut which made me double up. I put on a brave face and awaited my turn. Then with uncontrollable force the pumped in air found its way out in the form of a huge loud fart followed by lesser dribbles lasting for about half a minute. No-one neither turned a head or flinched as everyone thought that everyone else would think it was them if they made any movement. I placed a tightly rolled up scarf in the centre of the driver's seat for the drive home where I immediately ran a hot bath, sat at the top of the stairs on the edge of the top tread and shouted 'BASTARD' at the top of my voice.

During the next two weeks I had six hot baths a day. My wife couldn't believe how clean I was and how much our gas bills had increased.

Needless to say I was off work for a while and after two weeks spending a lot of time sitting on the edge of chairs and having hot baths things started to improve. I thought that I had sufficiently recovered to do a little shopping at the local supermarket. The drive in was fine. I grabbed a trolley and proceeded to work my way up and down the aisles when the pain started. I needed an edge to sit on. I tried resting against the corner of the trolley but it was too high and it kept rolling away anyway. There was nothing to use until I spotted the freezer chests. I hitched myself up and sat on the cold edge next to the frozen veg. This was bliss. I pretended to study my shopping list so as not to attract attention by sitting on the freezer. After five minutes I made a hasty dash for the checkouts. Unfortunately there was a queue at every one of them so I joined the shortest.

"Hi Dave! Been doing some shopping? How's things?"

The voice belonged to a neighbour who I hadn't spotted in the queue in front of me due to concentrating on the severe pain I was experiencing.

With gritted teeth, "Mmmmm!" was my answer every time he asked me something.

I couldn't get home fast enough to run yet another hot bath.

I shall bear it in mind that if ever I become afflicted with piles ever again then a ride on the bike might be a useful temporary remedy.

I fell asleep instructing myself that never again must I suffer from piles!

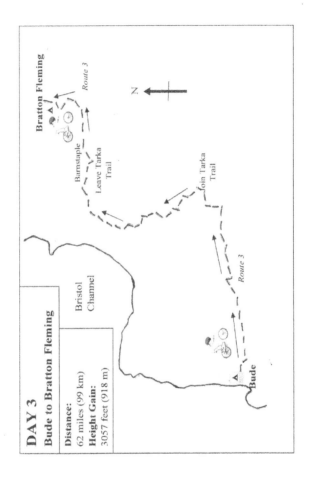

Day 3 – On the trail of the Otter

I was off at seven as usual to mixed cloud and blue sky. Fortunately the newsagent come general dealer was open so I had a chance to replenish my emergency food store. There was another roller coaster ride for the first twenty five miles before a wonderful downhill stretch of about two miles to the Tarka Trail.

Just before the downhill stretch I passed through the little village of Sheepwash with its quaint houses and thatched roofs. The local general dealer sold warm pies and cold drinks. A stop and rest was called for to refuel. I started to enjoy the refuelling stops as sampling the local pies and pasties fast became an addictive habit but I kept this pie for later! The clouds had all but disappeared and another warm day lay ahead.

The Tarka Trail is an old railway track, named after Tarka the otter and runs between South and North Devon. I joined it about twenty six miles south of Barnstaple where I would eventually leave the Tarka Trail to once again join the hills. The gradient was slightly up for about three miles and just before the summit there was another tea shop. I nearly missed it but caught sight of a little advertising board through the corner of my eye which read – *Teas and snacks for Cyclists.*

But it was only a few miles ago that I bought a pie and soft drink. Anyway I didn't need my arm twisting, turned around, parked my bike and went inside.

The building which incorporated the cafe was old with lots of junk lying about. Another old building was being renovated into a bunk house and the garden had miscellaneous plant pots here and there. A couple of tents in the long grass must have been the accommodation for the workers. The business looked as though it had only just opened and the owners were still finding their feet.

A young man, whom I assumed to be a student doing some vacation work, asked me what I wanted and put the kettle on. He made a huge fuss over me and showed a great deal of interest in my adventure then chucked a tea bag, which he presumed was ordinary tea because he wasn't sure, into a pot and asked me if I took milk. He passed me a half full small jug; I chose a piece of very crumbly but delicious homemade flapjack off a plate; gave him about £2 for the lot and retired to a picnic table outside. The table wobbled on the newly laid surface which wasn't as level as it should have been and slopped tea in the saucer every time I laid an elbow on it. A stone kicked beneath one of the legs remedied the situation.

It was a glorious day, lots of other cyclists began to arrive and the young man appeared to be by himself. This caused him to become flustered and a bit pushed to cope. I poured my tea and topped it up with some milk out of the jug which unfortunately came out accompanied by large white lumps. However it didn't taste sour and I didn't have it in me to ask for some fresh milk.

The tea didn't taste too bad and I was soon on my way. I'd now reached the summit of the old railway and it continued gently down for the next fifteen miles. About every mile or so there was a mosaic sculpture, made by local school children which depicted various prehistoric animals. The sculptures then gave way to wood carvings of people sitting in random positions on benches. Lonely figures looking sad, courting couples with their arms around each other and mothers with small children on their laps.

A few miles down the Trail I came to a small car park. As I waited to cross the road which led into the car park the Google Street View car passed with cameras on the end of a huge telescopic pole sticking out of its roof. I may now be on Google Street View for people throughout the world to see! I could have been somewhere I shouldn't have been or with someone I shouldn't have been with. Big Brother is definitely watching us all now!

The going was now very fast as I took full advantage of the gentle descent towards the coast at Bideford. As I passed through a gate, three young men were cycling towards me and waited for me passing through. The first two acknowledged my 'thank you' but the third stared in amazement, pointed and shouted '*King of the Mountains*' , he'd recognised the Tour de France shirt I was wearing. I acknowledged his observation and punched the air with a resounding 'YES' in acknowledgement!

I couldn't resist stopping at a mobile snack bar next to a building site. My plan was to buy a cup of tea, in a polystyrene mug with lid, cycle to the next available seat and have the tea with my now cold pie bought in Sheepwash a few hours earlier. I wedged the madly hot mug of tea in my handlebar bag and started to ride off. Unfortunately the tea just slopped all over inside the bag containing my valuables so I made a quick decision to sit on one of the chairs supplied by the snack bar and sip my way through the tea. I left the pie until later and chatted to a young apprentice electrician from the building site waiting for 24 burgers and 24 teas he'd been sent out for. We chatted for ages about his aspirations for travel and how he would love to cycle LEJOG. He wished me luck as he disappeared into the building site with a box full of burgers and teas. I found a seat half a mile along the track to enjoy my cold pie.

I seemed to fly towards Barnstaple and the Tarka Trail was now just a memory. On the other side of Barnstaple I could see the hills again. It was now almost up all the way to Bratton Fleming, a small village on the edge of Exmoor.

I crossed the river on the wrong bridge which took me away from my planned route. However the signs were good and pointed in the right direction for me to meet up with my planned route. I cycled along a promenade and in amongst cafes where people sat enjoying tea and scones. I wasn't tempted having just satisfied my lust for food and fluid.

I knew that near my next campsite there was no pub so I needed to make sure I had enough food to cook a meal that night. As I entered Bratton Fleming I looked around for a general dealer but couldn't see any. I asked a lady pruning her roses where the shop was. She looked in the direction – downhill – pointed down and said, "Just past the garage! It's steep mind!"

She was right, the hill was very steep. I stocked up with milk, a can of lager out of the fridge, because they had no cold bitter, and a few other luxuries. Why I bought a can of lager I have no idea because I can't stand the gassy stuff. I asked the owner which was the quickest way to the campsite.

"Only a couple of miles along the main road."

The only trouble was that the main road was about half a mile at the top of this very steep hill. I pushed all the way to the top passing the lady pruning roses on the way up who smiled and said, "I told you it was steep!"

I'd stuffed all the provisions I'd bought under the flap on one of my panniers which made the back of the bike a little heavy on one side. The rear end swayed which was worrying when freewheeling at speed down the hills. The whole pannier moved from side to side which unnervingly knocked me slightly off balance.

A couple of miles along the main road I spotted the sign for the campsite. Unfortunately it only displayed a caravan and not a tent but was only two hundred yards down the lane to the left. There was also a second sign, which displayed both tent and caravan but read eight miles. I opted to try the one two hundred yards away.

The owner was sympathetic to my cause and showed me to a quiet little spot in a corner. When I removed my pannier bags I discovered why the bike had an uncanny sway. The nuts and bolts securing the pannier to the bike frame had worked loose and the whole pannier was in danger of falling off. A quick fix with a screwdriver and Allen key remedied the problem. This is something else I'll need to keep my eye on!

I asked the couple in a nearby caravan if they would charge my batteries, had a wonderful shower and thought it was time to wash my socks, 'King of the Mountains' shirt and cycling 'paddypad' underpants.

I did my washing by taking it into the shower with me. If I was at the campsite before 4pm there was enough warmth in the sun to dry them. However this particular afternoon there was no wind and the sky had long since clouded over. Rain was forecast for tomorrow.

Tomorrow will be my last day in Devon and thankfully goodbye to the roller coaster countryside. The owner of the general dealers in Bratton Fleming informed me that the route over Exmoor involved a long gentle climb then several level miles across the top of the moor before heading down into a valley.

After my meal of Pasta 'n' Sauce I spent some time reading, collected my batteries then turned in. The rain started almost immediately.

Unfortunately my socks, shirt and inner shorts were still soaked after being washed and there was no way they would dry before morning. I laid them out under my karimat, placed my towel over them then placed the karimat on top. This was in the hope that the weight and heat of my body would dry them as much as possible. I was asleep just after 9pm.

Since I started the ride three days ago I'd been fortunate enough not to have needed to go to the loo in the middle of the night, probably due to being dehydrated. At about 3am with the rain rattling off the tent without any consideration for the occupant I woke up desperately needing a pee.

Now I always sleep totally naked in a sleeping bag the theory being that the heat from your body warms up the sleeping bag more efficiently than if you wear clothes. Anyway, that's what I'd read somewhere and it does work as long as you have a good quality sleeping bag.

Normally when it's dark I'd just kneel out of the tent away from the door to find relief or slip on a pair of shorts, a T shirt and some flip flops and take a trip to the loo. Unfortunately the loo was about a hundred metres away and there was no way I was sticking anything out of the tent in that rain.

In the absence of a pee bottle there was only one answer, have a pee under the fly sheet. I would be gone in the morning so wouldn't have to live in a 'loo' for any length of time. The big problems were that to pee as far away from the inner door as possible I would practically have to lie down as the roof slopes away to the front of the tent and also I store my bike under the fly sheet at night.

I searched for my head torch but had foolishly forgotten to put it in an easily obtainable place in case I needed it. I couldn't spend any time searching in the dark as I was now really desperate.

I unzipped the inner door and crawled naked over my bike trying to avoid the oily and sharp parts. To get the bike under the fly sheet I had to lie the bike down, push it in backwards then stand the front wheel up which partially blocked the inner door. There was no problem getting in and out under normal circumstances but trying to position oneself around the bike and to avoid peeing on it, especially the seat and handlebars was a contortion.

I eventually managed to get myself into a successful position, leaning on my left elbow to lower my head and naked back away from the cold wet fly sheet. My left knee was on the ground and resting behind to lower my groin and my right leg was on the other side of my bike with my right foot on the ground to raise the essential parts about twenty centimetres off the grass. I used my right hand to guide the procedure away from my bike seat. What a relief, all I needed to do now was to reverse the contortion and return to the warmth of my sleeping bag. The backwards crawl into my tent was infinitely easier.

I'd thought about taking a pee bottle but that just meant something else to carry and it wasn't an essential part of the equipment, just a bit of luxury.

Several years ago I was the support team driving a minibus for the Billingham Branch of Sunderland Supporters Association. About sixty members of the Association, aged from eight upwards, each year towards the end of the season walk from their home town of Billingham to The Stadium of Light, about 40 miles, to raise money for a nominated charity. They were short of a support team one year so I volunteered to drive the minibus to carry their bags and supply them with a brew and snacks every few miles. Also to pick up anyone who was struggling to keep up the pace.

Three miles from their destination they always stop at a local pub to change into their Sunderland regalia and oil their stomachs with a few pints. I also managed a few pints of orange juice, since I was driving, which flows through the body in exactly the same way as ale.

From here on my task was to shadow the walkers in the minibus and pick up anyone unable to progress any further. Having just walked almost 40 miles overnight, legs start to stiffen up and the whole body becomes a little weary especially after an hour or more sitting around in a pub at ten in the morning.

I parked in side streets bustling with shoppers and waited for the group to pass. My final temporary stop was on the southern outskirts of the city centre. There was no parking for a minibus between here and the Stadium car park on the north side of the city. I was now desperate for a pee. There was nowhere to go except at the Stadium and the walkers hadn't passed me yet. The desperation turned to agony. It was now essential that I use the loo.

'A bottle! That's what I need.' The only bottles in the minibus were unopened except for those in the rubbish bags. I rummaged through the rubbish and found that there were only empty 330ml bottles. I retrieved one and knelt down behind the piled up bags when there was a knock on the minibus door. It was one of the boys. Terrifying thoughts ran through my head – I'm going to pee myself – he's dropped out of the walk and needs a lift – I can't last another twenty minutes before parking at the Stadium.

I opened the door and asked him if he'd had enough.

He said "No! I need my season ticket out of my bag." I smiled and gasped with relief!

He retrieved his season ticket and rejoined the group. I was now bent double with pain. Resumed my kneeling position, unscrewed the cap on the bottle and felt the greatest release of pressure that I have ever experienced. The flow continued and I had no feeling whatsoever of it diminishing. I watched the empty space before the absolute top of the bottle shrink rapidly.

I needed another bottle, but the rubbish bag was over six feet away from me and I'd need to pinch myself to stop the pee, crawl on three limbs, open the bag with my left hand – I'm right handed – retrieve another bottle – unscrew the cap with one hand then continue to fill it.

There was now 3cm...2cm...1cm of space left when the final drops filled the original bottle to the absolute brim. I wouldn't need the second bottle. The cap was screwed on tightly and the bottle returned to the rubbish bag. I gave a huge sigh of relief, sat back in the driving seat and continued to The Stadium of Light with a huge smile on my face. I am now confident that whenever I need a pee bottle that I should ensure that it is in excess of 330ml!

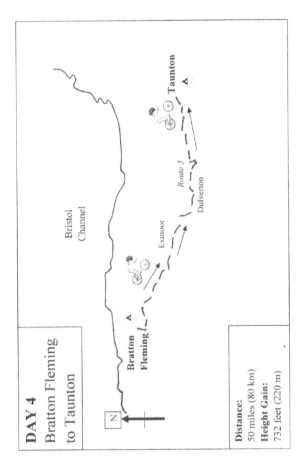

DAY 4
Bratton Fleming
to Taunton

Bristol
Channel

Bratton
Fleming

Exmoor

Route 3

Dulverton

Taunton

N

Distance:
50 miles (80 km)
Height Gain:
732 feet (220 m)

Day 4 – Lonely Terrain

The rain was still pounding off the tent when I awoke at half five. I knew the first part of my journey would be difficult. The highest climb I would make so far, nearly up to five hundred metres across the top of Exmoor, although Bratton Fleming sits at more than half this height. I lay half awake for about ten minutes then forced myself to leap into action, well gradually sat up and unzipped my sleeping bag. I slept with my new silk liner inside the sleeping bag last night and wore my spare pair of dry socks. It was cold. The theory about sleeping naked doesn't seem to apply to feet. I rolled over and took out my clean shirt and socks from beneath the karimat. Much of the moisture had been absorbed by my towel but they were still wet and cold. I just had to put them on. If this is done quickly, like plunging into a cold pool or stream, then the shock is immediate and minimal and it's over and done with much quicker.

Shorts, shirt then jacket and waterproof jacket then socks and shoes were very quickly put on and in next to no time I felt invigorated then warm. I went through my usual routine and was ready to go by quarter to seven. My shampoo was beginning to run out so after a top up from the soap dispenser in the loo I was on my way.

Just before I set off the rain decided to give me a break and stop. It held off for about half an hour. As I gained height onto Exmoor I could see more of the hills all around. Clouds were forming over them all. The road began to steepen and after only four miles I was walking. I must have walked for about two miles uphill before the gradient began to ease. I checked the altitude on my GPS; it read 492 metres at its peak then gradually started to reduce. I couldn't believe that I had reached the top, the hard part for at least the next twenty miles was complete. The rain now meant business and judging by the dark clouds ahead of me it looked as though bad weather would dominate for a few hours if not for the rest of the day. The road was now fairly level across the top of Exmoor. I felt really exposed to the elements. A few ponies nibbled at the grass by the side of the road unconcerned by the bleak weather. Years ago when on holiday in Devon we enjoyed a BBQ washing it down with the help of some scrumpy cider. I allowed my thirteen year old son a glass full which encouraged him to partake in some strange activities. One of which was to lean over the gate of a nearby field and kiss a horse full on, on the lips. He's never ventured anywhere near scrumpy cider since. That reminded me that my next campsite is on a cider farm!

Later during the same holiday my niece's husband stood behind an Exmoor pony. He patted it gently on the rump and it gave him an almighty kick in the balls. He's never stood behind a horse since.

Thunder rumbled loudly overhead which added to my need to get off this exposed road. There was no shelter at all for about twenty miles. I passed a workman sitting in his truck by some crossroads, no doubt waiting for his mates to arrive. He gave me a confused glance! The time was nearly eight o'clock. There were no buildings or houses, just me, my bike and my belongings battling against the torrential rain and the rumbles of thunder.

Some of the puddles were now small ponds. Any incline in the road developed a flood of water. I kept pedalling hard. Almost every minute I thought, 'What if I got a puncture? What if I had an accident?' The road ahead beckoned me to follow it for mile after mile. There were too many negative thoughts going through my head. I must concentrate on the task in hand and forget about these disagreeable daydreams. I knew nothing about what might lie ahead. There were no trees, not a wall or a fence or even a derelict building anywhere. Fortunately what little wind there was pushed me along and the road had a gentle descent to it. Even though the curtains of rain made sure I got a thorough soaking I felt as though I was making good progress. Eventually lone trees began to grow by the side of the road and a few stone walls appeared; a barn then a farm. I was approaching civilisation. The road started to descend quickly as I headed down towards Dulverton. I had covered almost thirty miles in two and a half hours. It was time for a rest but not until I reached civilization.

Unfortunately Dulverton was a little off the route so I pressed on until I came to Bampton, the next village directly on my route. The sky continued to ensure the day remained thoroughly miserable with relentless rain and the odd clap of thunder just to remind everyone who really was in charge.

A Spar shop shone out in the darkened village, fantastic, they'll have sandwiches and biscuits and all sorts of things to eat and drink. However, this particular one turned out to be a real bonus, hot pasties and hot drinks from a machine. I stocked up with sandwiches, cake and biscuits then bought a hot pasty and a cup of hot drinking chocolate. This was a very pleasant village to have found a quiet seat and soak up the local atmosphere while enjoying a snack. That wasn't an option under the dark, wet skies and I needed to find somewhere dry out of the wind and rain. Across the road from the Spar shop was an old Coaching Inn with a covered entrance designed for coaches and horses to stop and off load their passengers under cover from years gone by. This was my sanctuary for the next twenty minutes while I enjoyed my hot pasty and drinking chocolate.

The pasty was delicious but I mentally criticised the quality of the drinking chocolate for being watery. On finishing the liquid I noticed that I'd foolishly forgotten to stir it and ended up with a cup half full of chocolate sludge. I raked it out with my finger and ate it. After all, I needed all the calories I could consume, but truthfully I hate wasting money!

After a well earned rest and now re-fuelled I headed off along Route 3 which was yet again uphill struggle. However I knew that as down meant up to follow, then up meant down to follow and I was soon relishing the delights of tearing down a narrow lane which curved from side to side totally enclosed by an eight foot high hawthorn hedge. I was flying once again and leaning from side to side made me think of skiing down a cat track in the Alps. It was fantastic. My speed increased as I took full advantage of the descent and also the rain had stopped which added even more pleasure to my folly.

The wind whistled through my helmet when without any warning, as I rounded a bend, there pounding towards me were a dozen cows of all shapes and sizes totally blocking the lane. In fact they were squashed into the eight foot wide road. On seeing me they stopped dead in their tracks and stared at me with an evil yet puzzled look in their eyes. They made no sound, just stared. At the same time I squeezed my brakes and skidded to a halt and stared at them. We were about twenty metres apart and it was a showdown. There was no way that I was going back up the hill to find a cow free route and they weren't showing any signs of moving voluntarily. Whilst farmers handle cows on a daily basis and know exactly what to do, I am no farmer and am absolutely clueless as to the correct procedure to move a dozen cows blocking a narrow lane. Normally if I crossed a field with cows they would be content eating and chewing grass so wouldn't be bothered, but these critters just stared! Were they thinking 'Get him girls?' Or were they as uncomfortable with the situation as I was?

I decided that I must be strong and daring for timidly shouting 'Shoo! Shoo!' at them would undoubtedly have little effect. I asked myself, 'What do the professionals do to get cows to move?

They shout 'Harrr...Harrr', aggressively towards them.' I feared that any aggressiveness shown by me might backfire on me and force them to attack.

I plucked up courage and without sounding feeble shouted 'Harrr.....Harrrr!'

I was astounded; they turned immediately and started ambling off in the direction they came from. I felt in charge now so I shouted again and they moved faster. I released my brakes and freewheeled downhill after them. I shouted again, this time a little louder and they started to run. This was fantastic; I wouldn't have to make a detour. I kept up my bravado and continued to shout louder. The slimmer cows were now way out in front but the fat one at the back was definitely having trouble keeping up. There was a fork in the road ahead; I noticed a blue Sustrans Route 3 sign on a post pointing towards the left. I shouted at the cows. "**Harrr.....Harrr.... but not left, do not go left**," as if they would understand, but I was hopeful. They were now running and as sod's law dictates, turned left when they came to the fork. The road went uphill and the fat one at the back started to wheeze.

'Bloody hell' I thought, 'I hope it doesn't collapse.'

They were now at full gallop, udders swinging in all directions. I was pedalling normally but still had the upper hand and continued shouting cowboy style. There was a right hand turn in the road ahead which also had a Sustrans sign on it, this time towards the right. If they turn right I could be stuck behind them for miles. I had visions of following a herd of cows all the way to John o'Groats. Suddenly they disappeared to the left and went through an open gate, which I presumed was where they'd escaped from, back into a field. I felt both victorious and relieved that the cows were now safely back in their field and that I'd managed to get them there. After securing the gate I smugly continued to the right and along the lane singing the chorus to Rawhide, ' Head 'em up, move 'em out...................Yee—Haa!'

The road now disappeared through a dark gorge where any sunlight couldn't penetrate. At least I thought it was dark until I realised that I was wearing my dark sunglasses with the combined bifocals. I removed them and magically the gorge became much lighter.

The route dropped down into Taunton. I was now free of the hills of Devon and Cornwall and could now look forward to several days without any significant climbs.

I joined a canal towpath and kept a lookout for my next campsite at Tanpits cider farm. The route I'd programmed into my GPS should take me directly to the campsite. Unfortunately when it ran out there was no sign of any campsite. I looked around and decided to search the area by leaving the canal. Fortunately I bumped into a small group of cyclists heading towards me so asked them if they knew of the campsite. Unbelievably they had once stayed there and directed me to it.

They told me that they were on their way to Bristol to take part in an overnight challenge from Bristol to Exeter, a distance of 200 miles which has to be completed in twenty four hours.

I thanked them and headed off on their directed route only to have forgotten most of their instructions after our conversation. I managed to find the pub they mentioned but after that my mind was just blank so I ventured into the pub and asked some people sitting near the door where I could find Tanpits Campsite. The regulation middle aged drunk wearing a tweed jacket and cravat, who spoke with marbles in his mouth, looked at me as if to say 'Any fool knows where that is!' Stood up, swayed around a little while waving his arms about then rudely asked, "Why? Who the hell wants to know?"

Fortunately his colleagues weren't so obstinate and pointed me in the right direction for Tanpits Farm Campsite.

When I found it, it wasn't obvious that the place was a campsite but looked more like a working farm. The campsite sign was hidden high up in a tree covered by the season's new foliage. I cautiously rode in and looked around for a suitable door to knock on. A sign on a probable door read:

Knock and wait. If no answer ring the bell.

I knocked several times only to awaken and annoy a few scruffy looking dogs inside. I then tried the bell and waited. I find it's always frustrating to press a doorbell when you can't hear the outcome. No 'Bing Bong' or 'Buzzzzz...' or any evidence that the person at the receiving end has heard you. I pressed the bell again and about ten minutes later a grumpy looking teenage girl appeared, dressed in horse riding gear and wearing green wellies covered in horse muck. Neither a smile nor any information about where the showers were situated or if I needed to pay for them were forthcoming, so I asked. She pointed to the shower block, recited off a few rules about not using the showers or wash-basins to wash your dishes in then said the showers only take tokens which are 50p each. I asked for two. She took my money and told me where to camp.

The farm yard was full of rusty old farm machinery and a few dilapidated cars, but tidy, as was the camping area. The grass had been cut around the masses of rusting metal objects placed in random places around the campsite. There was one field for static caravans and tourers and another field over a bridge for tents and tourers. I counted about a dozen peacocks wandering about in all sorts of locations. They were on top of roofs and walls and rummaging around the dilapidated cars and machinery. There were also about the same number of cockerels as well as about twenty rabbits at home running and playing around the camping area.

I found a suitable spot which hopefully wouldn't collapse in the middle of the night due to underground workings and unpacked my soggy belongings.

Everything except my sleeping bag and spare clothes were wet. Even my matches that were wrapped in a plastic bag were wet. The GPS had condensation on the inside as did my camera. My mobile phone which was switched off suddenly started switching itself on, that too must be wet inside.

I removed the batteries from them all and that night slept with the phone, camera and GPS inside my sleeping bag. I remembered doing that on our expedition to the Himalayas when my video camera got wet. It worked and dried out overnight so I was optimistic about my camera, GPS and phone. If the GPS stopped working then I'd have a difficult job finding many of the routes as it was all programmed in and to save weight I wasn't carrying any detailed maps.....Fingers crossed!

My bike and pannier bags were thick with mud from the day's exploits and I luckily found a hose attached to a very powerful water supply beside the shower block. A good five minutes blast brought a shine back to them.

After a good hot shower including muddy laundry for which I only needed one token I found a local shop for milk and biscuits then walked round to the pub for a bar meal. The irritating drunk had left, probably to sleep off his afternoon's binge. A welcome meal and drink relaxed me just enough for the gentle walk back to the campsite before being well tucked in before 9 o'clock.

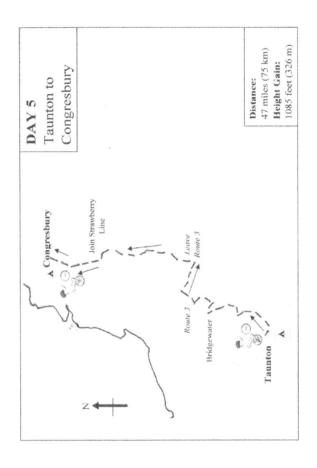

DAY 5
Taunton to
Congresbury

Congresbury

Join Strawberry
Line

Leave
Route 3

Route 3

Bridgewater

Taunton

N

Distance:
47 miles (75 km)
Height Gain:
1085 feet (326 m)

Day 5 – Canals and Strawberries

I've never been woken up by so much noise! If you've ever heard a peacock at five in the morning then you'll know what I mean. They make the loudest penetrating sound of any bird I can think of. Add to that the other eleven then add to that the cockerels competing with one another and you can guess what a din it was. I did not doze this morning. The farmer, his family and the resident campers must be immune to the noise. I followed my routine then emerged from my tent. The air was still, after the deluge of rain yesterday and throughout most of the night. The sky was thankfully clear of cloud. The twenty or so rabbits I'd seen merrily prancing around the campsite yesterday had multiplied over night. There must have been almost a hundred of them. They were everywhere. Surprisingly though, my pitch had not been undermined and I hadn't disappeared into a maze of warrens.

The first few miles of my journey today was on the Taunton to Bridgewater canal towpath and altogether I only had about fifty miles to cover.

I'd planned each stage to fit in with where the campsites were. I generally tried to plan each campsite to be on average about 100km (60 – 70 miles) journey but some of the stages were either much longer or much shorter than I would have liked. Originally I wanted to camp at Clevedon but on making enquiries at the tourist information office all of the 'Campsites' around Clevedon only took caravans and not tents. *See Table 2 for planned stages.*

By quarter to seven I was all packed and on my way. Having worked out where the campsite was in relation to the canal towpath it only took about five minutes before I was heading east beside the Taunton to Bridgewater canal. The tow path out of Taunton was well kept. The reflection of swans slowly gliding along the canal provided a perfect mirror image. I desperately tried to take a photograph, but as soon as I stopped they swam towards me thinking that I had some tasty crumbs for them. I passed a cob and his mate with five cygnets on the nest. It was a pleasure to see nature being allowed to develop without some irresponsible morons feeling the need to destroy it.

This canal must be one of the best kept secrets of Britain's Waterways. It's well off the busy canal routes around Bristol then north to Gloucester or around Bath then east to London. The towpaths are well kept and maintained by local volunteers who obviously take pride in their project. The sound of canal boats is barely audible as their speed, complying with waterway rules, is barely 3 miles per hour. When overtaking one I felt that I had supreme advantage over the crawling craft as I raced along at 12mph. Leaving them far behind often exchanging a wave and a smile as I passed.

Crossing the canal are many bridges. The modern design is comprised of iron girders resting on pillars on either side of the canal. This provides an easy underpass over head height for all towpath users including cyclists, whereas the original bridges are arched and low. Where the towpath goes under them, the canal narrows and the towpath drops to almost water level. This is to avoid towpath users having to duck too much. The towpath surface is also cobbled under the bridges to enhance grip at the most perilous part. However these wonderful original bridges and underpasses were designed for small ponies accompanied by their bargees over a hundred years ago and not for modern day cyclists. I remember encountering my first arched bridge, confidently cycling along with a good yard or two of grassy bank between me and the murky canal when the towpath dropped steeply and narrowed to about a yard to squeeze under the bridge arch. My wheels were now only a foot from the water's edge unnervingly wobbly on the well worn cobble stones beneath the bridge while I needed to duck down at the same time to avoid bouncing my head off the stone arch. I had to keep my speed up otherwise an overbalance would have definitely resulted in me, my bike and belongings taking a deep cold plunge. I needed to fight hard to keep the bike moving straight before emerging out of the other side breathing a huge sigh of relief having held my breath throughout. In future I must slow down before a bridge, survey the situation then get off and walk if it looks too dangerous. It's also impossible to see if anyone is coming the other way, so if two cyclists found themselves face to face under the bridge, there is little doubt that one of them, if not both, would take the plunge.

Before cycling on canal towpaths a permit is required, although it is freely available over the internet from British Waterways, one of the rules clearly states:

Dismount before bridges and walk.

Although I had a permit well before the ride, I only read this rule several weeks after the ride. I would have been wise to have read and absorbed the rules beforehand. They are there for a reason.

The peace was broken by the sound of the engine belonging to a strange Heath Robinson invention paddling towards me. It reminded me of something welded together to partake in a scene from the film 'Waterworld'. It looked a bit like an adapted World War II landing craft and was designed to rid the canal of encroaching weed. Further back along the canal I'd noticed copious quantities of weed piled high at the side of the canal. I now knew how they got there. This contraption was propelled by paddle wheels at the side. At the front was a rotating cutter, similar to that on the front of a Combine Harvester but rotated the other way, scooping the weed out of the canal then depositing it via a conveyor belt into the open vessel which stored the unwelcome growth. When the container became full, the contraption parked up at the side of the canal and the whole container lifted up and tilted to the side depositing huge piles of weed on the canal bank.

It was eleven and a half miles along the towpath before I had to turn off to avoid cycling into the centre of Bridgewater. I was totally engrossed in the beautiful surroundings and ease of cycling along the towpath and cycled straight past my turning.

When I checked my GPS and realised that I'd cycled about two miles too far I thought the best plan would be to retrace my tracks. The Bridgewater part of the canal towpath was not as well kept as the Taunton part. It was overgrown with long grass and weeds all about three to four feet high and full of seeds all ready to depart from their stems. The recent overnight rain kept the undergrowth very wet and as I cycled along I was quite often engulfed by the encroaching jungle.

I met a local out walking his dog coming towards me. He almost broke down laughing at me as I approached him.

He said, 'You'll be sprouting in a minute!' I wondered what he meant.

I was covered in wet seeds from my waist down. As I pushed my way along the path, the millions of seeds on the undergrowth had stuck to my wet shorts, legs, shoes and socks and I looked a bit like a giant sprig of millet. I couldn't even brush them off because everything was wet. I just had to wait until I had dried out.

The local asked me where I was going. I told him that I'd missed my turn and should be heading towards Glastonbury. He offered plenty of options to help me find a route out of Bridgewater, none of which I understood. I thanked him and started to get on my way until he thought of a better way .... which I didn't understand either. I thanked him again at which point he stopped me and offered a different alternative. Eventually I managed to politely prise myself away and followed the planned route on my GPS.

I continued following the GPS route down a lane for about a mile which ran parallel to a canal but not next to it. Unfortunately the lane came to an abrupt end at a field but the route on my GPS continued. I asked a passing dog walker if there was a path over the field and he assured me that there was a path by the edge of the field and would bring me out on a road. I walked for a couple of hundred yards but I could only push my bike. This can't be right. I consulted my GPS again and magnified the scale. I couldn't believe my incompetence. The route shown on the GPS was on the other side of the canal. I now had two options to cross the canal. Walk along the edge of the field for a further two miles to reach a road which eventually crossed the canal or retrace my trail once again and hope to find a bridge nearby.

I turned around and retraced my tracks. I was in luck. A few hundred yards after I rejoined the dead end lane there was a wall on the canal side with a gap that led to a bridge with a cycle channel by the side of the steps. I crossed the bridge and to my great relief spotted the NCN sign which read Route 3 to Glastonbury. I was, after losing the way twice, back on the correct route.

I spotted Glastonbury Tor in the distance which rises steeply from the Somerset Levels and knew that I needed to turn left before I reached it. Visions of thousands of people descending on these parts in a few weeks time for the Glastonbury Festival seemed out of place in this beautiful rural region.

Coming towards me were other cyclists of all ages, first in small groups of two or three, then in larger groups, then in a continuous line. Once the continuous line started it never seemed to stop or break. There must have been about two thousand cyclists altogether. People of all ages and all sizes were taking part in whatever this event was. I noticed the British Heart Foundation motif on lots of T- shirts. This was obviously their annual national fund raising event. When I phoned my wife that evening she confirmed that a similar event had taken place in the North East.

Almost everyone who passed waved and shouted 'Hi!' all with a smile. I must have returned the greeting for well over an hour. I felt like a celebrity.

Eventually I found my planned route and turned off NCN Route 3 and headed north towards Congresbury. I made the decision to bypass Bristol to the south as I didn't particularly want to cycle through the city.

I picked up my route passing through many very pretty villages which eventually brought me to Axbridge, the home of King John's hunting lodge built around 1500 and restored by The National Trust in 1971. Having not encountered any tea shops yet I was in need of an injection of energy from my supplies so I parked my bike next to a seat which I shared with another cyclist overlooking the lodge. Being Sunday, he was just out for the day, exploring The Strawberry Line.

It was just after this that I also joined 'The Strawberry Line', the route of an old railway which takes its name from the transportation by rail of the famous Cheddar strawberries many years ago.

At one stage the route passes through a long curved tunnel where one end can't be seen from the other. However it is lit by cats-eyes set into the track itself. Towards the end of the tunnel a family was walking just ahead of me when the man who I presumed to be the father, stood to one side and instructed his family to also stand to the side as he shouted, 'Make way for the 'King of the Mountains''. He was the second person to recognise the white shirt with red polka dots. We chatted for a while and he and his family were impressed that they had met someone who was actually cycling from Land's End to John o'Groats. Once again for no particular reason I felt famous and important. They asked how they could sponsor me as they hadn't any money on them. I gave them a blog card and hoped that they would. He was a keen cyclist and was travelling to the Alps to watch the Tour de France in July.

This area must be popular with keen cyclists because further along the track I encountered someone else who recognised the shirt and shouted the exact same phrase to his son – 'Make way for the King of the Mountains'. There was no way that I could come anywhere near to being 'King of the Mountains' but wearing the shirt was certainly a talking point and became a focus to meet many different people.

The Strawberry Line crosses a road at Congresbury which was my destination for the day. This village is apparently named after St Congar who travelled across the Bristol Channel from Pembrokeshire in 500AD. He reputedly thrust his staff into the ground on Cadbury Hill, behind the village, where he founded a monastery. The resulting Yew Tree that sprouted from his staff can still be seen to this day! The campsite at Oak Farm was easy to find, as it is on the Line, and I checked in at about half one. It was a warm, breezy day which was ideal for drying out my wet gear from the previous day. The grass around my tent became strewn with my wet belongings. I even managed to dry out the matches.

I asked the owner if the pub I passed did bar meals for which he answered favourably. I felt as though I'd had an easy day, no hills, good weather and lots of tow paths and old railway tracks to cycle along which kept me away from traffic.

After a good rest and a leisurely drying and sorting of gear it soon turned 6pm so I made my way along to the pub for a bar meal dressed in my evening wear; shorts, Great North Run T shirt and flip flops. Sandwich boards outside advertised speciality dishes which was encouraging. I asked at the bar if they served bar meals.

The waiter looked at me with a puzzled, questioning, stare. 'Bar Meals?'

'Yes! Do you do bar meals?' I answered with another question.

'Yes sir! This is a Greek restaurant and we do meals!' he replied. 'Do you want a meal?'

I replied 'Yes' and he showed me to a table.

There were couples having candle lit dinners after a hard day at work or indulging in a secret romantic interlude while others were celebrating special occasions in this classy restaurant. And there I was dressed in my camping clothes looking for a cheap bar meal.

Up until now I'd either eaten bar meals or cooked my own pasta in the evenings and usually spent no more than about £8 in a pub for a meal and a pint of beer.

The cheapest meal on the menu here was £12.95 for what looked like fried potato, sausage and scrambled egg mixed together with a few herbs thrown in for good measure and to add an exotic flavour plus £3.10 for a pint of bitter. Now that I was seated at a table I supposed I'd better order as long as I didn't walk into a Greek restaurant every night.

The waiter was quite friendly and quizzed me about my T shirt.

'What is BUPA Great North Run?' he asked with a Greek accent.

Whether he was Greek or not was debateable but the accent made the restaurant feel more authentic!

I gave him a run down on the Great North Run and BUPA.

And 'Where did you get that strange accent?' he quizzed!

He obviously recognised that I was not from Somerset and maybe nor was he by the sound of his accent!

A group of children appeared from a different room dressed for a birthday party. This was a far cry from the birthday parties enjoyed by my children many years ago at home with sausage rolls and egg sandwiches for tea.

Tonight is my sixth night under canvas and tomorrow I will have been cycling for a week. The time has flown by and because I've been getting up early the days have seemed full. I've enjoyed the cycling even though through Devon and Cornwall it has been hard at times, I've also enjoyed the rests and have never been bored.

It's a longer haul tomorrow, from Congresbury to Norton, north of Gloucester. The whole journey seems to be mostly quite flat. I collected my rechargeable batteries, kindly recharged by the campsite owner and it didn't take me long to doze off just after 9 o'clock.

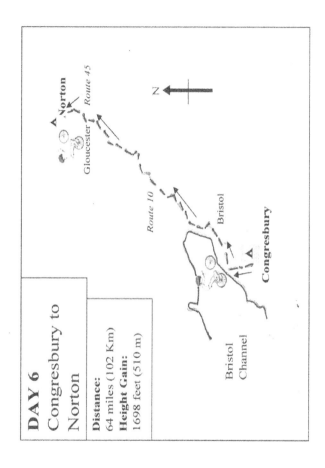

DAY 6
Congresbury to
Norton

Distance:
64 miles (102 Km)
Height Gain:
1698 feet (510 m)

Bristol
Channel

Congresbury

Bristol

Route 10

Gloucester

Norton

Route 45

N

Day 6 - In Bore Country

A perfectly clear and cloudless night made the early morning rise a cold one. For six in the morning there was a lot of traffic on the nearby road. I was on my way by seven and replenished my food stock at a nearby garage shop before rejoining the Strawberry Line. I asked for some 'meths' and the man behind the counter gave me a puzzled stare and uttered the word made famous by Manuel in 'Fawlty Towers'... 'Que?' He was foreign and obviously hadn't a clue what I was talking about. I told him that it didn't matter and left.

After only ten minutes I arrived at the end of the Strawberry Line at Yatton station and now needed to follow the route on my GPS towards the Avon Cycleway which is Route 41.

Once on this route it was well signposted taking me over the Avon Bridge which is also the M5 motorway. When in a car travelling over such huge bridges there is neither a feeling of height nor exposure as all you see is the road and possibly the distant view well out to the side. However, when on a bicycle there is a totally different aspect. The cycle track was on the right hand side of the bridge going from south to north; I was facing the oncoming traffic which was on the opposite side of the barrier to my left. The noise was quite deafening. The cycle track was about six feet wide. There was a railing to my right with open vertical bars followed by fresh air for a few hundred feet down to the River Avon. The bridge was almost a mile long and at that height there was an unnerving cross wind.

The exposure to fast oncoming traffic and the noise it generates plus a violent cross wind and the exposure created by the height are very daunting and not for the faint hearted. I was pleased to get over even though I had to stop and take a few photographs. A cyclist passed coming towards me with his head well down. No doubt he felt the same as me even though it looked as though he crossed the bridge regularly.

The sun was bright now so I wore my dark sunglasses with the clipped in bifocals which unfortunately made the map on the GPS a little dark. This worked fine out in the countryside as it was easy to follow the yellow line which showed the route I had programmed in. However in the towns and more road congested areas the yellow line just seemed to mingle with all the other colours, especially 'A' roads which are coloured red.

I was now in very busy Shirehampton, East of Avonmouth at about half eight – morning rush hour. I followed the route on my GPS with conviction and kept a constant look out for Route 41 signs. The little blue dot in a circle which represented me followed what I was convinced was the GPS route but hadn't spotted any Route 41 signs for about two miles up a long hill. I came to some very busy crossroads but couldn't see any Route 41 signs at all. After dodging traffic to cross the road I became rather concerned about being in the wrong place. I removed the dark sunglasses and put on my reading glasses. Sure enough, I was completely off the correct route and I'd been following an 'A' road which under the dark sunglasses looked very much like the programmed GPS route. I altered the scale of the map and opened it out and eventually my programmed route appeared. I should have turned left about a couple of miles back down the hill. The planned route actually skirted around the bottom of the hill and I'd cycled up it for nothing. After working out a new route I was back on track in about a quarter of an hour.

Route 41 took me through some delightful country villages. As usual around 10am I started to feel hungry and as though by magic 'The Village Store' appeared within the next ten minutes in a village called Easter Compton. The people who worked there were very helpful and friendly and a warm pasty and cup of hot chocolate, this time fully stirred, went down a treat. When I mentioned I was cycling LEJOG they looked really privileged that I'd chosen to ride through their village and buy something at their shop. One of the ladies washed out my water bottle and filled it with fresh water. After thirty miles nonstop cycling, the village seat provided a welcome rest.

I could sense a community spirit within the village, portrayed the friendliness shown and the well kept village seat which is always a sign of pride. Each year this village organises a carnival with floats towed by lorries loaned by local businesses, providing enjoyment not only for everyone who designs and makes them but also for the hundreds of visitors who come along to admire. Unfortunately due to Health and Safety Regulations and insurance the use of lorries had to be withdrawn and only non motorised transport could be used for the floats. The traditional throwing of flour and water was also banned. I wonder if they bent or even dispensed with the rules as they had on Cross Country Trains.

I continued along Route 41 and as I rounded a bend I was greeted by a fox standing in the middle of the road staring at me. It ran into the bushes.

After a couple of hours I came to Berkeley, a small town raised up above the surrounding countryside revealing the western edge of the Cotswolds in the distance. I managed to replenish my 'meths' here at a very cheap hardware store and also my own fuel supply at the bakers next door.

Since I started on this adventure I have been a thorough convert to local tea shops, cafes and snack bars. They are the saviours of hungry and tired cyclists all over the country. Also if there's a seat outside their shop, then that is a sure way of increasing their business tenfold.

What more could a cyclist ask for? A local baker's shop which sold first class sandwiches to order, mugs of tea for 60p and a magnificent vanilla slice to finish off which could all be enjoyed on a seat in the sun directly outside their shop where the world can be watched struggling by.

Mothers pushing babies in prams loaded up with the daily shopping; businessmen in suits parking their shiny cars confidently taking their portfolios through what appeared to be random doors and a man with a tape measure who wasn't wearing a fluorescent jacket, measuring the distance of drain covers from the curb! He must have been flouting Health and Safety Regulations because I could see him without having to protect my eyes from any fluorescent glow. This was a busy small town or maybe a large village but it seemed to have everything you could ever want. It was so clean that you could tell everyone who lived here had great respect for their environment.

I finished my feast and looked down; I'd made a terrible mess on the path with grated cheese that had fallen out of my sandwich. I looked around with embarrassment, un-crumpled the serviette I was given with the sandwich and picked up every bit of grated cheese then deposited it in a nearby bin. I must have had guilt written all over my face.

Route 41 continued north then east and at this point I turned left where I waved goodbye to Route 41 for Route 45 to Gloucester and then Norton, my next stop.

I wasn't looking forward to finding my way through Gloucester after my fiasco in Shirehampton and Bridgenorth but after a few miles I joined the Gloucester and Sharpness canal towpath and rapidly made headway towards Gloucester. The towpath and canal was very popular with cyclists, walkers and narrow boaters. This meant that there were lots of refreshment stops like tea shops and pubs. Unfortunately my stomach didn't have enough room to sample yet another tea shop and time was marching on so I reluctantly gave them all a miss.

Narrow boats, luxury motor launches, houseboats and river vessels of all description were moored alongside the towpath. Many of the narrow boats were decked out with brightly coloured flowers in highly decorated tubs of all shapes and sizes. The boats were brightly painted to match the flowers with designs that would reflect any generation since the birth of narrow boats. Names such as 'Chattydachs', 'Cinders', 'Cariad' and more traditionally 'Lady Olivia' had been proudly painted on their bows. The canal was equipped to moor hundreds of boats with mooring posts positioned every few yards. The grass verge between the towpath and the canal was mowed short enough to play bowls on. The whole canal represented an entirely different environment from that experienced in many urban areas. The cycle route continued along the tow path for several miles, not only into Gloucester but right through following the canal all the way. I was through Gloucester in record time for me, passing through towns and cities.

On leaving Gloucester, Route 45 was incomplete when I did my research but the signs led me directly onto a brand new Route 45 on a recently renovated old railway track. I followed this for a few miles but it unfortunately took me on the wrong side of the River Severn to reach the campsite at Norton.

I needed to get off this track and head towards my programmed route shown on the GPS. I noticed that the programmed route crossed a dual carriageway, the A40, not too far from where I was, so when I came to a gate I managed to get through and make my way to a roundabout on the A40 dual carriageway which is an access road to the M5 motorway.

I was only about half a mile from where my route crossed the A40 so I set off in that direction. The road was busy and not enjoyable. This was a far cry from Berkeley where I sat on a seat enjoying my rest in the sun and the relaxing rides along the canal towpaths.

I kept an eye on my GPS, not wearing the dark sunglasses with the clipped in bifocals, which would have been a huge mistake given the situation. The programmed route got nearer on the GPS but there was no sign ahead of any crossroads. Traffic was passing me at speed showing no sign of slowing for any junction or crossroads. Fifty metres, forty, thirty, twenty, ten and I was there, but there were no crossroads. I stopped and looked down. My programmed route looked like a crossroad on the GPS but was in fact a road that went under the dual carriageway that I was on. My immediate reaction was to emit a few unprintable swear words. I stood on the narrow hard shoulder gazing down over a bridge at my escape route.

I couldn't go on to the next junction because this road led directly to the M5 motorway. I couldn't go back because I would have to cross the dual carriageway. It was far too busy and there was a barrier down the middle. Fortunately at the end of the bridge there was a steep bank down through some young trees to the other road, my programmed route, protected at the top by a barrier.

I laid my bike down on the road side of the barrier, jumped over then dragged my bike through. Pointing the bike downhill I grasped the brakes and gently made my way steeply down through the trees and undergrowth. This was easier than I thought and in only a few seconds I would be on my programmed route, until that is I was confronted with a five foot fence at the bottom of the bank.

From a standing position there was no way I could lift the bike and its attachments up and over the fence but might be able to if I removed the tent and pannier bags. But then I wouldn't be able to lower the bike far enough over for it to reach the ground on the other side.

I decided on a different approach. I squatted down, grabbed the bike by the lowest part of the frame and front fork then stood up. I managed to lift the whole lot high enough to rest the bike on the top of the fence supported by the pannier bag nearest to the fence. I held it balanced in place with my left hand while I climbed over the fence. Once over the fence I grabbed the frame and fork on the other side of the bike and lifted it as high as I could over my head, stepped back and lowered it to the ground as gently as I could. Fortunately I used the fence as a brake and it slid to the ground. At last I was once again on my programmed route with only about five miles to my next campsite.

The road was quiet with a lot of bends. About half a mile further on there were two teenagers sauntering down the road going in the same direction as me with a free roaming 'bark and snap at anything' Scotty dog.

I slowed down and cautioned the lads that I would pass them on their left. The Scotty dog ran in front of me and made a beeline for my heels, growling and snapping viciously.

I put my legs into overdrive and accelerated off. There was no reaction from the teenagers as what I assumed to be their dog tore after me. I could hear its claws tearing and scratching at the ground along with its fearsome husky growl as it desperately tried to grab my right heel. I remembered the escapade on a training trip with Julian a few weeks earlier when he said 'You can't be sure of dogs!'

The irritating little dog was now only about a foot behind my pedal. Perhaps if it got close enough it might suffer an upper cut from my spinning feet. If I stopped it would have certainly taken a chunk out of my bare ankle – I wasn't prepared to stop and find out!

I shifted up a gear and increased my speed. Fortunately there weren't any hills. Fifty metres, a hundred metres, one hundred and fifty metres and still there was no respite. The lack of depth and strength in its bark and growls suggested that it often made a habit of chasing unwary cyclists. The husky growls and barks started to weaken and became more of a wheeze. I sensed victory looming. The sound of the scratching claws on the tarmac and wheezy growls started to fade and began to slow down. I was victorious. I could just about hear it panting like an old steam engine fading into the distance as it finally gave up. I didn't slow down and was a mile away in next to no time. Thankfully it wasn't a Rottweiler!

I followed my programmed route until about half a mile from my destination. The last half mile was on a bridleway over a field which unfortunately was deep in mud due to the heavy rain a couple of days ago. A quick look at the GPS and a longer route was taken to the campsite at The Red Lion Inn in Norton. The narrow road swept down towards the river where on its banks The Red Lion came in to view. I had arrived at my destination for the day.

The lady who owned the campsite was tending to her many flower tubs and hanging baskets and invited me into her office to get my details. She filled out the usual form which seemed to be standard with all campsites. Name....Address.....Date...... and in this case £10 fee for the night.

She asked me if I was cycling for charity and I explained about the school in Nepal. She immediately crossed out the £10 fee and wrote FREE. Her husband also charged up my GPS batteries.

The Red Lion Inn and campsite stand on the banks of the River Severn which in June 2007 suffered from severe flooding. A horizontal line drawn four feet up the wall on the site office showed the height of the flood that year. There were other lines which showed the height of floodwater in previous years but 2007 beat them all.

The bar meals here were not only good value but were also substantial and after a long day in the saddle – very welcome. £8 bought me steak pie, chips and peas, and a pint of bitter. Thankfully it wasn't a Greek restaurant!

The landlord told me about the flood and explained why the bar room had bare floor boards and a bar of just plain wood. The seats and chairs were all bare wood without cushions. I suppose you could say that the ground floor was 'flood friendly!'

I took a walk down to the river and being the first time that I'd seen the River Severn I was very impressed by its size. It is after all Britain's longest river stretching over 200 miles from over 2000 feet high up in the Black Mountains of Mid Wales down to the Bristol Channel. After the previous days of rain it was flowing fairly rapidly and about three feet from the top of the bank. The power of this water cannot be underestimated as I watched a huge tree being carried with ease past me to disappear down towards the estuary. I began to try and visualize the enforced terror on flood victims watching their homes and possessions being mercilessly engulfed by an unstoppable mass of filthy muddy water. I wondered if I might witness the Severn Bore but realised that I was too far upriver and higher than high water mark but it was also the wrong time of the year.

My drooping eyes and uncontrollable yawning was trying to tell me that it was once again 9 o'clock and it was time to snuggle up in my sleeping bag. It had been a long day and I didn't need a hot drink to coax me into dreamland.

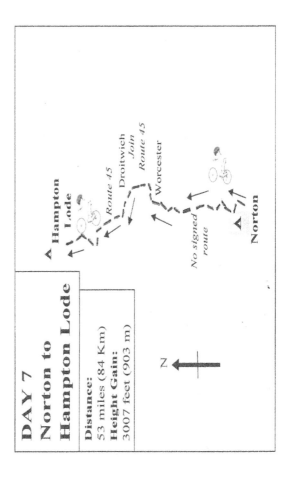

DAY 7
Norton to
Hampton Lode

Distance:
53 miles (84 Km)
Height Gain:
3007 feet (903 m)

N

Day 7 - Sauce, Salt & Vinegar

The morning was overcast and not too cold but produced a cold wind when cycling. The site at Norton seemed to be used a lot by workmen who were either working away from home on a project or permanently living in the static caravans. There seemed to be a mass exodus between half six and seven.

I'd planned my own route to Worcester as Route 45 was not signed for this stage and only proposed. After turning right out of the campsite I eventually made my way onto the B4211 which appeared to be an alternative commuter route between Gloucester and Worcester avoiding the M5.

I think that if I had to cycle LEJOG entirely on busy roads, I would have surrendered by now. Although during the day I should think the traffic flow would have been low, it was the opposite during this peak time between 7am and 9am. There is no rest, no respite, no enjoyment and no just stopping to soak in the view or more importantly, for a pee. I'd been desperate for miles and there wasn't anywhere just to hide in the bushes beside a field gate or a quiet two minute lull in the traffic. Although I can honestly say that I need more than two minutes these days. Mile after mile of constant traffic and not even a lay-by, then without any warning or information signs there was a left turn into paradise, a haven of pain release, a deserted picnic area. If I'd been driving a car and was unaware of this stopping place I would have driven straight past it. I pulled in, parked the bike and knew that I was about to experience a feeling of great relief behind a boulder when a car pulled in and out got a man with his dog. I had to wait. The dog immediately cocked its leg on a neighbouring boulder and released a full gallon. I sat on my boulder and crouched into a cycling position to hinder the impatient flow. They say that 'A watched kettle never boils' but also a watched dog never finishes peeing. It seemed to take ages to release that gallon before they disappeared with the dog bounding ahead into a nearby wood. I must get the balance right between being dehydrated and hydrated to bursting point!

After a few minutes I was back on the rat run accompanied by constant traffic noise and fumes. There would be cars waiting just behind to overtake when traffic was coming the other way so concentration was imperative to cycle in a straight line. There was no weaving about to avoid the odd pothole. Most drivers were generally patient and waited until there was plenty of room to overtake but there were always those who would risk my life to save a few seconds of their time like the Volvo lady in Devon. It was often difficult to hear a vehicle behind, especially a car as the wind noise in your ears was generally louder than a car quietly waiting behind to overtake. It was always quite a shock when they revved to overtake. There was always the odd worn out engine that produced noxious black or blue fumes as its driver overworked it to get past before a vehicle came the other way. Fortunately with stricter regulations there aren't many of these polluters on today's roads.

After almost 30 miles of torture my first sight of Route 45 came just before Worcester – what a relief, I could exit this arterial misery. It took me directly onto the canal towpath that guided me right through the centre of Worcester. The canal environment was very similar to that in Gloucester. But here there was a more industrial feel. I was surrounded by many run down warehouses which had spent their best years, probably a couple of hundred years ago, when canals were widely used for transporting goods. These were now going through a renovation stage being reborn as apartments and offices. The marinas were being cleaned and in a few years the whole area will have been transformed into a very desirable environment.

As I cycled along the towpath and around the marinas I pictured the life here over two hundred years ago when Dr Wall started to make fine porcelain and labelled it Royal Worcester. Chemists John Lea and William Perrins used herbs and spices brought from India to manufacture Worcestershire Sauce which they started to sell in 1837. Barges would have been loaded with crates of these more famous labels from Worcester together with lesser known products of vinegar and gloves to transport nationwide and eventually overseas.

The Route 45 signs through Worcester disappeared for a while but then reappeared on a series of minor roads heading towards Droitwich Spa.

This is a wonderful little town which I walked through looking for – a tea shop. I couldn't see one at all. There must be at least one here somewhere but if there was it was not easy to spot. I looked around for someone who might direct me. It's interesting to find yourself weighing up people to see if they can help or not. The teenager possibly playing truant - give him a miss; the man wearing a posh suit and carrying a briefcase in a great hurry - probably not from these parts and probably doesn't use tea shops for refreshment anyway; the old lady struggling with a shopping trolley - will probably get frustrated if I couldn't understand her directions; the workman halfway up a ladder - not an option. Where's the policeman when you want one?

I stopped a passing middle aged looking lady who had a full shopping bag. She must be local. She pointed me in the direction of two tea shops. I must have looked a little confused after I left her because she ensured that I got to the tea shop by following me and taking me directly to it. I obviously looked lost and desperate for a cup of tea. She pointed out a tea shop where I could sit outside and keep an eye on my bike. Yet again I have encountered friendship and help from everyone I have met, except for the toffee nosed drunk!

I ordered the usual pot of tea and toastie and took a seat outside in the sun. Just like in Berkeley I sat and watched humans of all shapes and sizes peacefully tackle their everyday mundane but essential tasks. People with their shopping, popping in for a chat and a cup of tea. Two local unemployed men on a table next to me chatted about when they were last employed. But there wasn't anyone measuring the distance of drain covers from the curb.

The cafe tables were situated in a small pedestrianised square which incorporated a memorial to Droitwich Spa's growth. A large water pump painted green. Most towns are built around an industry which attracts people to live there and hence a town develops. Droitwich Spa is situated on a massive deposit of salt and Droitwich Brine contains two and a half pounds of salt per gallon of water, ten times more than normal sea water and is only surpassed by the Dead Sea. The salt has been extracted and the brine bathed in since Roman times; hence the name Droitwich Spa. This town made its fortune from salt.

My tea and toastie consumed I returned to Route 45 which now followed a maze of quiet country roads. I passed a group of cyclists going in the opposite direction and we exchanged waves as they sped past. I guessed that they might also be following Route 45 but in the opposite direction to me. I stopped at the next village of Hartlebury to post some redundant maps home and stock up on a few things which I'd forgotten to buy in Droitwich Spa. To my surprise the same group of cyclists tore past me, this time in the same direction as me. We acknowledged each other. After I'd secured my provisions I followed in the same direction which went steeply downhill towards Stourport. The road was shaded by huge trees on either side which made it quite dark and probably because the road never saw the sun seemed to be constantly damp. These conditions had loosened the tarmac on the road's surface and produced many large potholes. With the combination of semi-darkness and sunglasses the potholes were only partially visible. As the hill went steeply down I reached a fearsome velocity until I hit the first pothole, then the second and third. In fact it was almost impossible to miss them. Fortunately I managed to steer around most of the more severe ones and finally reached a junction at the bottom of the hill where the group of cyclists were waiting. They had encountered the same potholes as me but one of them hadn't been so lucky as to avoid the larger ones and was busily mending a puncture.

Now I know that I'm carrying gear to support me for three weeks, apart from food, and need two medium sized saddle bags and a couple of smaller bags for all the gear, but this cyclist only had a midget saddle bag measuring six centimetres by six centimetres by four centimetres and in this he had all the tools and spare inner tube to mend a puncture plus his waterproof jacket and a packed lunch! I always feel inadequate amongst seasoned athletes.

I stopped and chatted to them for a few minutes while they asked me about my ride. The female in the group said that she had cycled LEJOG on a tandem but her partner had been an elderly man and they had to take it easy as he was forty two. She talked to me as though I was the same age as them, middle to late twenties. After all, it was dark under those trees and she was wearing her sunglasses.

The group confirmed the direction I was headed and I left them with the puncture almost mended.

True to form I got lost, ending up in a cul-de-sac surrounded by houses on the outskirts of Stourport which is built on the junction of the rivers Stour and Severn. The Sustrans signs had disappeared or I had missed one at a vital junction. A referral to the GPS was required and sure enough I'd missed a right turn about half a mile back.

The next town on my route which I arrived at was Bewdley, about 4 miles North-West of Stourport.

I couldn't resist resting a while, taking my time to eat an orange. It was so peaceful, clean and well cared for. On the other bank ducks and swans were gathered around people who had food for them. I was now only about twenty miles from my next campsite at Hampton Lode. It was only about one o'clock so I had a little time to soak up the tranquillity of this delightful little town. I sat on this beautifully kept seat in a small flower decked park overlooking the river and an arched bridge with a balustrade along the top. By the 14th Century the town became known as Beau Lieu, French for beautiful place and it's not difficult to see how Bewdley has been derived from that.

I was soon to learn that my rest at Bewdley was needed with it being situated on the river Severn meant that all routes out of Bewdley, except down river, went up, which was certainly true of Route 45 thankfully now well sign posted. The route out of the town rose gradually as the Severn valley started to rise into mid Wales.

After a few miles the route took me into Wyre Forest which followed an old railway for about three miles. It then turned sharply right, went downhill for a while then continued steeply uphill on a rough forest track for another three miles. I was determined to tackle the whole hill without walking and fixed my target on the next bend. As usual once round the bend the route continued uphill even steeper. My thoughts were - '*Just to the next bend, perhaps the gradient will lessen around the bend.*' Such optimism was futile because yet again there was a further upward struggle. I gave in and walked for about half a mile.

While in the forest which was well sign posted for family bike routes, mountain bike routes of all grades and walking routes I only saw three people, all walking. Wyre Forest is obviously a popular place at weekends and holidays, but like most places was deserted mid week in early summer.

I finally emerged from the forest and once again on to country lanes. Unfortunately this countryside was reminiscent of Devon and Cornwall which I was so relieved to have left behind. The roller coasters had returned. This went on for about five miles until I heard the whistle of a steam train. I couldn't see any railway but my GPS map indicated that the Severn Valley Railway was nearby. As I headed down a steep bank and over a bridge, there it was, passing under the bridge which overlooked Arley station.

I stopped on the bridge and looked down at the station. The whole scene could easily have taken place a hundred years ago. The high pitched whistle from the approaching train made everyone on the platform look excited as they all faced in the direction from which it came. A man in hiking boots with bright red socks who may have been a walker; a couple obviously on holiday, both with cameras pressed against their eyes waiting in anticipation to take a photograph of the approaching steam engine; a lady on a seat next to a pile of old trunks used as a station prop, looked as though she was off on a long journey and a middle aged man wearing a long navy blue raincoat which fitted in with the era depicted by the station but looked out of fashion in 2009. He may also have been a prop. Dark grey plumes of smoke approached through the trees up line. I took a few photographs and waited for the train to arrive. A mother with her small boy who looked as though he was desperate to use the toilet arrived on the platform through a door. The path to the toilet which was situated on the other side of the line was blocked, because of the approaching train, by some old milk churns. The guard allowed the child and his mother through. They had returned before the train arrived. Finally the engine appeared through the tree lined track. It was much smaller than I'd imagined pulling four dark red carriages more suited to the early nineteen hundreds. A few passengers leaned out of the windows in customary fashion. The engine driver blew his whistle to add to the nostalgia. It stopped at the station and even for early summer lots of people got off but only the handful waiting got on. I didn't wait for it to leave and continued with my journey.

Route 45 now took me on to an off road path recently renovated to take bikes as well as walkers. This was now exciting as it weaved and dodged its way around trees, bogs and boulders. There were long sections on boardwalks and steep little sections through narrow gaps. I was about three miles from Hampton Lode. As I approached a bend in the path I was confronted by a Saxon Warrior partially hidden by the long grass, only about four feet tall but looking fearsome while he guarded the route. He was not real of course but an iron statue to mark the Mercian Way which Route 45 follows to commemorate the western border of the ancient Kingdom of Mercia which stretched from the eastern border of Wales to the east coast. This short ride would provide lots of excitement for families out for the day which could include a train ride back to the start.

I left the off road track and headed downhill into the campsite at Hampton Lode, The Unicorn Inn campsite. There was no-one around except for three men in their early twenties packing their tent and belongings into their car. There wasn't another tent on the site although further down the campsite were lots of static caravans and a few tourers.

I parked my bike against a fence on the patio of the Inn and looked around for the office.

A sign on a door read:

When closed call at the Pub

This locked door was also part of the pub so I looked around for another door. There must be someone around as I'd just seen the group who had been camping.

I found a door that opened into the bar and walked in. There were about ten people at the bar all merrily drinking and putting the world to rights at four o'clock on this midweek day. They all laughed and were very friendly towards each other. The men were mainly unshaven with stubbly beards and the women, who I assumed to be their wives, appeared to be drinking as many pints as the men.

I asked about a pitch for the night and was directed by many pointing redundant arms, (the others holding glasses of beer to their lips), to the lady who administered the campsite while they continued their humorous conversation. She made out the usual forms, accepted the fee and seeing that I was kitted out in bright clothing asked me what my mission was. When I said that I was cycling from Land's End to John o'Groats to help fund a school in Nepal, all conversation ceased, half full beer glasses were gently lowered from their mouths and their attention turned towards me. I became their immediate hero. The five pound notes towards my sponsor money seemed to come from all corners and as more of them heard of my venture their attention was also channelled directly towards me. They wanted to hear about the Expedition to the Himalaya and about my bike ride so far. I held their attention for almost an hour. I was overwhelmed by their friendship and by the interest shown in me. One of the women couldn't wait to inform her sister on her mobile phone that there was a man in the pub cycling from Land's End to John o'Groats. I certainly felt important.

I asked if they served bar meals, which was a silly question because 'Meals Served All Day' was advertised on a board outside and opted to call back after 6 o'clock after I'd pitched my tent and worked my way through my afternoon chores.

I was given a choice of pitch anywhere on the three acre site. I thought it wise to camp near the pub and toilets.

Later back at the pub I ordered chicken and mushroom pie with chips and veg. which arrived in a dish packed to the gunwales with succulent chicken and brushed with gravy. I passed a comment that usually with chicken pies you're lucky to find a couple of withered up pieces of chicken drowned in watery gravy! The landlady said that with her cook it's the other way round – too much chicken and not enough gravy. She offered to charge my batteries in the bar and opened up the lounge for me to watch TV.

Around about seven o'clock the clientele drifted off until only the landlord and his wife occupied the bar. The landlord told me how crowded the campsite became during weather friendly weekends and holidays even though today it was void of happy campers apart from the ones who after a few late afternoon beers merrily saunter off to their mobile homes permanently anchored to the ground further down the campsite.

As ever a couple of hours later I also sauntered to my tent and crawled into my sleeping bag at around nine o'clock for another early start the next morning.

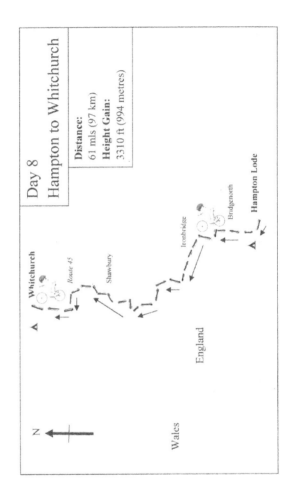

Day 8
Hampton to Whitchurch

Distance:
61 mls (97 km)
Height Gain:
3310 ft (994 metres)

N

Wales

England

Whitchurch

Route 45

Shawbury

Ironbridge

Bridgenorth

Hampton Lode

Day 8 – Famous Pies and Iron Warriors

Awake at twenty to six and on the road by ten to seven. This part of the country is beautiful but like all beautiful places, very hilly, and being next to the river that only meant one thing – from here it was always going to be up. At this time in the morning there was no sound from the Inn or the caravan park. Everyone was probably still sleeping off their merriment from the previous teatime as they most likely do every morning. They were a great bunch of people who showed a genuine interest in my venture and heartfelt friendship which gave me a great sense of importance. I was disappointed that there was no-one around to say goodbye to.

I found myself cycling steeply uphill under a dam to a reservoir and sailing club. The route on the GPS looked easy but when I arrived at the empty sailing club car park there was no way out. The ghostly clubhouse surrounded by mist rising from the mirror still reservoir and rows of sail boats, asleep and covered over for the night lying on their sides were protected by a high fence all round except for the way I'd come in. I felt trapped. I explored every nook and cranny to find a way out. Around corners to find dead ends and along the foreshore to find that it gradually disappeared into the water. I studied the route on the GPS and sure enough I'd followed the route into the sailing club but was now physically only ten metres from the yellow line shown on the screen. But where did I miss a turn or gate. I could just make out a track through a fence so I retraced my route steeply downhill until I was definitely on the programmed route. I spotted a gate with a large red sign which read:

'PRIVATE'

Could this be my route? On further scrutinising the sign which was partly hidden behind some foliage there was a Route 45 sign. Now I knew why I'd missed the route.

With difficulty I managed to wangle my bike through the kissing gate, (probably installed to discourage bikes) and continued up what I knew was going to be a steep hill. It was muddy and well overgrown although it appeared to have been used by some horses. The track was now less than a foot wide, steep, muddy and overgrown with brambles. I was forced to get off and push but had to push from the back of the bike as the path was not wide enough to accommodate both me and the bike side by side.

As it was still quite early, the foliage was soaked with dew so once again I became coated with wet seeds. The track eventually widened but continued up. It was far too rough and steep to ride. I pushed uphill for about two miles. At last a road appeared which continued downhill all the way to Bridgenorth.

The town was just waking up. Delivery lorries waited outside locked shops. Lots of people were busily making their way to work. Route 45 signs had once again vanished. I rested outside what appeared to be the old town hall dating back a few hundred years to study the route on my GPS. Straight ahead, turn right then continue downhill to a fork in the road. I decided to stop there and study the route again. When I reached the fork in the road it was a little confusing as there was a double fork and it was difficult to follow on the GPS. I took the first left hand fork and headed off for about a hundred metres. True to form I was heading off route and needed to turn around. I waited for a gap in the traffic and was in the process of manoeuvring my way through a U turn when I was aware of a man's voice respectfully trying to attract my attention...

"Excuse moy!".. in a very broad west midlands accent. "Excuse moy!" he repeated.

"Is that an Active 10 you have there moyte"?

"Oy've been watching you use eet and wondered what eet was loyke in the field"

Not that I was in a field but I knew what he meant. I looked up to be greeted by an obvious enthusiast for electronic gadgets who had probably never actually used one for what it was meant to be used for but knew everything about them. He was a gadget enthusiast who read all the magazines and studied all the new gear but didn't actually own any himself.

"Have you used the 'syncopated geolog cache drop' function yet?"

To which I replied, "The what?"

I've been using my Satmap GPS for several months now and felt totally ignorant of many functions on it. To me it was an electronic map with a route programmed onto it to follow. I couldn't answer anything he asked with conviction.

He was now standing over me and I noticed that in his right hand he was holding his breakfast. A bowl of cornflakes full of milk sprinkled with sugar then securely covered with cling film. No doubt to stop the milk from slopping out as he walked to his destination.

He continued to fill me full of technical jargon about its capacity to pick up signals with its 'Super Interstellar High Frequency Aerial' enhancing its ability to keep you on the right route.

"I've had no problems with the Active 10," I said with confidence. "It's just my lack of ability to use it properly. However it always gets me out a jam, one of which I am in now!"

He asked me about my challenge after he spotted the 'Land's End to John o'Groats' signs displayed on my pannier bag covers. I replied by telling him that I was cycling from Land's End to John o'Groats to help build a school in Nepal.

With an apologetic glance he said. "Sorry I haven't got any money on me but I'm working like an immigrant at the moment."

Looking down at his bowl he said, "My cornflakes are looking a bit soggy now! Must be off!"

He wished me good luck and I headed off, hopefully in the right direction. The route went downhill and turned into a lane parallel to a golf course.

When I planned the route I noticed that Route 45 was not complete for this section but there was a track marked on the map along an old railway. However I didn't know whether or not this was a right of way but it followed the river and was therefore on reasonably horizontal ground. I must have missed the turn because the road I was on started to rise fiercely. I stopped to study the map and the only other way took me a further fifteen miles over a hill towards Ironbridge. As I studied the map a lady walking her dog appeared on the brow of the hill. I asked her about the track on the old railway. She confidently told me that she had cycled along it many times to Ironbridge when she was younger although it was a bit rough in places but it was a right of way. She said the lady who owned the land had put up a Private sign during the Foot and Mouth outbreak in 2001 but had just not taken it down so I could ignore it. She told me where to turn off the road and if anyone stopped me who looked officious just to plead ignorance and talk about the weather.

I thanked her, turned around and headed off downhill then within a mile found the track. Once again I was following my planned route. After the rain a few days earlier the track was very muddy although someone had been along with a machine and had levelled it out. The whole track was shaded by large trees as most old railway tracks are. It was fairly straight and level but very wet and rough. I had to walk on several occasions due to the non friendly cycling conditions. It went on for miles and never seemed to end. With a cycle friendly surface this would have been a dream to cycle as there wasn't a hill throughout its whole length. My 'ignorance speech' was well rehearsed in case I was confronted by an irate farmer.

Very nearly at the end of the track I heard the unwelcome sound of a tractor up ahead and prepared myself for the worst. The farmer was just getting into his tractor as I approached. Before he could glare at me and shout 'Oy! Git off moy land!!' I smiled at him and greeted him with.. 'Hi there, I'm heading for Ironbridge and seem to be lost a bit. Is this the right way?'....Coward!

He smiled back and it was then I realised that he was not the farmer but a farm hand so was naturally more pleasant towards strangers.

He answered and told me that I was going the right way and I would come to Ironbridge about two miles further on. He even asked me about my challenge and wished me luck!

About a mile before Ironbridge I came to a junction of cycle routes - The Severn Valley Way and the Silkin Way. Because Route 45 was not yet finalised between Bridgenorth and Ironbridge it was not shown on this sign. Near Ironbridge my attention was drawn to a huge face carved in a tree. Whoever had carved it no doubt got their inspiration from Lord of the Rings! The carving was magnificent and looked real enough to be able to jump out at you and enfold you in its woody arms. Further along the road a house built under a cliff looked like a parallelogram from the front. It looked as though a powerful force had pushed the normally rectangular shape over to form a parallelogram leaning over at a very noticeable angle. Even stranger, the windows and doors were also parallelograms. Does that mean the window panes were also parallelograms? How do you hang wallpaper on parallelogram shaped walls and are the pictures that are hanging on the parallelogram walls also parallelograms? The list of enforced abnormalities in the house could be endless!

At last....Ironbridge. I entered the famous town cycling along the level towards a roundabout. There were another three roads onto the roundabout, two went very steeply uphill and the other went straight ahead downhill. None were at ninety degrees to each other. Two were in a V shape on my approach; I was on the left hand road. I was looking for the town centre and not having been there before thought the town would be fairly small but bigger than just a few shops. I stopped, looked at the road sign but *'Town Centre'* was not on the sign, so I referred to my GPS map. Unfortunately when I stopped the map spun around and it was easy to become disorientated. I have since found the correct setting to avoid this.

However I managed to sort out which exit to take, or I thought I had, and headed steeply uphill to the right. After about two hundred yards of hard slog the buildings started to run out. It seemed obvious that I was going the wrong way so I asked a couple walking uphill where the town centre was.

"Back down to the roundabout and turn right".

"Thanks! – Trust me to take the wrong route uphill!" I remarked embarrassingly.

I did a U-Turn and sped back down to the roundabout and turned right onto the other road which headed very steeply uphill adjacent to a row of terraced houses. About half way up I was forced to dismount and walk to the top due to the precipitous nature of the hill. There was no sign whatsoever of the town centre. Some workmen digging a hole became my next 'Lost Cyclist Information Desk'.

'Back down to the roundabout and turn right' which was in fact the very same answer that I got from the couple on the other hill.

There was only one other road to try so I turned round and sped off down the hill – well, took it a little more gently as this one was very steep and ended abruptly at the roundabout. A quick scoop around the roundabout and a right turn then hopefully I will eventually come to the town centre. After about thirty yards from the roundabout there they were; the shops of Ironbridge, directly opposite the famous Ironbridge itself, which included, yes you've guessed, a tea shop. But this was no ordinary tea shop, this was Eley's World Famous Pie Shop, which I'd never heard of before but a mug of tea and a world famous pie would definitely make up for taking the wrong road twice, and uphill at that.

I parked my bike and settled down at an outside table with my mug of tea and hot pie; I can honestly say it was delicious. I just sat there and soaked up the relaxed way of life all around. A group of elderly people (probably the same age as me) with fully laden bikes were standing on the Iron Bridge reading about its history. They must have been stopping B&B as they didn't have any tents. As all roads out of here go up, they'll probably be doing a lot of pushing today. It was only ten thirty in the morning and I still had many miles to cycle but I could have sat there all day consuming a few more pies.

A passing lady commented with a smile, "What a life!"

"This is the good bit. It's the bit on the bike that's hard," I jokingly replied.

I took a few photographs of the Iron Bridge; the first iron bridge in the world built in 1779 and then headed off along the road.

Route 45 signs appeared again and very soon they pointed uphill. I pushed several times before reaching the top of the hill, but once there I could see miles ahead and at last the hills started to gradually disappear and the countryside became more rolling farmland. Before the hills completely disappeared the four huge cooling towers of Ironbridge power station stood out like a sore thumb expelling hot air and water vapour amongst the trees in the Severn Gorge. They looked totally out of place.

At last there were now long downhill stretches sweeping gently around low hedges. I was once again simulating skiing downhill on a recently piste bashed blue run. The wind whistled through my cycle helmet and I felt elated. Suddenly about five metres in front of me a mother duck and her two chicks waddled out onto the road from under a hedge. I was too close to swerve or brake fiercely to avoid them. I managed to slow down a little and can still see the fear on mother duck's face when she saw this red and white rocket bearing down on her and her two ducklings. Before seeing it I could never imagine how a duck could show fear on its face. However, she unleashed her wings and flew out frantically quacking with great speed right across the front of my bike missing it by only a few inches. I blew a sigh of relief and my attention was now taken by the two ducklings but because they were slightly behind their mother couldn't follow her without becoming a cloud of downy feathers in my spokes. They started to follow her but at the last second veered off to their left which meant they were now flying in front of me. As they picked up speed they rose up to about handlebar height but were within touching distance of my hands. What an experience to have. I was now doing about twenty five miles an hour freewheeling down a country lane with a couple of ducklings flying in front of me leading the way.

I was very nearly touching them. A wildlife photographer couldn't have wished for a better shot. Unfortunately I was in no position to get my camera out and film the action. After about thirty metres they decided to part company and each flew off to either side of me. Thankfully none of the ducks were hurt and I continued thinking how lucky I'd been to have witnessed such an event.

The cycling to Whitchurch was straight forward with neither hills nor route finding problems. I had the first rain since Exmoor, gratefully only 'normal rain' but it was enough to warrant wearing a waterproof. I was now feeling hungry and desperately needed some replenishment. The energy intake from the world famous pie must have expired. At about half past one I passed through the busy little town of Shawberry where there was a wonderful baker's shop that also sold cups of tea. A pasty, cake and cup of tea fought off the hunger and was a good excuse for a welcome rest. Not wishing to stand in the rain to eat I looked around for a shelter to enjoy my food. The pub nearby offered the usual regulation outside covered smoking area. In this case it was a picnic table with a parasol sticking out of a hole in the middle. I found a dry spot under it and enjoyed my snack in the unfortunate company of a smelly ashtray overflowing with stale fag ends. Fortunately no-one came out to smoke.

I cycled into my destination for tonight, Mile Bank Farm campsite, Whitchurch. After informing me that I was the only camper apart from a single caravan, the farmer's wife must have felt a little sorry for me and would have offered me Bed & Breakfast but her rooms were fully booked. She was very kind and showed me to the newly appointed but temporary toilet and shower block then showed me to the camping field. I was spoilt for choice. The campsite was brand new as were the toilets and showers. I had them all to myself so must remember to keep them clean as there was no-one else to blame for any mess! The weather was due to be stormy with thunder and lightning through the night so I needed to remember to batten down the hatches and put all guy ropes out. She left me to erect my tent and I set about my task before the rain came. The lightning was flashing in the distance as were the rumbles of thunder. I laid out the tent as usual and pegged the back. I clipped the rear pole together and pushed it through the slot. Clipped it into the hole on the right then held the left end of the pole, bent it down to insert into the hole on the left when there was a hideous sounding crack. I'd snapped the pole right at the very top.

How could this be? I'd erected this tent hundreds of times. Perhaps it wasn't slotted together correctly? Anyway, enough of wondering why this had happened, what I needed to do now was to do a quick fix on the pole before the storm arrived. Gaffa tape was the answer. In with my repair kit I had a small roll of Gaffa tape. I very carefully extracted the pole so as not to detach it or split the tent material. When it was totally withdrawn I wrapped the broken part with tape and carefully threaded it back through the slot. As I bent it down again, the same thing happened. More tape was required. I wrapped several layers around the break and re-threaded it. This time it held and I continued to erect the tent, making sure the other two poles were fully fitted together before bending them into their slots.

I was pleased to be comfortably settled into the tent with the bike under the fly sheet before the storm arrived. I cooked some pasta for tea as there was no pub within easy walking distance. Anyway it was now pouring. Tomorrow will be my longest ride so far, about eighty five miles to Southport.......Goodnight!

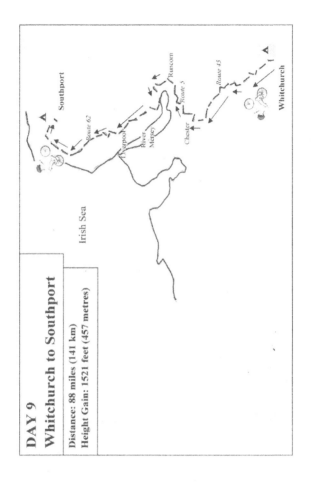

DAY 9
Whitchurch to Southport

Distance: 88 miles (141 km)
Height Gain: 1521 feet (457 metres)

Day 9 – Through Legions and Legends

I awoke to clear skies and wet ground. The rain had been relentless throughout the night and had stopped about an hour or so before I got up at five thirty. I remember that it had been very cold during the night, probably only about three degrees, so the tent was thoroughly wet through with rain and dew on the outside and condensation on the inside. Thankfully the broken pole remained intact with the Gaffa tape and there were no leaks.

The most direct route on the A41 to Chester is about 20 miles but the thirty five mile ride sticking to Route 45 involved a zigzag trail which should have taken me about three and a half hours, so when I arrived on the outskirts at nine thirty I was pleasantly surprised. The route was well signposted and there were no real hills to slow me down, although with the huge number of junctions there were many stops and starts on the largely quiet country lanes.

I thought a lot about the route through Chester which has evolved over the last two thousand years or so from the Roman settlement of Deva and wondered whether or not the signs would disappear as they had done through several of the towns I had been through. I needed to be on the other side of Chester as quickly as possible as the next fifty miles was through the most built up part of my whole journey: Frodsham, Runcorn, Widnes, Liverpool and Southport.

The signs led me directly onto a canal which continued through Chester and to my great relief it also coincided with the planned route on my GPS. The canal was quite stunning in places, passing through a deep man made gorge, past several locks where the land dropped dramatically and marinas, where there were many canal boats moored. I found myself on the other side of Chester in less than half an hour and on to the Shropshire Union Canal heading towards Ellesmere Port. At this stage I needed to be careful not to waste any time getting lost with such a huge distance to cover ahead of me today. Thankfully there weren't any real hills today so as long as I could keep on the route I should reach Southport before five o'clock.

The route left the canal and followed the A5117 dual carriageway, with cycle track attached, to Elton where I got carried away enjoying the unbroken haste and missed a left turn which bypassed the town. Fortunately this was a blessing in disguise because at half ten my stomach was in the initial stages of severe complaint. A quick look at the map to avoid totally retracing my tyre tracks led me to a row of shops with a baker that sold cups of tea and hot pasties. As I enjoyed my break an elderly gentleman stopped for a chat. He was very envious of my task as he had been a lifelong cyclist only having to stop last year when he turned seventy six. That gives me another fourteen years I thought!

Batteries recharged I continued along Route 5 which joined a rough track for several miles. The track itself was made up of straight stretches between half a mile and a couple of miles, all traffic free. However, it was infested with potholes and this whole section involved constant weaving from side to side to avoid the deep flooded depressions none of which formed a symmetrical pattern. I would get into a comfortable weaving rhythm when a random pothole appeared out of sync with the others. I thought it unwise to cycle through them to travel in a more direct line because I kept having visions of Dawn French disappearing into a flooded pothole in one of her comedy sketches. Due to the track being rough and the constant swerving I managed to lose a few odds and ends off the bike. The back light fell off at some stage as did the reflector off my left pedal and the plug out of the left side of the handlebars. I also lost the wind deflector peak off my cycle helmet. How I missed seeing that fall off makes me wonder if perhaps I'd dozed off at some stage. I checked my luggage plus the nuts and screws on the pannier and they too had worked loose even though I'd only tightened them a few days ago in Bratton Fleming. I imagined without a regular check, odd parts could fall off the bike without me noticing. The cogs and chain had also started to make a grinding noise having picked up lots of grit from the rough track.

The track brought me out at Frodsham, a bustling little town, on the edge of the Merseyside metropolis. There was a friendly atmosphere about the town and I would have loved to have spent an hour or so browsing round, especially as there was a market on, but with the long journey still ahead, and as I wasn't half way yet, I was forced to find the route to Runcorn. This was another part of the journey I was anxious about. The maps I'd downloaded via the internet several months ago showed only partial haphazard routes through the town which looked difficult to follow. However I'd planned a route as well as I could and hoped that there was some degree of signage. I was heading for the Runcorn-Widnes Bridge which I understood to be quite a landmark. Also I was following Route 5 and as long as I was going in the right direction, sooner or later I would end up at the bridge. Once over the bridge, I would be joining Route 62 which is the Trans Pennine Trail that runs all the way to Southport, my destination for the day.

On the outskirts of Runcorn I spotted a sign saying Route 5, Town Centre. This I followed. It was a breeze, all on a relatively new cycle track and very well signposted. It ran parallel to the main road that led to the Runcorn-Widnes Bridge and it was all off road. At times it crossed over the road on bridges and went through parks. This was fantastic, why did I have any concerns?

As complacency usually creeps in when things are running smoothly I became aware that I'd cycled past the same place twice, it looked very familiar. Anyway, I continued and followed the Route 5 signs. I was convinced that I'd already been on the route and it took me round in a circle once again back to where I'd been five minutes before. Confusion set in. There must be another way, a side route I hadn't seen. Once again I followed the signs just to be brought back to my original position. There didn't appear to be any way out. The route just came to an abrupt end and circled back on itself. One more attempt then if I'm still stuck in the same circular route I'll have to find a different way or ask someone.

This time I explored every gap and still saw no way out until hidden behind a wall was a ramp heading down to a shopping centre. There was no sign and I'd totally missed this several times. The ramp took me down and in the right direction through the shopping centre, then up a ramp on the other side where I spotted a Route 5 sign with an added bonus. Underneath the sign was a second sign labelled Route (62). This meant that within a couple of miles I would be at the bridge and on to Route 62.

From the shopping centre a well used and route marked cycle track took me directly to the Widnes-Runcorn Bridge. I saw the top of this enormous structure appear over rooftops and realised that my concerns about cycling through Runcorn were unfounded. A ramp took me up onto the cycle lane over the bridge. I remembered being on the M5 Avon Bridge four days ago and how it was quite intimidating. While the traffic was not as fast on this bridge it was noisier and there was more of it. The bridge itself was a massive structure, high above the Mersey, which was in desperate need of a paint job. There was rust and flaking paint everywhere. Not a good advert for the region.

Once over the bridge, a ramp took me down, through a tunnel under the bridge filled with graffiti then directly on to Route 62. I headed west along the north edge of the Mersey. The tide was out and miles of mud and sandbanks were revealed. After a good two hours since my last rest I enjoyed sitting on one of the seats that looked over the Mersey towards Runcorn and the oil refineries that I'd cycled past on the rough track some hours previously, although they were hidden from the track by a high bank so I was totally unaware of them at the time. The view inland towards the bridge was a far cry from the noise and fumes created by traffic crossing it. There was peace and tranquillity here.

I continued along Route 62 skirting the coast for a few miles and gradually rising above the sandbanks of the Mersey Estuary. This was dream cycling, traffic free, fantastic views, no wind and almost flat until I came to a fence and a dramatic drop into a mud banked ravine carved by a stream a hundred feet below. There was neither bridge nor long gradual ramp, just hundreds of long wooden steps leading down to a metal bridge which crossed the stream. Fortunately I was descending these steps which meant that gravity took the weight of my bike and its load whereas ascending the steps would have presented an entirely different challenge.

After a few miles I turned away from the Mersey and headed inland cycling through the pretty village of Hale. Within a couple of miles I was now on the edge of the Liverpool Conurbation and next to John Lennon Airport. The cycle route on the map followed the edge of Speke but there was no signed route here. I continued heading west but realised that eventually I would have to head north in order to rejoin my planned route. Speke looked to be a rough area.

Although there weren't any hills, the going was difficult as a strong head wind had sprung up in the last hour. After a couple of miles I arrived at a dual carriageway that headed north towards my planned route and joined the cycle track on its edge. The wind was not directly in front of me now which made progress much easier. My planned route was now a short ride through an industrial estate. At last I was back on track rejoining Route 62 on the edge of Halewood. From here on to the northern edge of Liverpool at Sefton, Route 62 follows an old railway with hardly a bend or a curve for almost twelve miles. There was a strange atmosphere along the route. It was clean and well kept with plenty of people using it but didn't have the same appeal as other routes I'd been on. Every mile or so there was a barrier across the track to negotiate. Unlike the usual barriers made out of wood or tubular steel, these barriers were made out of iron girders as strong as railway lines. Nowhere along the entire route was there a seat nor anything to sit on. Not even a log or boulder. There was no encouragement for anyone, no matter what their business, to linger. The head wind became increasingly stronger and even on the level I was just managing to average about ten miles an hour. Hardly anyone acknowledged me which was in direct conflict to everything I'd experienced since I started; apart from the drunken toff, although he did acknowledge me.

I was getting close to the end of the track when an elderly man walking towards me put his arm up and stopped me. He asked if I was continuing on Route 62 and if I knew the route at all. I answered "Yes, and No!"

Then he explained that due to vandals and riffraff, the route ahead was impassable and had been barred off by Sustrans. I would have to make a detour. He gave me directions which involved memorising the equivalent of finding your way through Paris. Turn right at the end when you come to a road. Take the first left, second right, go over a wooden bridge which you will need to walk over, right, left and so he went on. I was clueless. I didn't remember any of what he said so I thanked him anyway and continued to the road. I spotted a Route 62 sign which took me right, then another and another. This was definitely a detour but fortunately it had been well sign posted. The detour took me around the back of some factories. Rounding a corner there was a burnt out motorbike and various burnt out bits of car and furniture. This reminded me of one of my training sessions while cycling on Route 1 around Stockton and seeing burnt out cars still smouldering. It appears that Merseyside and Teesside have something in common – useless destructive yobs!

Within a couple of miles I was on the old Cheshire Link Line that was also amazingly straight through fields ending up on the southern edge of Southport. I was now less than ten miles from my destination – the leisure park which was on the northern side of Southport. At last I found a seat where I took a rest and snacked on a Mars bar.

Before embarking on this adventure a friend, who had been to Southport, told me that the beach was massive. It was a favourite place for land yachts and surf kites. As I approached Southport, I could see the sails in the distance, not far now. What I hadn't expected was the length of the promenade. It was miles; a sign on the beach read - 'Parking £3'. The car park attendant must have had a quiet day today as there were only two cars parked on this vast expanse. Being next to the sea, the head wind was now quite fierce but the cycle track was very flat and wide. This would be a fantastic family ride on a calm day. Depending which end of it you start at, Route 62 starts and ends along the promenade at Southport.

Route 62 is also called 'The Trans Pennine Trail' and can be cycled almost entirely off road to Hull then on to Hornsey, a total distance of 215 miles. The route can be extended into Europe by catching a ferry from Hull to Zeebrugge or Rotterdam then joining one of the many European cycle routes to Latvia, Southern Russia, Turkey or Switzerland. Now that could be a challenge to bear in mind for the future.

I kept a look out for an all important sign which stood out and read 'ROUTE 62' or 'TRANS-PENINE TRAIL' but must have missed it - perhaps there wasn't one! I have two SD cards for my Satmap GPS containing the whole of Scotland, England and Wales on 1:50000 maps. If there had been a sign here it would have marked a very significant milestone for me where I changed the southern SD card for the northern one.

As I approached the end of the promenade the whole of the Ribble Estuary came into view and there in the distance I could make out Blackpool Tower with the huge precarious looking roller coaster next to it and just faintly in the distance behind them the hills of the Lakes were just visible. For me this was a giant step as from there on I would be cycling on fairly familiar territory. I felt elated and spurred on knowing that tomorrow I would be in the Lake District. All the pain and agony of today's ride seemed to disappear even though I was absolutely well and truly knackered!

I followed the promenade to its end, turned inland then followed the main road towards a dual carriageway. Fortunately there was a cycle track set back, on both sides of the road. After a couple of miles I spotted a direction sign for my chosen campsite. Such relief, in less than half an hour I would have my tent up and be relaxing in the shower before having a well earned meal and then sleep.

The campsite looked well kept and organised. I parked my bike outside the reception and went in. A smart, well dressed young blonde woman, probably in her early twenties, was on the phone at the time so I waited until she was free. She finished her call and without a smile and very unwelcoming manner said 'Yes?'

I answered, "I would like a pitch for a tent for the night please!"

She placed her pen on the open regulation booking form and asked me, again without a smile or any positive communication, "How many children are there?"

Now I don't know how observant she was because she would have noticed me parking my bike, alone, unless she thought there were some children hiding in the bushes somewhere.

I answered with a smile and a little chuckle, "Only me - just one!" thinking that that would make things much easier for her in calculating the charge and administration.

Without a pause or a thought she almost looked pleased as she said, "Sorry we don't take lone adults!"

I must have looked totally dejected and hoped that this was a wind-up possibly depicting a Monty Python sketch. I'd just cycled eighty six miles against a strong head wind for most of the day, was absolutely shattered, hungry and tired and just needed to put my tent up, have a shower and a meal then go to sleep.

I explained this to her but she answered with the same phrase – "Sorry, we don't take lone adults".

I couldn't understand this rejection. Since starting my ride over a week ago I'd experienced only friendship and cooperation; (Apart from the drunken toff!) Here was someone who was undoubtedly a law abiding citizen but due to a ridiculous rule had been turned into a 'Jobsworth Ogre'. Was this another 'Health & Safety Regulation'?

I asked if she could telephone someone in charge, explain the situation, and get a more acceptable answer from the powers above.

That she could not do. Instead she said that there was another campsite about two miles up the road near some lakes and they might be able to accommodate me. However, she made me feel even more dejected by telling me that they also had the same 'No lone adults' policy. It seemed to please her that I could be left stranded.

I left, letting her know that I thought their rule was pathetic and went into the camp shop next door to stock up with something for a meal, in case I needed to camp rough for the night. The lady in the shop had never heard of this rule in her twenty years working there. I couldn't wait to vent my anger and over the next few months told everyone who asked about my bike ride. Afterwards, I wrote a letter of complaint to the owner who wrote back and apologised. He offered me a free night at their other camp site.

I found my way to the other campsite and stopped at the reception. The office was in fact closed for the night but the young woman still working accepted me anyway and told me where to camp. I asked about the showers and she said that I needed a key for which I would need to leave £10 deposit, refundable when the office opened in the morning at nine o'clock.

I explained that I would be leaving before seven. She thought for a while and told me to forget about the deposit and leave the key under the doormat when I left. A little different from the reception I received from the 'Jobsworth' blonde at 'That Other Campsite'.

There was a cafe here, which was within two minutes of closing when I turned up desperately in need of some food. The lady, being a little more experienced and human than her counterpart at 'That Other Campsite' asked me what I would like from her vast menu. She then told me to go and put my tent up and come back in about twenty minutes when my meal would be ready and I could also eat inside.

I found a quiet spot about a hundred metres away and set about my nightly routine to pitch the tent. I needed to check the gaffa tape wrapped around the broken rear pole. It was the first pole to be inserted and after a quick check the gaffa tape looked intact. I pushed the pole through its sleeve and bent it down to lock into place. I did the same with the middle and front poles and looked up towards the back of the tent to see bright orange near the top of the rear pole. But the tent's green, I thought, only to realise that the broken pole had torn through the gaffa tape then through the tent roof to put a six inch split in it. Just something else to test one's mettle!

I carefully withdrew the broken pole and inspected the tear. There was only one answer – gaffa tape it up and spend the night without the rear pole inserted.

As it was a fine night and my meal would be ready by now, I threw everything inside the half erected tent and cycled around to get my meal. I would have to mend the tent later.

She had made me fish 'n' chips with mushy peas and a pot of tea. She also threw in a couple of slices of bread and butter and had very kindly put a double portion of everything on the plate – it was massive. I'm pleased I was hungry.

She told me to sit down and brought the overflowing plate across to me. Her husband, who I assumed to be a general handyman on the campsite, also had fish 'n' chips and as we were the only ones in the now locked cafe, came over and sat next to me. He absolutely smothered his meal in tomato sauce and we chatted about my adventure.

He managed to get half way through his meal when he put his knife and fork down and said he'd had enough. I must admit that I was also a little more than half way through when I began to struggle and really could have done without the extra portion.

His wife gave him a stern glance shouted over to him with venom in her voice, "What's wrong with that?"

To which he replied, "There's too much tomato sauce on it!"

Her eyes bulged as she glared at him.

"That's an absolute waste of good food, and you know it!"

He made a quick exit and said that he might see me later in the bar.

His wife saw that I was maybe struggling a little and jokingly commented, "You'll not dare leave any of that now!"

Being an absolute coward and utter chicken in the face of aggression my feeble voice answered,

"No, I'm absolutely starving!" and was determined to eat the lot.

A few minutes later her husband returned with a couple of bottles of lager for her presumably as a peace offering.

I finished my meal, thanked her for her hospitality, and went off to find a hosepipe to clean the chain and cogs on my gears. There were two lakes attached to this campsite, one for quiet fishing and the other for jet skis to zoom about on. I asked if I could use their hosepipe to clean down my bike. Again a friendly face showed me the hosepipe and left me to it. It was powerful and I gave my bike a thorough clean.

I brought out the gaffa tape, and ensured that the tear in the tent was well and truly sealed. I put my bike to bed for the night in the front of my half crumpled tent then went off round to the bar for a couple of beers. I crawled into my flattened tent just after nine.

105

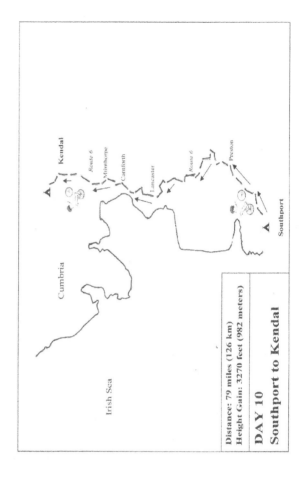

Kendal

Route 6

Milnthorpe

Carnforth

Lancaster

Route 6

Preston

Southport

Cumbria

Irish Sea

Distance: 79 miles (126 km)
Height Gain: 3270 feet (982 meters)

DAY 10
Southport to Kendal

Day 10 – Halfway to Victory

My planned route to Preston would take me on a criss-cross route with the A565 then the A 59. As there was only a proposed Sustrans route between Southport and Preston I planned my route on roads designated as cycle ways on the 1:50000 OS Landranger map. When I made my way to the campsite with the lakes, via 'That Other Campsite' I'd rather not mention, there was a cycle path on both sides of the main dual carriageway, the A565. I saw a few cyclists on this route at my normal morning time of 7 o'clock and wondered if it went all the way to Preston, about fifteen miles away. I asked the first person I passed and he said that he thought it did although there was a short section where you had to cycle on the road. Following this road would save me about ten miles and about an hour; also it was mainly a designated cycle route so I decided to follow it.

The wind from yesterday had disappeared and today was cloudless and almost wind free except for a very light breeze helping me along. I felt that I was flying towards Preston. I passed lots of signs which read *'Southport to Preston Cycleway'* and just before 8 o'clock was at a busy junction on the outskirts of Preston. The only drawback was that I hadn't followed my planned route on the GPS and even though I'd been following the *'Southport to Preston Cycleway'* there were now no signs to guide me to Route 6 which would take me to Lancaster then Kendal, my next destination. I spotted a sign to the Town Centre so followed this until the planned route on my GPS appeared on the screen. I needed to turn right to join it. I cycled through some back streets then eventually came to a park. I was there, Route 6 was now signposted. It went up a steep hill, continued through the park and then at a junction the signs disappeared. I was still on my planned route so followed it by turning right. Unfortunately this took me straight up against a twenty foot brick wall, but at least I was somewhere near the correct route. I skirted the wall until I came to a gate. My planned route was now way off the GPS screen and the only way seemed to be the wrong way down a one way street. I asked a bloke on a bike on his way to work. He also complained about the lack of signs but sent me in the right direction towards the centre of town where I should once again pick up Route 6.

I thanked him and followed his directions. I became trapped on the main bus route into town and was forced to stop at a very busy junction. I pulled onto the path and looked around for any cycle route signs. There were signs everywhere, all sorts of signs at varying heights from waist height upwards. Every available space and convenient pole or post seemed to have a sign attached to it. Arrows, directions, distances, One Way, No Entry, Public Toilets, Museum, Exhibition, Dogs on Lead, No Fouling, Fines for Littering, Bus Stop, No Parking and signs to give an instruction, some information or a warning to every conceivable section of the community they could think of; but no blue NCN sign with Route 6 printed on it. Then through the confused muddle of signs I spotted a blue NCN Route 6 sign about twenty metres away at waist height across two roads. It seemed like a playing card that had magically jumped out from a shuffled pack. At first I couldn't see it at all then it stood out like a sore thumb. All I had to do now was to wait for the lights to change in my favour and head for it. I kept it permanently in view until I reached it just in case it decided to disappear. I spotted another, then another and now they came along thick and fast. Within ten minutes I was out of Preston and in the countryside on my way to Lancaster. The going was good. The hills were gentle although sometimes quite long and the route almost wrapped itself around the M6 and the main west coast railway.

Not having stopped for over 3 hours I was in desperate need of a tea shop. I passed a road sign which read:

GOOSNARGH 2 MILES

I'd read in some information about Route 6 that Goosnargh is famous for '*Goosnargh Cakes*' which have been made there for centuries. Never having heard of them before, I looked forward to sampling one with a cup of tea. As I rounded a corner, there was a shop with a signboard which read '*Hot Pies/Pasties, Tea*'. That'll do me I thought, ditch the fancy cakes, so stopped, bought a hot pasty and a cup of tea, parked myself and the bike on a seat across the road and totally forgot about the Goosnargh Cakes. After I'd finished and got underway again I passed the shop that sold the famous cakes but it was closed. I'm pleased that I decided to ditch them otherwise I would have had to cycle back to the pasty shop!

I'd never been to this part of the world before and was pleasantly surprised at how beautiful it was. As I freewheeled downhill into the very pretty village of Scorton I noticed a shop on the left with a sign which had a magnetic attraction.

'Locally made Ice Cream on sale here'.

My hands seemed to grip the brake levers without any electrical impulse from the grey matter between my ears. It was as though I had developed a second brain to take immediate action when surprisingly confronted with a tea shop or ice cream shop. I parked the bike next to an ancient tractor which was well passed its 'use by' date but was doing a very useful job now as an attraction outside the shop. I walked into the shop expecting it to be the usual village shop selling groceries and of course 'Locally made ice cream' when I couldn't believe my eyes to see an absolute wonderland of gifts and glitter of all sorts. It was like a gold mine or an Aladdin's cave. From the outside it looked quite small but inside it was like the Tardis. You could spend an hour in here just browsing. However, my thoughts right now were not for souvenirs but for ice cream.

"Rum and Raisin and Toffee Fudge please - all in the same cornet!"

I sat outside next to the tractor precariously holding the cornet with two huge dollops of ice cream balanced on top. I don't know how I managed it but I bit my tongue on the first lick so had to be content with a few drops of 'raspberry sauce' to mix with the flavours. I must say it was some of the best ice cream I'd ever tasted.

Ahead, lay another city to negotiate and the chance of cycling through without getting lost was about 50/50. Unfortunately the ice cream came to an end and I needed to head off again along Route 6. The route crossed over the M6 and railway a few times before heading towards the River Lune. It joined an old railway track and headed north for several miles to the outskirts of Lancaster. Since the 'Jumble Signs' in Preston centre, Route 6 has been very well signposted. Before I had time to think about any confusion I might encounter cycling through the centre of Lancaster, I was on the towpath of the beautiful Lancaster canal and pedalling away from the city.

It meanders for miles following the contours of the surrounding hills with the added bonus that the towpath has a wonderfully smooth tarmac surface. The sun was beating down and the views over Morecombe Bay towards the Lake District were stunning.

Built on the opposite bank above the canal are lots of very desirable houses with terraces leading down to the canal, some with moored motor boats. These houses command a perfect position. A drive for your car at the rear, a mooring for your motor launch at the front and fantastic views towards the Lake District, plus one of the prettiest cycle tracks in the country on the opposite bank.

The canal twisted and turned, its route just flowed into tranquillity. I had an immense feeling of mystery and surprise. Always wondering what would be around the next bend. Ducks and swans were in abundance just paddling around searching for food. My wonder was fulfilled as I cycled into the next village, Carnforth.

Here I passed a wonderful looking pub aptly named '*The Canal Bend*' which was packed with people enjoying freshly made bar meals outside, taking advantage of the Mediterranean weather we were experiencing today. I stopped at a vacant seat overlooking the canal and tucked into some two day old sandwiches and a drink out of my water bottle.

I took some photographs of the pub and canal boats tied up alongside. This canal, and the weather to go with it, made me feel so relaxed that I could have cycled on it all day. In fact I hoped that it went all the way to Kendal.

I'd sat around for long enough and continued along the tow path. After about a mile the tarmac ran out and I realised that I hadn't spotted any Route 6 signs since Carnforth. I switched on the GPS and checked the route. Sure enough and true to form I was nowhere near my planned route. I should have turned off the canal tow path at Carnforth, which was now over a mile behind me. I retraced my tracks and turned onto the road which runs through Carnforth to reveal the sign – Route 6 – pointing north towards Kendal.

I was now unfortunately off the level and smooth canal towpath and back on to the usual potholed country lanes. The road went down from the canal and I began to pick up speed as I coasted down along the twisting lane. Coming round one of the bends there was a cock pheasant ambling along without a care in the world when I turned up to spoil his day. Just like all dumb animals, instead of just getting out of the way and hopping over a hedge, he decided to run along the road in front of me. I slowed down and followed. I remembered as a child watching the Road Runner cartoons. This was just like that. How far would the pheasant run before giving in? His legs went faster and faster but I kept three to four metres behind him. If I tried to overtake on his left he veered to the left and if I tried on the right then he veered to the right. He seemed to be playing with me always wanting the upper hand. He made no attempt to fly off for over two hundred metres then he managed to accomplish a vertical takeoff whilst running at about twenty miles an hour. On reaching the height of the hedge he veered off to the left, allowing me to pass through.

A few miles further along the road, a buzzard appeared from the side and flew along in front of me about five metres above my head. Its majestic glide seemed to send out a telepathic message that even if I tried I could not match its powers. Again after about two hundred metres it flew off to the side and landed in a tree.

There were now more hills to cope with, some of which I walked up. On reaching the top of one of the steeper hills there was a young woman cycling the opposite way to me who had also pushed up her side of the hill. We looked at each other as we mounted our bikes and simultaneously said "At least we'll both be going downhill now!"

It certainly was downhill once again and the twisting, winding roads through the surrounding pine forest once again reminded me of skiing. I experienced the beauty and excitement of skiing for the first time only twenty years ago at the ripe old age of forty two. For the first five years or so I constantly crossed ski tips to either fall or plough headlong into snow drifts. I remember one such incident when my wife and friends decided not to venture out onto the piste as visibility was down to about a metre in white out conditions. I'd managed to find the top of the piste, luckily some chair lifts were open, and spotted the dark shape of some other skiers ahead of me slowly progressing down the slope. Lumps and bumps in the snow were impossible to detect as were sudden drops in the slope. I was concentrating on keeping the other skiers in view when the ground disappeared beneath me forcing that wonderful falling feeling of butterflies to create a little fear. The tips of my skis buried themselves in a soft mound of snow catapulting me five metres head first to end up buried head down up to my shoulders in powder snow. There was no-one around to fall about laughing at the sight of a pair of skis sticking vertically out of the snow and their owner five metres downhill with his head buried in the snow with legs pointing skywards.

Then for the next fifteen years I probably only fell only a handful of times until I became the proud owner of a brand new pair of carver skis. What a difference they made. Turning was easier; staying on them was easier and I probably became too confident. On my last school ski trip to Courmayeur I managed to wipe out twice into snow drifts where no-one else was involved but on three occasions other skiers were involved. The first involved a jovial colleague, Kerry, who was waiting with the rest of the staff team for me to catch them up after having left my rucksack at a mountain restaurant. I spotted them all standing in a line half-way down the piste. I put in some long sweeping turns and thought it was a good idea to come to a resounding halt just in front of Kerry, and hopefully shower him with snow. I picked up speed, to the right, to the left and then headed down towards the group who were watching me in trepidation all the way. I was renowned for inaccurate stopping. About four metres from my goal I turned my knees to the hill to hopefully stop just in front of him but my skis didn't bite and I ploughed straight into him. Fortunately for Kerry, he is quite rotund, in a polite sort of way, and I only sent him on a backward slide for a few metres, whilst I bounced of him and ended up in total wipe out. There was silence until I sat up with snow packed into my ears and up my nose and a very shocked Kerry started to laugh, closely followed by the others. After taking a good ten minutes to control the uncontrollable laughter we set off again down the piste.

Also skiing in our group was one of our coach drivers who happened to be quite a good skier. The two of us started to criss-cross each other down the piste, just missing each other on the cross over, until one of us either turned too early or too late and as we turned looked straight into each other's eyes travelling at about twenty miles an hour. We collided head on and for the second time in less than quarter of an hour I found myself diving head-long into the snow. He almost mirrored my calamity but there was no uncontrollable laughter from him this time. He re-attached his skis and mouthed something about a buffoon, leaving me sprawled in the snow. I spotted that my other colleagues had noticed the collision and had resumed their fits of laughter at a safe distance.

Later that day, we skied off separately after arranging to meet at a restaurant half way down a narrow piste amongst the trees. I was on my final approach to the restaurant which involved a sharp right hand turn off the piste to stop and park the skis. I made a wide sweep intending to do one of my rapid stops when I caught the wrong edge of my ski on a lump of hard snow. I would have managed to stop in time, except for the fact that about twenty pairs of skis were left lying in the snow where their lazy owners had just stepped out of them. I was travelling at a fair rate when I hit the first pair, skiing right over them; then the second and third, scattering them in many directions. This contact with skis did nothing to aid my reduction in speed, nor my ability to turn. Straight ahead I saw an elderly couple enjoying a glass of vino calda (mulled wine), when I hit their deck chairs and sent them sprawling in the snow.

"Must be English – too fast!" one of them shouted shaking his fist.

I saw that they were uninjured, apologised from a distance and made a hasty retreat. It was the wrong restaurant anyway!

If I fall off the bike my landing will not be as cushioned. Perhaps a little slower downhill, especially with the heavy load I'm carrying would be a wise decision!

The signage for Route 6 was very good and after a few miles I cycled into Milnthorpe, which is right on the edge of Southern Lakeland. It was time again for a cup of tea and some cake. There was a small market in the square which I wandered around looking to buy some fruit when I noticed a couple about my age or slightly older who seemed desperate to talk to me. Eventually the man came over and we started talking about LEJOG. He seemed very interested in the route I'd chosen because, with his wife, they had cycled much of my route but in stages and over many months.

They had also cycled along Route 62 through Liverpool and like me had felt that there was a strange atmosphere along its whole length.

He pointed me in the right direction for the tea shop and asked me how he could sponsor me. I gave him a card and with my bike walked off for a welcome cuppa and whatever they had to eat.

He and his wife followed me into the cafe after a few minutes and wondered if they could sponsor me there and then. I should have jumped at the chance but recommended that they sponsor me using the Just Giving web site as the Government would also add 28% Gift Aid. They promised that they would contribute but must have lost the card before they could manage.

The waitresses in the tea shop must have been listening to our conversation, because when I went to pay the bill I was presented with a slab of fruit cake with £3.50 on the price tag. I kept it for later and must say it turned out to be the best fruit cake I'd ever tasted. It was now nearly three o' clock and with ten miles to go to Kendal I needed to get a move on as finding a replacement tent pole for the one I'd broken was a priority.

As I cycled into Kendal and crossed one of the main roads there were a couple of people on bikes waiting to cross the opposite way. Their bikes were as laden as mine so they were probably cycling long distance. They were in fact cycling from John o'Groats to Land's End – JOGLE not LEJOG.

LEJOG sounds distinctly French, probably because of the prefix LE... and implies that it is a proper noun naming a well known endurance activity like the Lyke Wake Walk (LWW) or Coast to Coast (C2C) or The Pennine Way, whereas JOGLE sounds like the noun, to joggle and suggests an action performed by men to adjust themselves to feel more comfortable. It doesn't sound quite as important as LEJOG, even though doing a JOGLE challenge is probably slightly more difficult than the LEJOG challenge.

The two people in question were married, cycling JOGLE for charity, but were cycling about fifty miles a day then stopping at the nearest B&B. They were following the same route as me but the other way of course and we exchanged vital information about what lay ahead for all of us. We said goodbye and wished each other luck.

On entering Kendal town centre I needed to find an outdoor shop that had spare tent poles. I tried all the major outdoor stores like Nevis Sport and Field & Trek but they only sold complete tents – no spares. My last option was Millets. The man in the shop was magnificent. They sold all the spares you could ever need for anything outdoors. He told me to bring my bike into the shop and show him the broken pole. After trying lots of old poles from the back of his shop he ended up having to raid an unopened packet then saw a piece off a new pole to fit. Once we'd managed to make up a new pole, disregarding the broken bit, he even asked me if I wanted to put my tent up in the shop so we could make sure that the new pole fitted. I convinced him that I knew it would fit. Anyway my tent was soaked after the heavy dew the previous night. He was so concerned that the pole should be right that he loaned me the hacksaw he'd used to cut the new pole to the correct length and told me just to drop it off at their store in Ambleside on my way through the next day. He gave me directions for the quickest way to the campsite at Staveley, about four miles along the road towards Windermere.

It was Friday and the weather forecast for the weekend was very favourable. The Camping & Caravan Club site at Staveley is very popular and extremely well run. I found the reception and booked in. I was personally taken to the exact spot on which to pitch my tent. The pitch was furnished with its own picnic table and parasol which I had all to myself but more importantly there was a restaurant and bar which I would make use of after making sure my tent was fully functional and waterproof.

I unpacked the tent and erected it. The new pole worked fine but the Gaffa tape had started to peel off the tent fabric. I stuck it down with even more Gaffa tape but realised that this could keep on happening so made a trip to the camp shop to see if they had any super glue. I explained to the lady in the shop what I needed it for and being a woman she said, "Why don't you sew it down?"

Good idea, I thought, but I didn't have a sewing kit. The one thing which I should have had on my list – I forgot probably because I'm a man.

She offered to lend me her sewing kit and would drop it off when the Friday evening rush had died down.

I was looking forward to tomorrow for several reasons. An old college friend who lives near Carlisle, whom I hadn't seen for a couple of years was going to meet me at the Carlisle campsite to catch up on old times and go for a bar meal. He went by the name 'Pukey Dick' at college for obvious reasons. Being a keen sportsman he had a few false teeth acquired after various sporting impacts. Every time he embarrassed himself by having to live up to his name he would remove his false teeth to avoid having to retrieve them from a pile of vomit.

I would also be cycling through the Lake District and starting the second half of my journey, plus Julian was going to meet me at the campsite near Carlisle and cycle with me to Glasgow. I was looking forward to four days of company. When I phoned home to report the day's activities to my wife, Gail, so she could enter it on my blog, she told me the bad news.

Earlier in the day, Julian was cycling home from work as part of his training. He was following another cyclist through Hartlepool and was in the act of overtaking him when the other cyclist without warning, turned right. Julian ploughed into him sending both of them flying. Unfortunately for Julian he put his hand out to save himself and broke a thumb. A visit to the local hospital, advice from the doctor, lots of strapping and severe pain, put Julian on the sidelines where cycling from Carlisle to Glasgow was concerned.

I phoned him to express my concern for his injury. Because he was looking forward to a few days camping he insisted on getting the train to Carlisle as he had already booked it together with a few days off work.

After a well earned shower, I headed off to the restaurant, enjoyed a filling meal and a couple of pints then returned to my tent to await the sewing kit. It didn't arrive before I dosed off for the night before 9 o'clock.

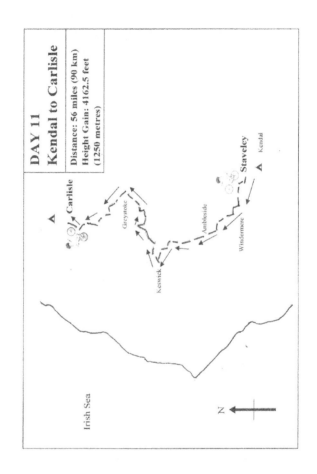

DAY 11
Kendal to Carlisle

Distance: 56 miles (90 km)
Height Gain: 4162.5 feet
(1250 metres)

Day 11 – Lakes and Mountains

As usual the tent was soaked inside with condensation and outside with dew. I unzipped the inner tent to feel the cool air on my head and shoulders and noticed a little white box, not mine, under the fly sheet. On close inspection, it was the promised sewing kit. Even though the lady had been hard pressed processing new campers until late into the evening she hadn't forgotten my dilemma. I thought I'd better set to and sew up my damaged tent. After a good ten minutes trying to thread the needle I gave up, mainly due to the fact that I was still half asleep, so I went through my usual morning routine, wrote the kind lady a note and promised to return the needle and green cotton that I had borrowed in a few days by post.

I was on my way before seven and left the note and sewing box on the step at the reception then rejoined Route 6 which took me towards Windermere. The route was well signed with a designated cycle path by the side of the normally very busy A591. However before seven on a Saturday morning it was quiet. The route was generally easy with only one roller coaster section giving me any trouble.

Route finding looked easy practically all the way to Keswick, although I would not be going through Keswick, as Route 6 followed the A591 most of the way but turned off at St John's in the Vale towards Threlkeld. I reached Windermere well before seven thirty and found myself yet again on a downhill 'ski run' past the station. I felt the wind whistling through my cycle helmet and imagined that I could be in Carlisle by early afternoon. Thoughts of when I was sixteen in 1963 pestered me after my father gave me his old racing bike (now called a road bike) which had been standing unused in the garden shed for years. He bought it second hand in 1935 and used it to get to work and back for almost thirty years. I was keen to take it for a spin and cycled to our local village which was accessed by a long descent into the village centre which then continued downhill for a further mile or so. My destination was along a left turn about half way down the hill.

Riding the 'racer' for the first time I became over enthusiastic and set off without checking it, a job which my father sternly recommended, testing it out on the long descent to see what it could do. I applied the brakes to prepare for the left turn resulting in both cables snapping leaving me powerless to come to a halt. My speed increased as I approached the turn but my dilemma was the busy village centre just two hundred metres straight ahead. I had to turn otherwise I would certainly have ended up being another passenger in an ambulance or even worse. My only hope was to swerve into the left turn. I looked around to ensure there weren't any vehicles overtaking me or coming towards me, moved into the middle of the road to widen the turn then swerved into the fast approaching left turn. I thought that running the rims along the kerb should slow me down but that idea was thwarted by a parked car within fifteen yards after the turn. About 50 yards further on the little road came to an abrupt end protected by a wooden fence with pointed slats and a sharp right turn into a narrow back lane. I hit the fence and catapulted over it ripping my chin and neck on it as I flew over the handlebars. The bike crumpled on impact bending the frame and front fork to render it only fit for scrap while I ended up with my bottom half attached to the top of the fence by my trouser waist belt and my head sharing the soil in someone's allotment with a row of onions. I hid from my father for days!

Back in reality the sun was shining through a deep blue sky and the air was starting to warm up nicely. Perhaps I was going a little too fast for comfort with such a heavy load. There was a sudden metallic snapping sound followed by a constant whirring which didn't sound too promising and my mind went wild with fear. I could see the steep descent continuing several hundred yards ahead. It's amazing how only thoughts of injury and destruction from the past fly through your head. I gently applied the brakes and came to a halt by the side of the road. I breathed a relieved sigh as I knew it wasn't the brakes. A few people out for an early morning stroll gave a startled glance as they witnessed the abnormal sound. That sound had come from somewhere at the back of my bike and on close inspection I found that the bracket which fastens the pannier to the bike frame near the rear hub had snapped on the right hand side. Fortunately the broken part was pointing backwards and merely produced the 'lollipop in the spokes' sound effect. Had it been facing forwards there would have been broken spokes and pandemonium galore.

I felt that the early and good start was about to be lost as I now needed to find some way of mending the broken bracket. I lifted the whole pannier up so the broken part was resting on its counterpart which was still attached to the bike. Gaffa tape to the rescue, I secured it by wrapping copious amounts of tape around the shattered parts. It worked, the pannier was now secure and I was off. I knew that I would need to replace the pannier and the nearest bike shop was in Ambleside, but I'd be there well before eight o'clock and they didn't open till nine. Perhaps I'd just have to hang around and be an hour later reaching Carlisle.

After a couple of miles I was conscious of an intermittent high pitched buzzing sound, a bit like an irritating gnat in your ear. The pannier had slipped a little and was leaning over to the right thereby catching the treads on the tyre. I would need to make yet another repair. I'd put the broken bracket on the rear side of the bolt that attached it to the frame and this caused it to slip, so I forced it onto the front side of the bolt, wrapped it tight with lots more Gaffa tape in the hope that it solved the problem. A cyclist on his way to work stopped to offer his help. He saw that I'd just about made a temporary fix.

'If you need any more Gaffa tape I work just around the corner!' he offered.

He said that Keswick was my best option for a new pannier as I would probably get there for about ten o'clock, if the pannier hadn't fallen off by then.

I thanked him and we went off in opposite directions.

With the hacksaw loaned to me by Milletts in Kendal attached to the top of my tent roll so I wouldn't forget it, I was on the lookout for Milletts in Ambleside so I could drop it off. It was easy to find as the store was situated on the one way system. Two miles gone and the new mend hadn't come away yet. Ambleside was quiet, considering that in a couple of hours it would be heaving with shoppers and tourists. Continuing along the A591 I passed Rydal then Grasmere. I knew that Dunmail Raise was ahead of me which entails a long climb up to the pass before it drops down towards Thirlmere.

As I looked ahead, it didn't look very steep, but I've driven over Dunmail Raise many times and it feels steep in a car. A couple of years ago I watched a fully laden cyclist struggle up the hill during a downpour. I remembered the distressed look on his face as he forced his way uphill with great difficulty and thought, 'That could be me in a few years!....Mmmmm!!'

The pannier bracket was still intact. I focussed on a gatepost about a hundred yards up the hill and was determined not to stop before it. I reached the gatepost then focused on a bush higher up. My thighs were now feeling the pull of the hill but I managed to make it to the bush. Just one more then I'll walk, but my legs rebelled and refused to be forced any further. I stopped and pushed. About a hundred yards from the top, the hill levelled out a little so I got on and pedalled again.

Cars passed me in both directions and a thought occurred to me that those drivers who hadn't seen me pushing the bike might have thought that I'd shown great determination and pedalled all the way up the hill. Perhaps the cyclist I saw a few years ago had done the same...who knows!

This was the weekend of 'The Bob Graham Round' which covers seventy four miles of forty two Lakeland Peaks with about 28,500 feet of ascent. It must be completed within twenty four hours. The official traditional start and finish is the Moot Hall in Keswick but in June an organised event starts and finishes at Seathwaite in Borrowdale due to the large number of fell runners. The route also crosses the A591 over Dunmail Raise and pitched at the top of the pass were several tents, surrounded by marshals and cars. I think that my challenge was the easier option as several runners who were taking refreshments were up to their eyes in mud, sweat and tears with just another forty or so miles to run. About the same distance as I had to cycle to reach Carlisle.

Once over the pass I knew that it was virtually downhill all the way to Keswick except for one small steep hill. I was winding my way through the crowds on this busy market Saturday within an hour. There are two cycle shops in Keswick that I know of so I made my way to the nearest one which I thought was next to the motor museum. I wasn't quite sure where it was so 'When in doubt don't mess about' and ask someone, preferably a local. So I asked the first person who I thought could help. He said 'Sure!' and beckoned me to follow him. He immediately disappeared down some steep steps then I saw him vanish around a corner. I couldn't follow very quickly due to having to negotiate the steps with a heavy bike. Fortunately the cycle shop was just around the corner. The Pedlar. I bought a new pannier and changed it over putting the old one in a nearby skip and guess what? The Pedlar was also the home of a fantastic tea shop.

There was a spare table on the sundrenched veranda which I commandeered, ordered my food, sat back in the chair, gazed up at the sky, closed my eyes and drifted into the land of nod with the knowledge that my bike and attachments were once again in A1 condition. Keswick is a wonderful town which I had frequented many times bringing many students to sample its intriguing atmosphere during school camps in June and Mountaineering Club Challenges with senior students. One in particular which drifted through my mind was on the weekend of September 29th in 1996 when I organised a two day challenge walking from Coniston to Keswick to raise money to buy a voice activated computer for a fourteen year old boy from the school, who had had the serious misfortune of breaking his neck to become permanently paralysed due to a swimming accident whilst on holiday.

Our challenge was to camp at Coniston on the Friday night of the Challenge, climb Coniston Old Man and walk across the tops to Wrynose pass where our support team would meet us with tents and cooking equipment. Continue into the head of Langdale then climb up to Sprinkling Tarn where we would camp on the Saturday Night. Then make our way to Seathwaite in Borrowdale on Sunday where we would deposit our tents and other surplus equipment back with the support team before finishing our journey on foot down Borrowdale to Keswick.

Everyone set off in high spirits to reach the summit of Coniston Old Man in two hours then cross the tops to meet the support team at the Three Shires Stone which stands over eight feet high on Wrynose Pass. Incidentally, three days later, this stone which had stood up to every type of storm and tempest that could be thrown at it since 1816, was knocked down and broken into three pieces by an old lady who lost control of her Morris Minor on the treacherous pass. I think it has since been mended and replaced.

We collected our camping equipment and set off for Langdale. The weather forecast was not good, high winds and torrential rain being on the cards for the afternoon and throughout the night. The rain started at the head of Langdale. Everyone quickly made use of their waterproofs except for one boy. A very intelligent sixteen year old boy who later went on to achieve nine A*s at GCSE and four Grade As at A Level but without an ounce of common sense. His excuse for not wearing his waterproofs was that he was warm enough and the rain didn't bother him. He was suitably reprimanded and had his waterproofs on before he could blink. Unfortunately his jacket was of the plastic sort worn by workmen who dig trenches and it gave him no warmth at all. He was given a spare fleece to wear under it before commencing on our journey. As we learnt later this particular weekend was the first time since Mountain Rescue teams were first established that all four teams in the Lakes had been called out at the same time. We passed two of the teams on their way down to Langdale carrying injured people on stretchers. Everyone had their heads down pummelled by the wind and rain.

At Sprinkling Tarn we found a partially sheltered spot and started to erect the tents. I managed to put my tent up as did three of the boys in one tent and another staff tent. Unfortunately the wind was too strong for the other tents to go up. The task was futile. Whilst everyone worked tirelessly to try and erect the tents I noticed that our sixteen year old with the inappropriate jacket was just sitting in the storm with his hood down and jacket open to the elements. This looked like the onset of hypothermia. I quickly managed to bundle him into my tent out of the weather along with his bag and got him into his sleeping bag. The staff gathered in a huddle to make a decision. The main problem was the boy with suspected hypothermia. The three lads who had managed to erect their tent were now inside it and in their sleeping bags. Apart from one other staff tent no other tents would go up. There were twenty five of us altogether.

A decision was made that I would stay with the boy along with another staff member in my tent. The three boys already tucked up in their tent would remain with us but everyone else would walk down to Seathwaite to the support team about three miles away. It was now dark.

Three staff and seventeen senior students set off into the darkness and storm whilst my colleague who is six and a half feet tall squeezed into my tent with the also six foot boy. I gathered heavy boulders and placed them on every peg on both tents then manipulated myself under the flysheet of my tent, arranged the three rucksacks so at least I could get in and out to check pegs in the night and slipped into my sleeping bag. My tent was a two person Vango Hurricane the same type of tent the other three lads were in so I knew that as long as we'd erected them correctly they should stand up to the weather. However space was a bit limited for me and two six footers meaning that the hypothermic boy was soon warmed through.

Whenever I'm in adrenalin fuelled situations the need to go to the loo seems to pass then as soon as I got settled down in my sleeping bag and found a comfortable position I was desperate for a pee. The tent was forced down by the wind and flattened against our faces. It was another three hours before I found the will power to get up and venture outside. It's such a chore getting out of your sleeping bag to leave the warmth behind, put on a waterproof jacket whilst in an unknown yoga position then go out into the horrendous wind and rain making sure not to allow the wind into the tent. I didn't bother with any boots and after relieving myself remembering to kneel down with my back to the wind replaced the boulders which had been torn off the tent pegs by the fierce wind. I noticed that a pole had snapped on the other tent which had torn through the fabric. The worst that could happen is that they would get wet a little. I returned into my nest.

The hypothermic boy was snoring loudly, totally oblivious to the frantic activity that had gone on around him. My colleague and I lay awake most of the night feeling the cold tent forced onto our faces throughout.

As it began to get light there was no let up in the ferocity of the storm. It had forced itself upon us for almost twelve hours when at precisely seven in the morning it stopped almost abruptly. We lay there in silence, the inner tent which had detached itself from the outer, draped over us like a soggy blanket. My six and a half foot colleague whose feet were protruding slightly at the bottom end of the tent whispered, "There's something nibbling my toes!"

I gently opened the outer zip and peaked through the gap.

"It's a fox!"

Our faces were only six feet apart as we gazed into each other's eyes. It stared at me, having had a good sniff at my colleagues feet then calmly turned round and trotted off over the hill.

"Hello Sir! You ordered chiabatta with sundried tomatoes and mascarpone cheese!"

I jumped up, looked totally confused for a few seconds, confirmed my order and was back in June 2009.

After my mini feast on the sun drenched veranda I wandered around the market looking for the hardware stall. I needed to replenish the Gaffa tape as it had been in great demand lately. They only had bright green in the small rolls or large rolls weighing 2 kilos and 6 inches in diameter. I opted for the small green roll.

I started to get carried away a little and forgot about the time. It was now after midday and I was barely half way to Carlisle.

I joined the old railway at Keswick station and cycled towards the A66 through the crowds of cyclists and walkers. After about a mile the crowds thinned out and before long I was yet again virtually alone on the route. The cycle path which runs parallel with the A66 alternates between a cycle path next to the A66 and the old disused A66.

Back in 1995, the C2C was the only previous long distance bike ride I'd attempted along with five friends. We cycled this section during a storm, heading towards Penrith. Just before Penrith the storm abated raising our spirits, so we stopped at the town sign by the side of the road to take a photograph as a keepsake. There were some road works with traffic lights about twenty yards after the sign. As we lined ourselves up for the photo next to the sign someone discovered that by covering up the letter 'R' on the sign it read 'PEN-ITH'. The occupants of a passing pickup truck towing a compressor noticed our humour and pointed with laughter. A second after they passed we heard the screech of brakes and an almighty bang as they hadn't noticed the road works and temporary traffic lights ahead! Our getaway was rapid!

At the top of the hill near Scales the cycle route makes its way onto a narrow lane which winds around Blencathra. It climbs gradually until it overlooks the A66 with fantastic views back towards the hills around Keswick. I passed an Alpaca farm which seems to be a growing breed throughout the country.

I continued on the lane which eventually came out at Mungrisdale, two miles up the valley from the A66. I would now have to cycle two miles back on another road to rejoin the cycle path alongside the A66.

The hill went quite steeply down so the cycling was easy. A young deer jumped out of the long grass next to me on my thrilling downhill ride. It was two hundred yards away before I could stop and get my camera out.

After a few miles on and off the A66 cycle route and the old road I arrived at Penruddock where a left turn would now take me along quiet country lanes towards Carlisle. The hills were now long and rolling, gradually working their way down towards the Vale of Eden.

'*Cyclists Tea Shop – 3 Miles.*' Did I just see an appealing sign I thought or was it a mirage? There was nothing here, just the odd farm house and no villages for miles. Then there was another. '*Cyclists Tea Shop,*' prefixing an arrow. I must be getting close. I was also following Route 71 now having left Route 6 back in Keswick. The tea shop must be on Route 71 which is part of the C2C (Coast to Coast) usually from Workington or Whitehaven to Sunderland, or anywhere on the east coast. A small posse of riders passed me going in the other direction. They weren't fully laden so must only be out for the day. Then more riders passed. Perhaps the tea shop had been their destination.

'*For Cyclists Tea Shop take the third right after about a mile*'

I kept my eyes open as an opportunity like this could not be missed. Then there it was. An old farmhouse converted into a wonderful little country tea shop. Tables and chairs filled the garden. There was a bike rack at the front which was unfortunately full, but I managed to find a parking place for my bike against a grassy bank.

A sign read.

'Car park at rear only for vehicles supporting cyclists doing events.'

The sign also welcomed all comers but they would have to park their cars elsewhere. The only problem being that all roads within half a mile were very narrow and had nowhere to park. Anyway, I was on a bike so I quickly grabbed the only spare table outside and placed my order.

In this place, a mug of tea *means 'A MUG OF TEA'* and a scone means 'A SCONE'. Everything they sold was huge and tasted fantastic. This cyclists' tea shop in the middle of nowhere is well worth the effort to get on your bike and sample their menu. It was near Greystoke.

Only about twenty miles now and it was virtually flat. I passed an intriguing piece of artwork.

Somebody had taken some time to make the signs out of iron but I couldn't tell whether they were meant to be part of an installation or just dumped – probably just dumped. Standing about six feet high in the long grass and covered in rust they read *'PEACE'* and *'LOVE'.* Perhaps they'd been there since the 1960s!

Dalston beckoned now and I cycled into the campsite at Dalston Hall around about four o'clock. The site was excellent with an abundance of red squirrels cautiously wandering around. The warden had a broad Cumbrian accent and like all of the campsite owners, except one, was extremely friendly. He explained that the showers were free but I would need a twenty pence piece to activate the shower then retrieve it out of the box below the slot and just keep on putting it in the slot as many times as I wanted. The only problem was that the box with the slot was not inside the shower cubicle and was located about three metres away around a corner. It also swallowed several twenty pence pieces without refunding them.

I was just enjoying a well earned ice cream when 'Pukey Dick' and his wife arrived. I mentioned that Julian was also joining us but would have to catch the train back from Carlisle at seven o'clock. This didn't leave us much time for a bar meal. Dick said he would return at half past five then take him to the station in time for his train.

My tent was almost erected, being very careful with the poles now, making sure they were properly inserted, when Julian arrived with Andy, his friend from Glasgow.

I hadn't met Andy before but he had sponsored me after Julian had told him about my ride. Andy is the sort of person whom everyone would want as a friend.

Julian met him in a bothy in a remote part of Scotland when they were both back packing a couple of years ago. They spent the night in the bothy and after breakfast Julian left to walk back to his car a good fifteen miles away. On reaching his car, Julian searched his pockets and rucksack for his car keys unable to find them anywhere. He realised that he must have left them back at the bothy.

'Are these what you're looking for?'

It was Andy. Well after Julian had left, Andy had noticed that Julian's keys must have fallen out of his pocket and even though he planned to go in a completely different direction had followed Julian to where he said his car was parked. They have been friends ever since.

Now just to confirm what a fantastic guy Andy is, he'd been reading my blog and had read that Julian had broken his thumb which rendered him unable to cycle with me from Carlisle to Glasgow. So he telephoned Julian, offered to pick him up at Carlisle station and spend two nights camping; the first night at Dalston and the second at Castle Douglas. This is to be my next stop. Andy also intended to cycle with me to the Scottish border at Gretna, cycle back to Dalston to pick Julian up then meet me again at Castle Douglas.

I spent the next half hour or so making a better job of my temporary patch on the tent. I used the new green Gaffa tape to secure the outside edge of the black patch. Just for good measure squeezed the last few drops of super glue under the green edge then finally managed to thread the needle and sew the edge of the green Gaffa tape down. Hopefully that will do the trick!

Camped next to us were a vicar and his wife. They seemed to be experienced cyclists and well equipped for their adventures. They had a trailer attached to their car with a tandem and bike trailer on it. Although they hadn't cycled LEJOG they had completed many parts of it including Lochs and Glens from Carlisle to Inverness. They assured me the scenery was fantastic throughout and made specific reference to the long ride down into Ayr which incorporated miles of uninterrupted downhill cruising where some excitement would certainly be experienced.

Dick arrived spot on five thirty and we all piled into his car for the short trip to the Bridge End Inn, the pub of his choice (knowing the area) in Dalston village. This was definitely top of my list for quality bar meals to date.

After being dropped off back at the campsite, Julian and Andy sauntered off for a walk while I turned in for the night. After all it was after 9 o'clock!

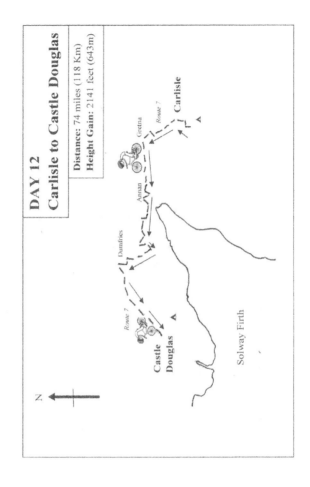

DAY 12
Carlisle to Castle Douglas

Distance: 74 miles (118 Km)
Height Gain: 2141 feet (643m)

Carlisle

Gretna

Route 7

Annan

Dumfries

Route 7

Castle
Douglas

Solway Firth

N

Day 12 – Across the Border

Oddly enough there wasn't a drop of condensation on the tent this morning. Everything was bone dry. Andy was starting to stir but Julian slept on. Since he wasn't joining us there was no need for him to get up early. There wasn't a cloud to be seen although the forecast, supplied by Andy's upmarket mobile phone, was for the sky to be overcast with possible drizzle, slowly heading north. Perhaps the forecast was wrong, or the rain had already moved north.

We were off at a quarter to seven and cycled towards the river. Pukey Dick had told us of a short cut which shortened the route by about a mile. It involved crossing the main west coast railway by using the self controlled gate. This was a first for both of us and we assumed that if there was a train approaching then we couldn't get access across the rail line. It worked but we both crossed with haste and caution. The cycle track along by the river was superb. Level and smooth. We soon established a good rhythm and were eager to get into Scotland. It followed the river and there were the usual NCN signs to guide us. We were on Route 7 now and I would be following Route 7 all the way to Inverness.

We passed the usual early morning dog walkers and joggers and rode with speed and confidence until the track came to a sudden end filling us with confusion. We found ourselves enclosed by a high fence on three sides. We stopped and pondered. Looked at each other and in unrehearsed unison asked each other!

"Have we missed a turn?"

Andy confirmed what I'd told him about signs disappearing and routes heading to what seemed like nowhere. A jogger ran passed us as we checked the GPS, acknowledged our 'Good morning' greeting and disappeared through the fence. We were bewildered because neither of us had noticed the gap but on closer inspection there it was. It was hidden by being at right angles to the line of the fence, so looking directly at the fence you couldn't see it. Del Boy would have referred to us as being a couple of Plonkers!

Within a few minutes we were in the centre of Carlisle and lost! We must have missed a sign. I switched on the GPS again and sure enough we were off the planned route. We found ourselves cycling through the deserted shopping precinct apart from a few street cleaners and tramps. It took us about ten minutes to get ourselves back on to the planned route and we were soon on a minor road out of Carlisle heading for Gretna.

At this stage in my journey, the routes seemed to be well signposted so I kept my GPS switched off in order to conserve the batteries. A set of three rechargeable batteries would last about twelve hours of constant use but the problem was getting them charged. I had managed to do this at Whitchurch but after that hadn't needed to as the routes were all well signed. However, as we had experienced in Carlisle there are places where the signs have disappeared or just aren't there. My GPS was an invaluable tool for unforeseen situations.

Yet again, we came to a T-Junction without a sign. We guessed and turned left which unfortunately took us into the middle of a farm yard swarming with cows. The farmer appeared wearing green wellies, green rubber dungarees and a long green rubber coat. Apart from his head he was entirely clad in green rubber.

He calmly looked at us and said, "I think you're lost!"

He was also covered from head to toe in sloppy brown cow muck.

We looked at him apologetically, pointed back the way we came, and said,

"It must be that way then!"

He nodded, so we turned, ensuring not to coat our wheels in the sloppy cow muck and headed back. Shortly after the T-Junction where we had gone wrong we spotted a Route 7 sign.

As luck would have it, the new stretch of the M74 which links the M6 at Carlisle to the M74 near Gretna had recently been completed and the plan was to use the old road as a Route 7 cycle path. This was now complete and avoided cycling to Longtown then back to Gretna, saving about nine miles. We stopped at the border to take a few photos then Andy headed back to Dalston to get his car and Julian. We'd meet again at Castle Douglas.

I followed Route 7 through Gretna then into the countryside and eventually to Annan which appeared to be a little run down.

It was here in the 14th Century where Robert the Bruce's family lived and in 1332 where his followers defeated Balliol's forces which ended the first invasion of Scotland by the English.

In the 18th Century, Annan made its wealth as a shipbuilding town constructing mainly clippers. There is little evidence of that wealth today as the town looks dreary and in need of some investment. A group of cyclists gathered in the town centre probably for their Sunday cycling excursion.

After Annan the route drops down to the coast until it passes through the tiny hamlet of Powfoot. As the time approached ten o'clock and I spotted a seat facing south towards the Lake District hills I felt that it was time for a rest. A row of fisherman's cottages behind me had the same view on what was now a gloriously sunny day. The overcast skies were just to the north, but to the south was unbroken sunshine. It looked as though I was destined to enjoy another fabulous day.

Continuing along Route 7 I passed through the tiny village of Ruthwell where the first savings bank was founded, then further down the road I noticed a sign referring to Brow Well which has a Robbie Burns connection. Apparently shortly before he died in the prime of his life at only thirty seven, he was ill-advised by his doctor to visit Brow Well, take its water and bathe in the sea. The doctor mistakenly diagnosed his condition as 'flying gout' whereas he was in very poor health due to a heart condition. Just one look at the well was enough to realise that anyone drinking from it would achieve a similar fate. It is reminiscent of the brightly coloured foul smelling liquid which oozes from the bottom of a pile of manure.

This part of Route 7 follows the coast then travels inland beside the River Nith towards Dumfries. Near the mouth of the river there is a small village called Glencaple which imported huge amounts of tea and tobacco from America a hundred and fifty years ago. Wooden ships used to carry the cargo were also built here; the first was called 'The Lord Nelson'. Seats set out by the side of the river are shaped like one hundred and fifty year old sailing ships as a commemoration to the village's seafaring heritage. The village was in fact the port for Dumfries as the river is only navigable up to this village except at high tide.

After a further six miles or so I was cycling through the very busy park in Dumfries. Then something near to my heart caught my eye – Grierson's Coffee Shop. It was warm and sunny, there were tables and chairs set outside and it looked very welcoming, plus it was about midday and this was the first tea shop I'd passed. The fact that it was labelled as a coffee shop was irrelevant.

I ordered a cheese and onion toasty with a pot of tea which came to the outrageous sum of £3.10 and sat outside to await my meal. My snack was with me within ten minutes except I'd expected a couple of cheese and onion toasties with a pot of tea which is what I got - plus a plate full of salad and chips to go with it. I didn't really want that much in the middle of the day but since it was there in front of me and I'd paid for it I had to eat it. Great value! I managed to become well and truly stuffed and spent a little longer than usual to finish the pot of tea.

Back on the bike I rejoined Route 7 which followed a recently surfaced old railway path for about two miles then onto a long straight road which made a gradual ascent for miles.

When on our C2C cycle ride in 1995, a few miles after we'd passed through Cockermouth we were all feeling a little peckish so stopped at the first pub serving bar meals that we came across. An hour later plus a couple of pints and a huge plate of pie, peas and chips we set off downhill and into Winlatter forest. The forest track started to rise and we all came to a united halt, got off and walked. We'd eaten far too much to be comfortable and I'd promised myself not to fall into the same trap again.

After that huge lunch in Dumfries I'd fallen into the same trap and was now feeling a little tired and longed to reach Castle Douglas. My stomach churned and I used any excuse to stop and walk a little. A road sign signified that Castle Douglas was three and a half miles and after a short steep climb, which I pushed the bike up, it was then virtually downhill all the way. I spotted some roof tops in the distance and just knew they belonged to Castle Douglas. I instinctively shouted out loud, 'There it is, that's Castle Douglas!' This phrase reminded me of when on the school trip to the Himalayas we took a flight to see Everest. When Everest came into view it was unmistakable with the plume of snow and ice crystals blowing off the top in the jet stream. I shouted to the others, 'There it is, that's Everest!' Not that Castle Douglas could be compared with Everest but the way I felt after that huge lunch, Castle Douglas was my Everest for today.

I found the campsite and checked in. A fellow camper, who was in the office, noticed my pannier bag rain covers which had printed on them – *Land's End to John O'Groats, to help fund a school in Nepal.* He was from Nepal and had links with a Sherpa community. He handed me a handful of change.

I set up my tent on yet again a lovely campsite set right next to the tranquil, Carlingwalk Loch, and pedalled off into the town to replenish my stores, but mainly for the usual litre of milk. A retired couple approached me and asked about my bike as he had a similar one. They also asked about LEJOG which they were thinking of attempting sometime in the future.

Julian and Andy arrived and after they'd set up their tent we wandered into the town to get a meal. Julian looked quite refreshed and pleased with himself. Andy told me why. After we left Dalston before seven this morning, Julian was left alone. Our neighbours that night, the vicar and his wife, must have taken pity on Julian and had cooked breakfast for him: Porridge with honey. He hadn't had to do a thing.

Camped next to us in Castle Douglas were four bikers from Sunderland who were now well into their fifties. As a boy, one of them used to come to this site every year during ship yard fortnight. That was a time in the sixties when shipbuilding was in its prime on the River Wear and the whole shipyards would close for their annual summer holiday for the last week in July and the first week in August. He told us that his father, who had access to very powerful magnets, would bring one on holiday with them, attach it to a strong cord then go out in a boat onto the loch. As they rowed along he would lower the magnet overboard so it just scraped the bottom. They were after the rowlocks which had fallen off the hired boats over the season. In return for retrieving as many rowlocks as they could the owner would give them free use of the boat for the duration of their holiday.

I turned in as usual at 9pm leaving Julian and Andy to stroll around the loch. I'd enjoyed the two days with some company but now would once again be on my own as I worked my way north through Scotland. It was Glen Trool tomorrow and our vicar friend and his wife made one comment when I told them I'd be camping at Glen Trool.........

"Oooooo!....The Midge Site!" They looked at each other with worried expressions.

Having camped in Scotland and the Lakes for years during the midge season I knew what to expect so wasn't too perturbed at the prospect of a few midge bites. I'd also camped in Glen Trool before at Caldons campsite by Loch Trool which is the one I'm heading for.

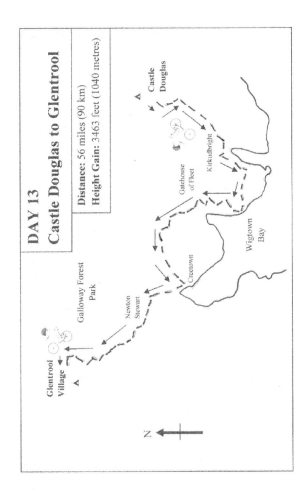

DAY 13
Castle Douglas to Glentrool

Distance: 56 miles (90 km)
Height Gain: 3463 feet (1040 metres)

Castle Douglas

Kirkudbright

Gatehouse of Fleet

Wigtown Bay

Creetown

Galloway Forest Park

Newton Stewart

Glentrool Village

N

Day 13 – Forests, Hills and Midges

The weather looked promising today as I lit the stove in preparation for my early morning cup of coffee. As I made my way back from my first visit to the loo at about 6am another camper was hurriedly trotting over to find some relief. I smiled and said 'Good Morning'; he gave a desperate looking acknowledgement as pain in some part of his anatomy forced an uncontrollable squirmed look on his face.

Andy and Julian were both awake when I returned; awaiting their porridge vigorously simmering on Andy's stove. We chatted as we ate breakfast; I packed a few things then returned to the loo about twenty minutes after my preliminary visit. Confusion and astonishment caught me to see the chap whom I'd passed twenty minutes earlier still trying to get into the loos. There was a combination lock on the door to deter non campers from using them. He was definitely having problems getting in and now had a worryingly strained expression – he was now challenging the restricted side of desperation. He was thumping the code in thinking that by hitting the buttons harder would open the lock but was repeatedly denied entry.

'Having trouble?' I asked. 'Let me try!'

I punched in the code I'd been given – CY0216 – turned the knob and the door opened. He showed me the code written down on his camping receipt. –CY0261- The warden had inadvertently reversed the last two digits and the poor chap couldn't get in. He was now relieved!.... A lot!!

Julian, Andy and I waved goodbye and I was off on the next leg of my journey to Glen Trool – 'The Midge Site'.

Route 7 took me over some rolling hills to Kirkcudbright, about ten miles away. I cycled into the quiet town before eight o'clock. There wasn't much activity around yet. Life around here seemed to be in a different time zone. At eight o'clock in the morning around the heavily built up areas of Britain on Monday morning, roads and towns are buzzing with activity. I only counted four cars actually moving, the rest were all parked up still waiting to be awoken by their sleepy owners. Hardly a handful of people were up and about. There were fishing boats tied to the jetty and others lying on their side anchored in the empty River Dee as the tide was out. There was a wood sculpture of a mother closely hugging her young daughter near the harbour to commemorate those lost at sea. Perhaps the peace and quiet reflected the fact that Kirkcudbright is the home to many artists and has been labelled 'The Artists Town'.

By main road it was only about six or seven miles to the next town, Gatehouse of Fleet, but Route 7 took me fourteen miles around the coast then through a forest to the town that got its name from the Gait House of the Sound of Fleet.

It took me about an hour and a half to get there, that made it more or less ten o'clock so it was time to find a tea shop. I asked a local to point me to the nearest one which he carried out with great pleasure. I knew he was local because in this part of the world at this time of the day in mid June I was probably the only non-local around and he was wearing carpet slippers and pyjama bottoms in the street. I followed his instructions without any problem down the only street with shops and locked my bike to a drainpipe outside a souvenir shop which also had a sign reading 'Tea Shop' or something that meant the same.

'Tea Shop' could also be interpreted as Coffee Shop, Coffee Bar, Cafe, Restaurant, Burger Bar, Refreshment Stall, WI or Village Bric a Brack sale (because they always sell tea and cakes), Village Fayre, Supermarket hot drinks machine and hot snacks counter. In fact anything where you can get a refreshing cup of tea and snack.

I went inside and walked through the souvenir section to a huge cafe at the back overlooking a large carpark. I noticed that there was even a covered bike park next to the car park, signed '*NCN Route 7 Bike Park*', which filled me with confidence knowing that I was on the right track and not lost again! The pot of tea and toasted sandwiches were perfect. I ensured that there wasn't a plate of salad and chips as accompaniments. It was still only 11am and with about thirty miles to go I should get to Glen Trool about mid afternoon. As I unlocked my bike a local came up to me, leaned over towards me and said with satisfaction with the same accent and charecteric quality of Fraser out of Dad's Army:

"Aye .... just the hills in front of ye noo laddie!"

I thanked him for that welcome piece of information and headed off towards Newton Stewart. The narrow metalled road headed up through Galloway Forest Park for about six miles until the summit was reached. There was a wonderful run down for about three miles into Creetown from here, a quiet village situated on the coast. A level disused railway path took me the extra seven miles to Newton Stewart. This path had been recently renovated. It had a new tarmac base with metal kissing gates where farm tracks crossed it. There was one in particular that I will never forget. The catch had been attached in such a position that it stuck out into the gateway and as I struggled through manipulating my weighty, cumbersome bike, I thumped my left thigh on it.

A resounding "Bollocks!" would have been heard a hundred yards away.

Fortunately there wasn't any lasting damage but my thigh throbbed and had little strength for a few hours afterwards. Some refer to it as being a dead leg!

Heavy clouds were now starting to build and the air felt heavy. I was soon in Newton Stewart and stocked up on a few provisions. The route out of the town took me on to a forest drive towards Glen Trool. At an opening in the forest I was looking ahead towards my destination when the most enormous flash of lightning I'd ever witnessed stretched across the whole sky from west to east. I've seen lots of lightning before but never one horizontal and so elongated. There was no sound of thunder and no recurrence.

The rain fell gently but never really amounted to much. Fortunately it was not accompanied by any wind. The forest was still, dark and damp with an eerie feeling about it. There was no-one else around and I hadn't seen anybody since Newton Stewart. There was no wild life around, no birds, just miles of dense conifers. I imagined aggressive wild beasts watching my every move from the thick bush. Tales of 'The Durham Puma' and 'The Beast of Bodmin' filled my mind. Perhaps this was retribution for a similar scary trick I'd played on my neighbours many years ago.

As part of the Christmas party season, some years ago, I was entrusted to hire a gorrilla outfit for use in a school production.

Looking after the costume overnight was too much temptation not to put it to some menacing employment. I'd arrived home at about half nine after the production with light snow falling and a couple of inches accumulated on the ground. The scene was perfect for the fun to begin. I climbed into the gorrilla outfit, practiced a few gorilla sounds and hunched leaps and bounds before venturing out into the silent street. My first victims lived next door. I knocked on their door with a scratching motion on the frosted glass. The door opened displaying three female heads followed by loud screams alternating with "You silly bugger!" The door slammed shut. I think they knew who the perpetrator was.

I leapt and bounded to a neighbour across the street. I got the same reaction. I continued further up the street to friends who are Godparents to our youngest daughter and knocked on their front door. Both being well respected in their chosen careers and throughout the community and neither standing for any nonesense. The hall light illuminated and I could see a blurred male shape unlock the door then push the handle down. He half opened the door to see a black gorrilla leaping about in the snow on his front garden. Without any communication he slammed the door, locked and bolted it then peered through the frosted glass trying to make out who it was. I rolled around in the snow a few times before disappearing around the side of his house to the back door. He beat me to it as I heard the key turn in the lock and bolts rattle. I returned to the front garden, rolled around a few times and uttered some gorrilla sounds. His wife approached from further down the street. She was on her way home from a Christmas 'Do'. Totally unphased by a gorrilla leaping around in the snow on their front garden she calmly put her arm around me, stroked my head and asked.

"Hello! Who are you?"

I tried to play the fearsome gorrilla for a while and noticed that my friend who was still peering through the frosted glass in the front door had spotted that his wife was on the front garden trying to console the rampant gorrilla. He opened the front door now showing great courage and verbally attacked me. I couldn't playact any longer and rolled about in fits of laughter. They both then realised who this fool was; she also broke out in fits of laughter and he submissively looked at me and mouthed loudly, "You Bastard!"

After eight miles of damp silence when all I could hear was the crunch of gravel under my tyres and no evidence of any hidden beasts, I emerged at Glen Trool Visitor Centre. It was still raining with a few early holiday makers in the 'Tea Shop'. However, this one was definitely a coffee shop because there was a wonderful aroma of freshly ground coffee. A mug of coffee and a caramel slice certainly perked me up after that long ride through the dank and lonely forest.

The waitress asked me with that wonderfully friendly soft Scottish accent where I was heading. I mentioned the campsite in Glen Trool stating that I thought it was about two miles along the road towards Loch Trool. She looked puzzled and asked, "You mean Caldons campsite?"

"Yes, that's the one!" Feeling pleased and impressed with myself havng given a correct answer.

'That's been closed for about two years now!' she said, 'You need the one in Glen Trool Village, about half a mile in the opposite direction.

This was even better for me because the site at Caldons was two miles in the wrong direction which meant that I would have to cycle two miles back in the morning. However, the site at Glen Trool village, which is not shown on any map is on Route 7.

I thanked her and headed for Glen Trool village. The site was mainly for caravans, both static and tourers, but there was a small tent site next to a pond. The owners were very friendly and charged both my phone and GPS batteries. They had told me that earlier in the day a thunder bolt had shook the whole site and frightened everyone. It was apparently so loud that they had all dived for cover, but hadn't seen any lightening. This was undoubtedly the thunder associated with the lightening without thunder I had witnessed earlier in the afternoon. It had in fact knocked off the electricity and they had difficulty getting the hot water back on tap but I was assured it was now working.

The warden told me about a camper who had talked about climbing The Merrick (the highest mountain in Galloway) all week when the weather had been perfect, but didn't have the courage to make the decision to do it until today. He left early in the morning when the weather was fine, left a diagram of his route and as yet hadn't returned. She didn't want to have to call Mountain Rescue so was hoping he would return within the next couple of hours.

I cycled down to the tent site and found a suitable spot beside a picnic table and not too near the pond. The atmosphere was perfect for midges and there were a few around. It was quite early in the season for the hordes of midges that are associated with Glen Trool so with a bit of luck they might not be too bad.

After pitching the tent and storing the bike I trundled off for a refreshingly hot shower. It was raining heavily when I returned so I zipped myself into the tent and cooked the usual meal of pasta in sauce under the fly sheet. With the remains of the slab of fruit cake given to me at Milnthorpe and a few biscuits to follow I settled down and read my book.

During the downpour four drenched backpackers from Yorkshire arrived on site. They were attempting the Southern Upland Way and one of them must have been having trouble with his boots and rucksack because two of them called for a taxi then disappeared to Newton Stewart for a couple of hours to buy new ones. The other two went for a shower. Before the others returned from the town the rain had stopped and I chatted with the two who remained about our different adventures. Two of them were sharing a tent and the other two had their own tents. The other two returned from Newton Stewart with new boots and a rucksack. The proud owner of the new gear showed them off to his mates before all four disappeared to the pub about half a mile along the road.

They had left their towels drying on the bushes, boots outside to air out and various other odds and ends lying around the outside of their tents. About an hour later the cloudless blue skies were once again blanketed in dark grey and the rain started once again. I grabbed their towels and other items and bundled them under the flysheet of the nearest tent then turned in for the night as it was now after 9pm.

Around about 10pm I was awoken by footsteps trudging through the grass next to my tent. They faded off towards another tent higher up the site behind a bush. I assumed they belonged to the lone walker on The Merrick as that was his tent. About an hour later voices woke me again and the first thing I heard was...

"Somebody's nicked my towel!"....

"And somebody's nicked my boots!"...In true Goldilocks style...Then there was the sound of a zip...

" They're here under the fly".....

"Bloody Hell, Tim's left his tent open and everything's soaked....his sleeping bags sodden!".....

"There's a huge puddle inside!"

Tim must have stopped off at the loo then appeared on the scene.

"What's up lads?".....

"You must have left your door open and your sleeping bag's soaked!"...

"Bloody hell, first the boots and now this, I've had enough, I'm off home tomorrow!"

Tim didn't appear to be a very experienced camper. I must have drifted off because the next thing I knew it was half five in the morning.

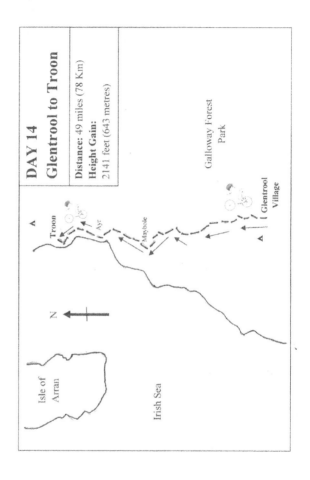

DAY 14
Glentrool to Troon

Distance: 49 miles (78 Km)
Height Gain:
2141 feet (643 metres)

Galloway Forest
Park

Troon

Ayr

Maybole

Glentrool
Village

N

Isle of
Arran

Irish Sea

Day 14 – More Forests, Hills, Midges and Sea

There was an eerie silence when I awoke at about five thirty this morning. Experience told me that I shouldn't venture outside until I was absolutely ready to do so and should dispense with my usual routine. The air was very still and damp. I got dressed, covered every part of my body except unfortunately from my knees to my ankles and my hands and face then packed everything into my pannier bags before opening the inner tent. I had worked out exactly what I would do next. Get out quickly, put the stove on, have some breakfast, pack then go. I opened the inner tent and was greeted by a thick cloud of midges just waiting under the fly sheet to pounce. Apparently they are attracted to carbon dioxide. So when in a confined space like a tent, the carbon dioxide accumulates, so do the midges. The only way to escape from their torment is to stop breathing. I should have perhaps eaten breakfast before opening the inner tent but the pan I was using as a bowl was under the fly sheet. You could almost sense what they were thinking. With the inner now open they moved in quickly to conquer the inner as well as the outer, although when the cloud moved it just seemed to enlarge and didn't actually move from one place to another. I grabbed the stove and matches, lit the stove to boil some water for a cup of coffee. While the water was boiling I took the tent down and packed it. While I was doing this one of the Yorkshiremen who was sharing a tent emerged to go to the loo.

With my water now boiled and my bike packed, I made a cup of coffee then poured a bowl of cereal. Throughout my vigorous activity packing I was constantly rubbing my face and legs to destroy the midges that were biting me to bits. It was difficult to keep calm with the constant aggravation. The stinging pain became unbearable. To try and avoid them I walked around eating my cereal but that didn't stop them. The Yorkshireman who went to the loo returned and tried to get back into his tent but he only succeeded in letting in more midges than he did when he originally emerged. He reversed out with his tail between his legs like a naughty pup. I could hear his displeased mate shouting...

"You've let all the bloody midges in!....Bugger off!"

The expelled mate grabbed his cigarettes on his backward retreat and lit one. The theory being that the smoke keeps them away. Not these, they were vicious. You could imagine when viewed under a microscope they would have teeth associated with the film Alien and also match their looks.

I'd now finished my cereal and coffee, so bundled the mug, bowl and spoon into one of my pannier bags and hastened to the loos. We both shouted "Best of luck!" to each other as I left the Yorkshireman and his mates at war with the midges. I stood the bike against a wall, grabbed my toothbrush and paste then ran in a few circles to try and fool the clouds of them gathering around me because I'd stopped moving for a few seconds. As if they could understand my thoughts I changed direction without giving them a hint, ran up the steps into the loo, opened the door and slammed it shut behind me. The atmosphere inside felt like paradise; no midges!

After more relaxed ablutions than my breakfast I was at last on my way, before half past six this morning – I was once again following Route 7. It was over twenty miles to Crosshill, the next village and twenty five to Maybole, the next town. The road was lonely, not a soul nor a vehicle in sight except the sound of forestry workers cutting down trees in the valley. I could just make out the drone of their machine. I watched from the road as it grabbed a tree, cut it through at the base of the trunk, rotated it through ninety degrees, trimmed off all the branches then cut it into six foot lengths. What an incredible machine.

I passed what looked like a purpose built or renovated building for bats. The windows and doors had been blocked up and pictures of bats painted on the side. Perhaps it was the home of the Glentrool Forest Vampire. With the spooky and eerie atmosphere I'd experienced over the last 24 hours it could be quite feasible. I took a photograph then didn't wait to find out!

The road rose steadily for nine miles but nothing too steep. I stopped after a couple of miles to remove my jacket. With cycling steadily uphill I was starting to get a little warm. The sun was starting to emerge but the air remained very still and cool. As soon as I stopped, they were there again; swarms of evil midges. My legs felt as though they'd been wrapped in stinging nettles then aggressively rubbed in. My legs throbbed with pain every time there was a heartbeat; the pain increasing with intensity on the beat and diminishing slightly between beats. Normally, for the first midge bites of the year I experience slight irritation and a few red dots where I've been bitten, but when I looked down at my legs they were covered in large scab like lumps which irritated constantly to the point where only severe scratching relieved the pain which of course made it worse. I had to keep cycling as that was the only way to relieve the agony.

I needed a drink so reached for my water bottle but unfortunately had forgotten to fill it in my haste to escape the midges at the campsite. It was empty. A couple of miles further up the road I found a clean flowing stream so I filled up my water bottle with extreme haste and continued to the top of the hill when I was conscious of my eyes watering and realised that I must have dropped my sunglasses on the grass near the stream a mile back down the road. I returned to collect them.

I cycled back over the brow of the hill and looked at the fantastic view that had opened up ahead of me. I could see the coastline and the Irish Sea beyond. The hill bordering the coast looked like a resting stage for Martian machines portrayed in the film War of the Worlds. They were the giant towers of a wind farm. The road descended, following the contours of the hill. It was narrow, only one lane wide with a barrier to the left, where the hill fell away steeply into the valley and to the right the hill rose to its summit which was beyond my view.

I was off, rapidly building up speed on the descent. This was a welcome relief after nine miles uphill. The road weaved its way round the hill, every corner being a blind one. I could feel myself leaning into the bends. The wind whistled through my cycle helmet and once again I imagined myself tearing down a narrow piste in the Alps. It was about three and a half miles to the bottom and at this rate I'd be there in a few minutes. This must have been the descent that the vicar and his wife had talked about way back in Carlisle.

After about half a mile I was thinking that this is fantastic and there's another three miles to go yet. When I leaned to tackle a right hand curve I had to apply both brakes firmly to avoid ploughing into more than five hundred sheep about thirty yards in front of me. They had just been gathered from the hillside by a couple of shepherds and their three dogs. Believe it or not they were going downhill, the same way as me. They filled the road from one side to the other and were walking...slowly. I came to a screeching halt and waited.

One of the farmers who was sitting on a quad bike greeted me.

"Hi there – hope you're not in a hurry – you may as well park up and have your breakfast. We're going all the way down to the bottom of the valley".

Great, I thought, disappointed at losing the long downhill thrill. However, I had enough time to spare and here, right in front of me, was an event that I'd only ever been forced to witness from a car window or watched the first few seconds on a television before turning it off. I could follow them all the way and see how they keep their sheep together using the dogs.

Mimicking my antics back at the campsite loos, three lambs suddenly ran off into the thick undergrowth to the left haphazardly dodging and weaving their way round the bracken but never running in a straight line. Two of the dogs were dispatched to retrieve them. With orders from their masters they circled the lambs to chase them back onto the road. The lambs had a different idea. They went everywhere except back onto the road. The dogs blocked off their escape and were hard pushed to persuade them to change direction. They separated and two of them were eventually coaxed back onto the road. The third disappeared into a ditch and couldn't get out. The farmer on the quad bike left it on the road and ran about a hundred yards down the hill to retrieve the lamb. I noticed something fall off his head, it looked like his hat, but he still had one on. He bent down, hauled out the lamb and carried it back onto the road. I told him that he appeared to lose his hat. His reaction to retrieve it was immediate.

"It's ma midge net – a cannay do wi'oot tha'!"

He asked me where and took his quad bike to retrieve it.

The flock reluctantly moved on until half a dozen lambs broke free, this time up the bank to the right. The dogs were ordered to retrieve them and ran right around to get behind them. A few more lambs spotted the commotion and decided to join in. There were now ten escapees and more started to tear away from the main flock. The mutineers seemed to be like a magnet, attracting even more. The rear of the flock turned and the shepherds now had a job on their hands. They needed to frighten those in the main flock to stay with it but the runaways needed to stay calm and not get too agitated.

There were now up to thirty renegades running back the way we had come but high up on the grassy bank. The dogs couldn't keep up. One of the dogs was ordered back to keep an eye on the main flock, the rear of which had stopped making any progress downhill. I could just make out the front through the bracken, about 200 yards ahead which was still progressing downhill on the road but slowing down. The farmer on the quad bike raced off up the road to get in front of the tearaways. He disappeared out of view and we all awaited his return.

The other farmer told me that the flock were made up of ewes and their lambs. They were off to market. Normally the lambs would just follow their mothers down the road and it was quite a straightforward job but this year the lambs just wanted to do as they pleased and wouldn't follow their elders.

"Bit like some school children," I remarked.

He smiled and agreed. Although I would think in this part of the world they wouldn't have too many problems from disobedient children. They could just stand them outside to keep the midges company.

The thought of midges and naughty children took my mind back over twenty years when camping in Borrowdale with thirty 14 year old boys. One of the firm rules laid down about noise was that there would be no talking or noise after 11pm and none before 7am. It was a very sticky night in July when I was awoken by three boys playing football around the tents at half four in the morning dressed only in boxer shorts. Smoke and steam poured from my ears and nostrils like a savage bull in a cartoon. I punished them by standing them against the dreaded midge wall to remind themselves of the rules. I thought I'd give them about 5 minutes of suffering before sending them back to their tents. Unfortunately I must have dosed off and was woken once again. This time it was from the continuous slapping sound made by many hands on bare skin that startled me just before seven o'clock. The following morning the boys slept solidly, well past the regulation 7am, as remaining quiet throughout the night is far more attractive than continuous midge torture!

After ten minutes the mini flock of naughty lambs returned along the road followed by the quad bike and the two sheep dogs. Again a couple of the renegades tried to break away but the dogs now had them well and truly under control. The open hill was soon separated from the road by fences and the lambs had nowhere to go except ahead. After a good hour and a half they finally reached their destination, through a gate and into a field next to the farm. The farmers wished me luck and once again I was on my way. Unfortunately I was now at the bottom of the hill and had a level ride for a couple of miles before the road began to rise again over the next set of hills before dropping down to Maybole.

This wasn't a nine mile ascent as tackled a couple of hours earlier and I was at the top in less than three. I could see Maybole on the hillside about seven miles as the crow flies directly ahead. For five of those miles the road descended gently to the village of Crosshill before a fairly level ride to Maybole. The time was after ten o'clock and it was definitely time for a tea shop stop. There's bound to be one in Maybole I thought and I even started to get excited at the prospect of sampling the delights of yet another different tea shop.

I could see that the road swept down before rising fairly steeply into the centre of Maybole and was in top gear quickly approaching a bus at the bus stop with a car stopped behind it waiting to overtake. There was no oncoming traffic so I prepared myself in anticipation of following the waiting car past the bus. The female driver hesitated, I braked to avoid ramming into her rear bumper but she pulled away. It was now too late for me to follow her through as I was now in the wrong gear and virtually stopped half way past the bus. I fumbled with the levers to change gear but couldn't maintain rotating the pedals when I heard an almighty crunching sound and the pedals became firmly fixed with the back wheel locked. I looked down to see the rear derailleur pointing upwards. It was broken. All I could do was to get off the bike and drag it past the bus. Fortunately the driver had noticed that I was in trouble and waited until I was out of his way before he moved off.

I stood the bike against a wall and just stared at the broken part for several minutes. I was gutted when I saw a bare break on what I assumed was the frame where the derailleur was fastened to it. The wheel was locked in place with the derailleur and chain sticking through the spokes. My first reaction was that my adventure was over and I'd have to catch a train home or get someone to collect me from Maybole. A passing motorist stopped and asked if he could help. He told me where I could find a garage but there was no cycle shop in Maybole. I needed to think about getting the broken part fixed rather than being defeated and taking the train home. I was now on Day 14 of my twenty day ride. I was feeling low now and certainly didn't feel like having to do the whole lot again, especially through Devon and Cornwall. I needed to think positively.

I managed to undo the chain from the derailleur and fasten the derailleur to the bike frame with some Gaffa tape. Yet another use for Gaffa tape. The small bottle of washing up liquid I'd brought along came in handy to clean my hands. Now I had to find the garage. I wandered off up to the town, pushing the bike past a wonderful tea shop and then asked around where I might be able to find a garage. I thought that someone might be able to weld the broken part. The garage was easy to find but the owner said he didn't have the skill to weld such a small part but thought that David at Redbrae Services was the man to do it. He had the skill to weld anything.

He gave me directions and I walked off in a sorry state pushing my injured pride and joy. Inside ten minutes I spotted the garage and faced the man in question.

"Excuse me please I'm looking for David"

"Aye! Who's askin'!"

I explained my situation and he said, "It'll be me you want then!"

He looked at my bike and shook his head.

"Can't weld that," he said, "It's alloy."

My heart sank and a return trip home looked to be on the cards.

"Hang on a bit – it's a small part. It's not part of the frame."

He showed me where the part was fixed to the frame. I must have looked really pitiful because he asked me into his office, made me a brew and offered me the tin of biscuits. I knew these tea shops could be anywhere that served refreshments but I never thought I could include the office of a garage in Maybole as one. I managed my tea stop in Maybole after all.

He thumbed through the Yellow Pages and phoned around for a cycle shop which might sell the broken part. He located one in Troon for me. I spoke to the owner and he said that it was the derailleur hanger that had broken and that he should be able to help. The time was only about 11am and he said the shop was open till five. It was about twenty miles to Troon and there was a station in Maybole, but if I got the train I would have to return either later that day or the next day to continue from where I'd left off. After all I didn't want to not cycle any part of the route. Apart from cheating I would not have felt fulfilled on completing the challenge and couldn't with conviction be able to say that I'd cycled from Land's End to John o'Groats.

David came to the rescue and thought that he could shorten the chain so that I could cycle to Troon with one gear.

After about ten minutes we managed to shorten the chain so it was on the middle cog between the pedals and the middle cog on the rear wheel. The chain needed to be in line and fairly tight otherwise it just came off. Eventually we got it to work without coming off. He said that the quickest way was to join the main road, the A77 to Ayr then join the NCN Route 7 to Troon. Again I was thanking yet another Good Samaritan and was on my way. He wouldn't accept any payment.

The A77 to Ayr was fairly level and I'd made the decision that if any hills became too steep then I would need to walk up them to avoid putting too much strain on the chain. Luckily there weren't any hills to fear and I was soon eating up the miles. Unfortunately with only having one gear I couldn't change up when my speed increased. This meant that as I got faster my legs were spinning as though they were involved in a scene from a Tom and Jerry cartoon. I needed to adopt a system in order to make steady progress even though it might be slow. I started counting pedal revolutions. Twenty turns to go as fast as I could then freewheel to a count of ten. I did this for mile after mile. Within ten miles of Ayr I joined a cycle path next to the road. I was being overtaken by children on mountain bikes and BMX stunt bikes and couldn't do anything about it. Why weren't they in school?

After about an hour and a half I reached the coast at Ayr and the sandy beach. The air was clear and warm and across the sea the mountains of Arran majestically stood out on the horizon. I'd only eaten a couple of biscuits since a midge infested breakfast at six this morning and was feeling a bit peckish. I found a couple of two day old sandwiches in my bag so parked myself on a seat and ate them. I could see Troon in the distance on the other side of the bay. The promenade was buzzing with mothers and toddlers out to take advantage of the glorious weather.

It was about eight miles around the bay to Troon and I could be there in less than an hour as long as the chain held.

I entered Troon following the directions given to me by the bike shop owner over the phone and soon found it. It was closed. My heart sank and I was now well and truly stuck. My mind was working overtime. What could I do now? Could I cycle all the way to John O'Groats in one gear? Where could I find another bike shop? The nearest one now was back in Ayr but they had told me that they wouldn't be able to get a part for a couple of days. Irvine was the next town but the bike shops there couldn't help. In desperation I went to look through the door then spotted the sign.

GONE FOR LUNCH – BACK AT 2PM.

I had about twenty minutes to wait. I should have guessed that people who work in small businesses away from the rat race still lead normal lives and close for lunch. I waited.

Spot on two o'clock the owner arrived and remembered me from my phone call earlier in the day. He thought that the job would take a while so asked if I could return at about four o'clock. I left the bike with him and piled my bags and tent in an unused corner of his shop then strolled off to look for the campsite, which, as luck would have it, was only around the corner from the bike shop.

I passed a row of crumbling cottages by the side of the lane leading to a rundown entrance with no sign of an enquiry office. The site looked well kept and clean, with plenty of caravans and people around. I asked some sun worshippers where the office was and they pointed me back in the direction of the cottages. I knocked on the door of the first cottage which had filthy net curtains at the window. There was no reply so I knocked on the next door which had similar decor at the window. The door opened and a very unkempt man poked his head through the opening. The few teeth that he exhibited were dark brown and half rotten, probably from years of smoking.

"Yes – what is it?" he questioned with suspicion.

"Do you have a pitch for a tent for the night please?"

"Where's your tent?"

Then I went through a shortened history of my broken bike to explain why I didn't have it.

He opened the door fully to display his full features.

He was hunched with tatty hair and clothes which looked as though they hadn't been washed...ever! His woolly jumper was full of holes and his slippers looked as though they had never left his feet. He walked on their sides with the soles sticking out to the side. They were probably originally soft slippers but now had shiny black regions of grease encrusted into them and were ridden with holes. His trousers were similarly dirty and also full of holes.

There were no other camp sites within miles; this was my only option especially with not having any transport. He beckoned me with his right index finger and showed me to the exact spot where I had to put the tent. There must have been someone camped there the previous night as the grass was still flattened in the shape of a tent. I asked how much for the night. He said ten pounds. I gave him a twenty pound note and he produced a huge bundle of dirty looking notes from his back pocket to give me the change.

It reminded me that before our trip to Nepal being advised when handling money to rub antibacterial gel into your hands as Nepalese money is filthy. Many Nepalese people don't have pockets and keep their money in the most undesirable places.

Just next to this spot was a lone camper. He was a man in his early fifties who was soaking up the sun. He asked what I was up to and I told him about my ride, the problem that I had with my bike and was waiting for it to be mended. He said that he was having a few days away for a rest. He was wearing shorts only and I spotted a vertical scar on his calf and another next to his heart which suggested that he must have had a heart bypass operation using a blood vessel from his leg. I returned to the bike shop to retrieve my tent and noticed that my bike was being dealt with in the workshop. I returned to the campsite with hope then erected the tent and chatted to my neighbour until four o'clock approached.

I was excited now at the prospect of getting a fully working bike back as the next part of the journey was virtually level all the way to Balloch at the southern end of Loch Lomond. I entered the bike shop full of optimism.

The owner just looked at me and said, "Sorry but I can't fix it, I haven't got that particular part." My heart sank!

He continued. "However, I have phoned around and Dooley's Cycles in Paisley will definitely be able to fix it for you. They are a Specialized dealer and have the parts."

He also mentioned that the back wheel was slightly buckled and he'd straightened it as a freebie.

I thanked him, got the phone number for Dooley's then rode my one speed bike back to the campsite. The lone camper asked me if the bike had been fixed and I told him the story. He loaned me his phone, as mine didn't work, to phone Dooley's. They informed me that they could definitely fix my bike when they opened in the morning at half nine. He gave me directions telling me that the bike shop was just down the road from Gilmore Street Station.

The campsite owner appeared and both he and the lone camper offered some help. The lone camper offered to take me up to Dooley's in Paisley there and then but since it was thirty five miles away there would be nothing they could do tonight. It was too late. He offered to take me up in the morning then I could continue my journey from Paisley when it was fixed. I said that I couldn't do that because I would feel as though I'd cheated and wouldn't feel fulfilled. They both said, "But who will know, only us two and what does it matter?" It appeared that neither of them understood the depth of fulfilment and satisfaction gained by successfully completing a challenge legitimately.

I couldn't take up his offer and said that if I left at half six in the morning, I could be there by 9.30. I'd cycled twenty miles in one gear to get here so I could cycle another thirty five to get to Paisley.

With all this commotion I needed a shower before I walked into the town for a bar meal. The shower and toilets were useable but had never been upgraded in perhaps fifty years or more. The taps were of a design I'd never seen before anywhere – perhaps they were antiques. The owner must have bought a job lot of toilet paper back in the sixties. It was the sort that as a schoolboy I used to use as tracing paper as the soft varieties that we have today had yet to be invented. It wouldn't have surprised me to have found torn squares of newspaper hanging on a nail behind the door.

After my shower I returned back to the tent to see clouds of blue smoke bellowing from the region of the lone camper's tent. He was cooking his evening meal in the boot of his car. He had the hatch fully open and the cooker was placed in the boot. The car was full of smelly fatty blue smoke; the sort that clings to your furniture, carpets and clothes for days. He was cooking sausages with all the accompaniments he probably shouldn't have been eating if he had just had a heart bypass. I told him that I was off into town for a bar meal and left.

I found a pub with a restaurant attached, ordered a pint and a meal then found a seat to await my food. In a corner I spotted a computer with internet connection and asked if I could use it. The bar maid said that it was free to customers. I hadn't as yet seen any of the entries my wife had put onto my blog so now was a good opportunity. Also, as luck would have it, she wouldn't be able to take my call tonight as she was out till late so I could enter the day's blog myself.

I wrote about the midges, the sheep and the broken derailleur and that I was setting off early in the morning to get to a Specialized cycle dealers in Paisley to get it fixed.

When I returned, the lone camper was sitting in his car reading with the windows open...I wonder why? I thanked him for the use of his phone and said that I'd be off at about 6.30 in the morning. He wished me luck and I told him to enjoy the rest of his holiday. I was tucked up in my sleeping bag just after half past eight.

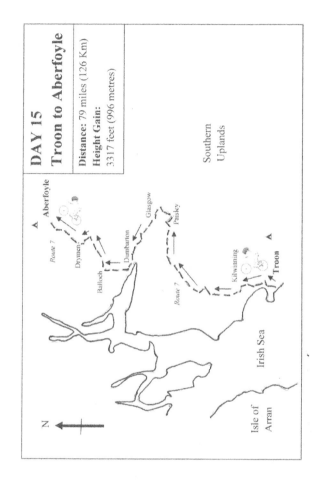

DAY 15
Troon to Aberfoyle

Distance: 79 miles (126 Km)
Height Gain:
3317 feet (996 metres)

Day 15 – From Lowlands to Highlands

The need to get my bike fixed must have been the trigger to wake me up. I found myself gazing at the roof of the tent at 5am to the sound of torrential rain hammering down. Something inside starts questioning whether or not you should get up. It's a bit like Monday mornings when attempting to get up for work after a pleasant weekend. Once my waking mind had started to function properly I resigned myself to the fact that I had to get up now to be in Paisley by 9.30. I emerged from my tent fully clad in waterproofs to notice the lone camper frying yet more sausages and filling his car with a further plume of fatty blue smoke. I'm not against sausages, in fact they can be very tasty but in moderation. Anyway, what was he doing up so early? I had a good reason but he said that he'd come away for a few days rest. I progressed through my usual routine but a little slower due to the heavy rain. Even the midges were having a lie in this morning although at Troon the midges are only in the Conference League compared to Glen Trool's Premiership beasts. The lone camper wished me good luck and I pedalled out of the campsite before six thirty.

My plan was to follow Route 7 along the promenade for about a mile then inland for another mile. At this point I would leave Route 7 and follow the A78 trunk road past Irvine, come off at the sign for Kilwinning then rejoin Route 7. Although I didn't like cycling on main roads, this would save me nearly three miles, navigation would be easier as I wouldn't have to cycle through Irvine. Also it was before seven in the morning and I reckoned that the traffic wouldn't be too bad in this part of the world so early. To avoid using my GPS I remembered that I would need to come off on the fourth junction along the A78.

When I reached the promenade the wind blowing off the sea was very cold. I needed to keep warm. I was wearing my 'King of the Mountains' cycling shirt, soft shell top plus waterproof jacket and fluorescent waistcoat and of course the usual cycling shorts which were now sodden. I stopped to put a fleece hat on, pull my waterproof hood over that then put the cycle helmet on top of the lot. Zips and cuffs were closed tightly and I was prepared for the worst.

Fortunately the route to Paisley looked fairly level on the map without any major hills. I felt strangely warm and cosy even though I was cycling through torrential rain. What little wind there was blew from behind and thankfully helped me along.

Within five minutes I was cycling along the A78. It was a dual carriageway and contrary to my thinking was very busy. Fortunately there was a one metre wide lane on the left which I stuck to like glue. I quickly got into the routine of twenty rotations of the pedals then a count to ten freewheeling. Spray from the traffic was thick and wet. I kept my head down and just concentrated on keeping my wheels within that one metre lane. A direction sign appeared ahead, this was the first junction – Irvine. I needed to take extra care when passing the off slip roads. It was dangerous just to continue past them as you would in a car. I needed to cycle along the slip road until I was opposite where the kerb started on the other side of it, cross straight over at right angles to the road then join the main carriageway again. Similarly I needed to cross the on slip road at right angles then join the left hand kerb whilst still on the on slip road. Back on the main road again a sign read, Kilwinning five miles. The traffic was now very heavy and fast. Lorries would give me a wide berth if there was nothing overtaking them on the outside lane. When they couldn't the wind coupled with the huge quantities of spray felt like a mini hurricane. Irvine Centre, one mile. I passed the second turn and tackled the slip roads as before. Only one more junction to go then I'm off this death trap. My legs were spinning as fast as they could until they weren't putting any energy into the forward motion of the bike.

There was a bridge ahead to cycle under where a mass of water had accumulated. The unwelcome pond spread out from my side of the road to well over the middle line of the road. It looked to be about four to six inches deep and was constantly rippling as traffic passed through it. I knew that I couldn't pull out to avoid it as there was too much traffic and I was only aware of its danger when almost riding through the pond. Then I heard a deep droning sound approach from behind. I knew that it must be something big and that the spray would be exceptional. Turning my head to see what approached was not an option as I may have inadvertently veered to the right and into its path. I entered the small lake and the white lines disappeared under the murk. I concentrated to keep the bike in a straight line and the wheels to the left of the now obliterated white line. The flood must have been about fifty feet long. The droning sound got worryingly loud when whatever it was also entered the flood. I was hit with a mini tsunami which washed right over my head. I was knocked off balance and struggled to keep the bike in the narrow lane. I daren't overcompensate otherwise I would have ended up in the road. I had a glimpse of the monster as it passed. The forty tonne mobile crane not only drenched me with a tidal wave but followed up with its own weather system. I was forced into the six inch wide rain channel to the left. I desperately tried to get out but my front wheel just kept rebounding of the sides of the two inch deep channel until I hit what could have been a dead rabbit, piece of exhaust or some other lodged debris. This stopped my front wheel from making any further forward progress. The back of the bike flipped up like a bucking bronco and I went flying over the handlebars thumping my right knee on them as I flew. Fortunately I fell to the left and on to the sodden grass verge. What seemed like hundreds of cars passed and I didn't notice anyone looking. They probably daren't because visibility was so bad. If anyone had noticed me they probably thought – "What's that silly old fool doing riding a bike on this busy road at this time in the morning in this weather?"

With only a sore knee and hurt pride, I checked the bike and its cargo, got back on and continued to the exit at Kilwinning. When I spotted the sign the relief was overwhelming. The tension seemed to drain out of me and I could relax once again. I was free of this artery to hell and was once again on the lookout for Route 7 signs. I followed the main road into Kilwinning which compared to the main A78 was peaceful and quiet. After zigzagging my way through Kilwinning following Route 7 I was finally into the countryside and had already covered over fifteen of the thirty five miles to Paisley. It was nearly 8 o'clock so I was just about on schedule to arrive at Dooley's by half past nine.

With fifteen miles to go, Route 7 was entirely on an old railway with a smooth tarmac surface. The rain still pelted down but there was no wind now and I made admirable progress albeit under reduced steam. If the bike had been fully functional I would have managed this section in less than an hour. Along this fifteen mile stretch I saw only one other cyclist. Nine o'clock approached with only five miles to go. I needed to look out for the signs. Then it dawned on me - which signs? I'd forgotten the name of the station. I needed to look out for ....? station but what was its name? Being on the outskirts of Glasgow, Paisley's probably quite a big place so I didn't want to spend an hour or so looking for Dooley's Cycles after getting into Paisley before 9 o'clock.

When I was on the phone to Dooley's, whoever I spoke to said that his shop was just down from '*Something station*'. Then just as I thought I may have problems finding which station I saw a sign pointing to '*Gilmore Street Station*'. That's it! Although I couldn't remember the name, it was there hiding in the back of my mind just waiting to be jolted to the front. A narrow lane transferred me from the quiet Route 7 onto the now bustling main street in Paisley. The street was wide with loaded buses everywhere. I chose to half walk and half cycle on the wide footpaths gradually making my way towards Gilmore Street Station. I saw the station ahead but there was no sign of a bike shop. A shining star appeared in the shape of two drenched police women who gave me directions. Dooley's was only fifty yards along the road. I was there at 9.25am and it was still closed. The windows were covered with thick steel shutters as was the door. Locks and heavy chains were in abundance fastening thick iron bars firmly in place across the door. There was a lady serving in a mobile burger bar just next to the entrance. A couple of people were enjoying a bacon sandwich and a mug of tea. I asked what time the shop opened. The lady who was probably only half my age answered, "Half nine hin. D'nae worry son he'll no b' long!"

Whilst cycling and pushing the bike I'd been warm, but now standing here waiting for the owner to arrive and open the door I began to shiver. I paced backwards and forwards to keep warm and kept checking my watch what seemed like every couple of minutes but it must have been every couple of seconds. I was getting a little anxious and impatient as it was now a full one minute past nine thirty. Then I became aware of one of the burger bar customers leave the relative warmth of its shelter then walk the three yards to the bike shop and proceed to open up. He'd been there all the time. He must have heard me ask the burger bar owner what time the shop opened. Strange that he didn't say that he'd open up in a couple of minutes but did now say "Be with you in a minute!" He started on the steel shutters protecting the two windows, unlocking the padlocks, removing the long steel bars then lifting down the shutters which he placed to the side. The door came next. He unlocked the outer steel door, to reveal the shop door reinforced with steel mesh. As he opened the shop door a warning alarm sounded giving him only a few seconds before the main alarm went off. He rushed into the back of the shop to deactivate it.

I wheeled the bike into the shop and he asked me what the problem was. I mentioned about the phone call the previous afternoon but he wasn't the one who had taken the call so he knew nothing of my plight. However he asked me to unload my tent and pannier bags so that he could have a look at the bike. He wheeled it into his workshop at the back of the shop, applied a few spanners and Allen keys then came back out and told me that he could fix it. A great feeling of relief passed through my body. The anxiety of wondering whether I would have to spend the rest of the day searching for a Specialized dealer to replace the broken part was whisked away from my mind in a short sentence. I handed him the derailleur which I had in one of my pannier bags. He took it to fasten it on then returned a few minutes later to explain that that too had broken and he didn't have a replacement for that. The relief turned once again into despair until he said that he thought he should have a different one that might fit. He had three different derailleur parts that would fit. The cheapest at £30 would fit but he said they were a bit like chocolate and probably wouldn't be up to the job for the journey I was making. The most expensive at £80 would work but were really meant for mountain bikes. That left the £50 model which would do the job and definitely get me to John o'Groats. He spent another fifteen minutes trying to attach it to the bike but found that it wouldn't function properly in the extreme gears; (the very top and bottom gears). The only option was the chocolate derailleur.

I was now beginning to shiver uncontrollably in the unheated shop. Even though I was out of the rain and inside, my body was wet with sweat which over the last forty five minutes had cooled. My shell jacket was also wet both with sweat and rain that had seeped through zips and any openings in my waterproof. Only one other person had visited the shop since nine thirty and it was now approaching ten thirty. My dream like state was jolted by the shop door bell clanging as someone had just opened it and walked in. Standing there in the doorway was Andy. The shop was quite dark inside and as he stood in front of the door with the light behind him he looked a bit like the silhouette of a guardian angel. How had he known I was here at Dooley's Cycle shop in Paisley? Unknown to me he'd come to ride through Glasgow with me all the way to Balloch at the south end of Loch Lomond, another thirty miles along Route 7. Although I was still shivering I felt as though I'd been given a shot of adrenalin. He said that he'd intended to cycle with me at some stage in Scotland and most likely through Glasgow. He'd emailed my wife to let me know that he would join me at the point where I had left Route 7 to come to this bike shop then had fortunately read my blog from the previous night. He had looked through the Yellow Pages for Specialized bike shops, made a note of them, got on the train with his bike and cycled from Gilmore Street Station to the nearest shop on his list. As luck would have it I was in that shop. After about ten minutes the bike mechanic emerged with my bike now fully functional. He did say that the chocolate derailleur would last for the rest of my journey but I would need to be gentle with it. I paid the eighty seven pound bill which included the new derailleur, a new chain and the replacement derailleur hanger plus his time then Andy and I were on our way. Our first stop was after about two minutes at a coffee shop on the corner for a hot drink and something warm to eat.

Andy told me that he'd cycled Route 7 through Glasgow the previous day so he could guide me through. He had even made a mental note of any obstacles such as sharp stones and metal spikes protruding in odd places especially through narrow gateways. Fully warmed through now, we were off. My task was easy now for the next thirty miles. All I needed to do was to follow Andy. We left the coffee shop and entered the main street. It was alive with buses which came quickly from all angles. Andy was only carrying a small pannier bag and had little difficulty dodging buses, taxis and pedestrians with great expertise. He soon disappeared into the distance, lost in the crowds. I found it difficult to dodge and weave, especially with a heavy load and the chocolate derailleur and every time I made the decision to join the road from the footpath a bus would turn up and block my exit. I got off and pushed. I knew that Andy was heading for Route 7 where I had left it so would join him there. He looked around and saw me walking through a gap in the crowds. He waited and we joined Route 7 together.

Now together and away from traffic we were flying. Anticipating approaching traffic at crossings in order to avoid having to stop we held on to the excitement. I felt power in my legs now that I could change gear and get the most out of my bike. It felt as though Andy and I were reliving our childhood playing follow the leader. We were on a non-stop mission to cross Bell's Bridge to the Glasgow Exhibition Centre, the venue of the next tea shop. We ate up the miles, there were no hills and our whole journey was off road apart from about a mile through Pollock. There was no respite from the rain but that didn't matter anymore. We were both warm yet wet but were thoroughly enjoying ourselves. The Exhibition Centre loomed, looking like an Armadillo up close or the Sydney Opera House from the distance. Once over Bell's Bridge we were in Northern Scotland and I knew that there were only five days left before I cycled into John o'Groats. We locked our bikes to the bike rack and went inside to enjoy a hot pot of tea and a recommended cinnamon scone.

Back on the bikes we followed Route 7 off road alongside the River Clyde and the Forth and Clyde Canal. There are many quirky things throughout the World that people have devised to make money, some strange and some quite funny, but anchored by the side of the river was an old ferry which had been converted into a fish and chip restaurant. It was labelled 'The World's First Sail Through Fish & Chip Shop.' There was even a serving hatch stuck on like a bay window a few feet above the surface where small boats could line up, tie up, order their fish 'n' chips then sail off into the sunset. Fishing boats on their journey out to sea could stop for a round of fish 'n' chips to sample what they probably caught the previous day without having to get off their boat. There can't be many, if any, other sail through fish 'n' chip shops.

Route 7 followed the canal all the way to Bowling where it joins the Clyde through a system of locks. The cycle path continued off road west to Dumbarton then follows the River Lovett to the North for about four miles until it reaches Balloch where Andy was to catch his train home.

We reached Balloch at about three o'clock, found a little tea shop and chatted over a snack before we parted company. Andy had cycled from Balloch to Aberfoyle a few years ago and warned me about the long hard climb out of Drymen about ten miles away which was half way to my destination for today.

The rain had at last stopped to reveal blue skies with the odd cumulus cloud drifting by. Waterproofs came off as it was warm enough to cycle without them. We shook hands and thanked each other for a great day cycling. Andy wandered off for his train about a hundred metres down the road and I set off for Aberfoyle a further twenty miles north. I thought I might get to the campsite at about 5.30 which would give me enough time to get sorted, showered and have a bar meal at the pub next to the campsite.

Back on my own again I needed to be more attentive to the Route 7 signs as Andy had taken that responsibility off me since half ten this morning. The signs were good; there were lots of them including stickers on gate posts and telegraph poles to confirm that you were on Route 7. After junctions there was always a confirmation sticker with an arrow pointing in the right direction, even in the other direction for anyone travelling south. Because I had lots of faith in the signage I left my trusty GPS switched off in order to conserve the batteries. The road climbed steadily up from Balloch and the view over the Arrochar Alps was superb.

I remembered that when I had planned this part of the route there was a short section of about two miles on a main road leading up to Drymen. I reached the main road, spotted a Route 7 sign and followed this main road until I saw the next Route 7 sign on the outskirts of Drymen, pointing right, along a minor road which climbed fairly steeply.

Thinking that this must the long hard climb out of Drymen that Andy had warned me about, I prepared myself for some strenuous pedalling.

I had to change down in gear but not right down and was up the hill in a few minutes. I felt quite proud but questioned Andy's judgement of a steep hill and a hard climb. I confidently followed the Route 7 signs for the next couple of miles and continued along this narrow winding road until I came to a junction with a main road. There were no Route 7 signs. I became confused. The only answer was to consult my GPS. I switched it on and waited for it to attach itself to the satellites. My planned route was nowhere to be seen on the screen so I zoomed out until it became visible.

I'd now cycled over seventy five miles today since half six this morning, been soaked through, had hardly anything to eat and the time was now approaching five o'clock and have just discovered that I've cycled five miles in the wrong direction. That means when I get back on track I'll have cycled ten miles more than I needed to. I couldn't understand where I'd gone wrong because I'd been following the signs meticulously then suddenly there weren't any. Where had I gone wrong? I grabbed a few biscuits out of my pannier bag, turned around and headed back for my planned route.

About four miles back along the route I spotted the first sign hidden under tree foliage, pointing back the way I'd originally come from, then next to it another sign pointing slightly to the left across a field. Now this really confused the situation. If I took the original road back it looked as though I'd be going back the way I came from Balloch and if I took the sign to the left I'd also end up going back to Balloch. My conclusion was that the signs must have been moved around, as they often were around the suburbs, but surely not here out in this beautiful rural countryside. As I may have mentioned before, the screen on the GPS swings around when stationary, which is something that I thought I'd remedied and this confused me even further. My planned route suggested that I needed to turn right. I looked around and believe it or not to my right, was a narrow track, fenced on both sides curving round by the side of a hill towards a gate, about a hundred yards ahead. Lots of the NCN routes do cross fields on tracks and follow bridleways, so I thought without any further confusion I would head for the track. At the next gate, about a hundred yards away, the GPS was showing that I'd come the wrong way and I should have followed the road back the way that I'd originally come. Besides, through the gate was just an open field and the track had disappeared. I'd now worked out what to do and turned the bike round when I heard the distinctive whistle of a farmer guiding his sheepdogs along with the sound of a following quad bike. It got progressively louder until around the curve in the hill and hemmed in by the fences, about fifty bleating sheep came trotting towards me. I was trapped. Oh dear! There I was dressed in white with red polka dots and a bright red and white cycle helmet in the unenviable position of potentially scaring fifty sheep back towards what would certainly become an irate farmer. My only answer was to sit down by the side of the track, keep very still and make absolutely no noise. The sheep appeared and hesitated for a moment. I made no motion. I didn't even look at them. They might think I was a large red and white rock wearing a helmet. There was more whistling and the sound of the quad bike got closer. The sheep moved and walked passed me followed closely by the dogs. The farmer appeared, looked at me with a slightly puzzled look on his face and calmly asked, "Are you lost?"

"Yes! I got a bit confused with the signs back at the junction there."

"Ah! Ay, they've just rerouted Route 7 off the main road and put it through the fields over there."

I was confused no longer and realised what had happened. From the main road to this junction I'd in fact been going the wrong way.

Having spotted Land's End to John o'Groats printed on my pannier bag rain covers he asked where I was heading today. He was quite chatty and told me that his sister had cycled LEJOG along with her boyfriend a couple of years ago. But when he told me about their venture last year I once again felt that LEJOG wasn't such a challenge after all, and to lots of people it's just a training jaunt for something greater. They'd cycled from the most southerly point in Europe, in Malta, to the most northerly point in Norway.

"And on mountain bikes," he boasted. "Not on one of these fancy things that you've got!"

"That's quite a challenge, bet that took them a while then!"

I thanked him for the information about the change of route, he wished me a safe journey and I was soon on the outskirts of Drymen once again.

At the main road I spotted the Route 7 signs now going in my direction and cycled through the centre of Drymen. The road out went up, very steeply and for a long way, for nearly three miles. This was the hill that Andy was referring to. I walked most of the way.

The campsite at Cobleland on the outskirts of Aberfoyle was a mere three miles away, all downhill. This was another fantastic run down. My thoughts were now totally fixed on a bar meal with a couple of pints to help it down. I was famished. I remembered back several years when my wife Gail and I camped at Cobleland in our caravan and used the nearby pub next to the campsite on several occasions. The meals were commendable enough to drool over. *Campsite ½ mile,* a sign informed me. I nearly went whizzing past it but turned in through the gate and it was exactly as I remembered it except that it had been refurbished with new toilets and showers.

I checked in at the reception, they had one bottle of milk left which I selfishly grabbed and asked if they still served bar meals at the pub over the road.

"The pubs gone," he said. "It was pulled down about seven years ago after the landlord hanged himself in the bar. They built a couple of bungalows on the land."

He told me that the next pub was about two miles along the disused railway track. I settled for pasta with sauce and a couple of pieces of cake then washed it down with a couple of cups of tea.

The time was approaching 8pm when I managed to erect my tent so after a shower and a meal I was straight into my sleeping bag that night. This had been my longest section to date covering ninety five miles, that's ten more than I should have. Only five days left.

When I started, I was ticking the days off until I got half way and wasn't really bothered about how many to go. Since half way I've been counting the number of days that are left and am not really bothered about how many I've done. Strange how the mind works – isn't it?

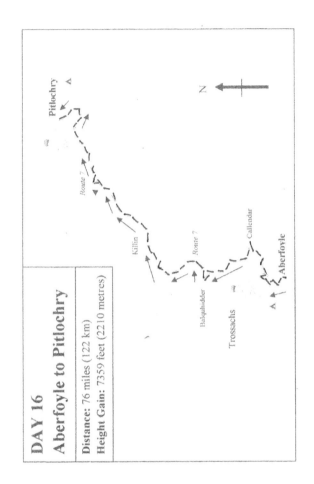

DAY 16
Aberfoyle to Pitlochry

Distance: 76 miles (122 km)
Height Gain: 7359 feet (2210 metres)

Day 16 – Through Rob Roy Country

The forecast was for sunshine and showers. It's amazing to find that when you are completely shattered after a full day of exercise and activity it seems more difficult to dose off to sleep. I assumed that the rain never stopped until after two in the morning. I knew that because I never fell into a deep sleep until after it had stopped. The weather seemed to be a mixed bag today. Damp air with clouds racing across the sky brought the threat of rain.

I left a quiet campsite well before seven this morning. The gate was still chained and locked but there was enough room to wangle my bike around it. The old railway track into Aberfoyle was level with a good surface through the forest. I knew that ahead lay a long climb, steeply up through Achray Forest and Queen Elizabeth Forest Park, home to one of the more exciting Go Ape courses with its two four hundred and twenty metre zip wires. We'd been on holiday here a few weeks before and sampled the delights of the course.

I was soon riding through Aberfoyle. The only sign of life being a delivery van at the local Coop. From the luxury of a level track from the campsite I was now destined to face a steep climb up through Queen Elizabeth Forest Park for the next four miles. As soon as I turned right out of Aberfoyle I faced the steep climb on the road but only for a few hundred metres before the route disappeared off into the forest. The tracks were narrow and exciting, being level and even slightly downhill for a while before rising steeply after the visitor centre. I remembered walking along this track during our recent holiday here and thought that I would perhaps just about manage to cycle up it. What a silly thought, I was pushing before the first bend and continued pushing for at least a mile. The forest was empty, only me and my bike around. I could see clouds streaming past high above the trees but from where I was on a track through the forest there was no wind.

The track levelled off and I was able to ride again and was soon back on the piste once again racing down towards Loch Venachar. I passed a loch strangely named Loch Drunkie. The views from here are intoxicating. Perhaps that's why it was christened with such a name.

The forest track continued to wind its way down but it needed care on the steep curves as the surface was made up of gravel and not tarmac. A skid and fall now would certainly end up with more than a grazed knee. The track gave way to a narrow road by the side of Loch Venachar leaving only four miles to cycle to Callandar.

This part of Scotland, also known as The Trossachs, is famous for being the home of Rob Roy MacGregor that well known hero and outlaw from the eighteenth century.

Next to the Rob Roy Visitor Centre in Callander is a lovely little tea shop in an old school. I remembered that the food was wonderful here from our recent holiday and couldn't miss out on their delights. This was to be my first tea shop stop of the day and it's not even nine o'clock yet. Fortunately the shop had just opened so I was lucky enough not to be too early.

The owner asked me about my adventure and gave me £10 towards my cause. I also remembered a cake and pie shop along the high street that sold haggis pies. I bought one, which was piping hot, packed it away in my pannier bag and kept it for later. This was also the last place to stock up on a few necessities so I called in at the Tesco Extra store on the way out of town.

Route 7 now follows the path of an old railway which is by the side of Loch Lubnaig and consequently level for about nine miles. It then rises slightly and heads off towards Balquidder where Rob Roy is buried. The railway which was closed along with hundreds of others by the destructive Dr Beeching in the 1960s was an artery leading to both Killin and Oban.

The threatening rain had now started to pound down as it had done over Exmoor and on my frantic journey from Troon to Paisley. The difference was that I am now in the highlands and the temperature is a few degrees lower being both further north and higher in altitude. I passed through Balquidder and the sign for Rob Roy's grave. It was beckoning me to stop and take a photograph, but the urgency to keep pedalling in the rain and keep warm had more appeal even though another rest would have been welcome. Had the sun been shining the outcome may have been different.

When researching this challenge I remembered reading that there is usually a snack bar situated at the top of the pass before dropping down to Killin. I challenged myself to reach that snack bar before stopping and hoped that even in this cold incessant rain it would be open.

Over the last few years the next section of the route has been upgraded to follow the railway and not the main road. A new cycle path heads up through the trees and eventually joins up with the railway as it passes over a spectacular viaduct skirting the contours of the adjacent mountain. Just as I turned onto this new path I met a couple on a return journey from Killin. They had cycled from Callandar to Killin the previous day in abundant sunshine to return today in torrents of rain. They thought that the journey to Killin was more difficult than the return journey so it looked as though I had some hard pedalling ahead. A few hundred yards along the path it turned left and zigzagged what seemed like a thousand times uphill very steeply. I pushed left then right and left again. When would it stop? At each turn there was another turn a few yards ahead. Emerging from the final zag, the view was stunning, even though much of it was lost in the mist and rain.

Ahead lay the old railway, dead straight but with a good steady incline. I now understood what the couple had meant. I looked down to my right to see the busy A84 what appeared to be a mile below in the valley. It was alive with lorries and cars which were lost in the haze produced by the copious amounts of spray being constantly manufactured.

The surface was good, although a steady stream was flowing against me as I laboured up the incline. My feet were now aching with wet and cold. They were quite painful. Although my body was warm, I felt wet through and knew that a lengthy stop at the top could induce constant shivering. I reached the old viaduct and the views down were worthy of a short stop and some photographs. Although unlike at Rob Roy's grave in Balquidder I convinced myself that I needed a short rest here. I could see the road rising steeply to meet the level of this old railway at the top of the pass. The cycle track crossed the main road and as I rounded the hill, there it was, *The Snack Bar!* It was open. Warm air spewed out from its inner soul. I parked the bike and got as close to the escaping heat as I could, sheltering under the supported hatch cover out of the deluge of rain. My feet were throbbing and painfully cold and I had hardly any strength in my fingers and hands to undo the zip on my handlebar bag to obtain my wallet. This snack bar was situated in one of the most remote spots I had cycled past and probably for that reason given the weather was the most welcome.

I ordered a mug of tea and a sausage sandwich. My body required heat. My hands clamped themselves around the hot mug and I leaned as far as I could into the warmth of the snack bar. I think the lady on the other side was pleased to have some company today as business had been poor. She had been in two minds whether or not to close.

"Do you live far away?" I asked

"No! Just across the road."

Her house was hidden in the trees about fifty metres from her little cabin on wheels. She and her family had moved here from England a few years ago for a less hectic way of life. A bold move that quite a few people from south of the border had made. She told me that she and her family love their new found paradise here in Scotland.

Sausage sandwich and tea consumed and the possible onset of hypothermia due to uncontrollable shivering was a signal that I needed to move. I was now at the top of the pass and a large bold sign in front of me warned about the steep descent ahead. The sign didn't exaggerate. The track descended rapidly in long waves like a long serpent weaving its way through the trees before levelling out on the outskirts of Killin about two miles away. I'd picked up a lot of grit on the wheels today and constant heavy braking was taking its toll on the brake blocks. I cringed listening to the constant scraping sound as I squeezed the brakes to control my steep descent. I was now on the single track road which runs alongside Loch Tay on its south side. Being a low classification road it just followed all the rises and falls of the hillside. The further I cycled along it the louder the scraping sound when I used the brakes. When I found a lay by to stop and check the brakes my worst fears were realised – brakes were rubbing metal on metal. There was no rubber left in the brake blocks. The brake blocks had lasted well only being replaced when I had the bike serviced before I set off for Penzance sixteen days and one thousand two hundred and fifty miles ago.

Luckily when Julian and Andy met me in Carlisle, they had bought me a spare set at my request which I now needed. I removed the well worn ones and fitted the new ones which should last me for the rest of my journey. I tested the new brakes before setting off and after a few adjustments thought I was in possession of a new bike, once again braking in silence – no scraping sound.

With a combination of my new effortless and quiet braking system plus the fact that it had now stopped raining to reveal deep blue skies I had renewed determination. My feet began to dry out a little but more importantly had warmed through. A fairly long climb brought me to the top of a hill and another rapid descent. I braked towards the bottom before a bend only to be annoyed by that infuriating grating sound from the brakes again. I checked, double checked and checked again. They were fitted properly, working correctly and stopped the bike without sound when I moved slowly. Another hill and the scraping returned. This time I removed the brake blocks and checked them. These new blocks were faulty. Hidden about a newspaper page thickness beneath the surface of the rubber was the sharp edge of a metal bar. As soon as I had applied the brakes with any force this metal edge had immediately worn through the paper thin rubber and made contact with the wheel rim. Fortunately it only occurred on one of the blocks. I used my pliers to bend the offending part away from the rim and refitted the blocks. Hey Presto! On the next downhill the problem was solved. I made a mental note that on completion of LEJOG I will return these faulty parts to Halfords for a refund.

As I was fixing the brakes an elderly couple in a camper van stopped and asked if they could help. I explained the problem and they gave me £2 towards the fund when they read my pannier bags.

This road was the full length of Loch Tay, about fifteen miles which took me slightly more than two hours. At Kenmore the route crossed from the south side of the valley to the minor road on the north side. Clouds were now streaming across the near clear sky driven on by a strong westerly wind. I was about twenty miles from Pitlochry and there were no hills to fight. I'd been bursting for the loo for miles and hadn't spotted any convenient gate or handy bush to hide behind plus I was feeling a bit peckish after two and a half hours since my sausage sandwich when I spotted a pull in hidden behind some trees next to a footpath which led down to the river. I was experiencing bliss and relief and exhaled a loud sigh of pain loss when I was aware of female voices just around the bend. I just managed to adjust myself respectfully and position the haggis pie in my mouth when three ladies appeared.

"Hello! You look as though you're doing something exciting?"

With half a haggis pie stuffing my cheeks I made gestures as to the reason I couldn't reply just at that moment.

It was the print on my pannier bags that caught their attention and fortunately not the sound of thankful relief.

One of the ladies had been to Nepal and ever since had wanted to donate some money to help these children. She produced a twenty pound note from her purse for my cause. It's always a kind gesture to hand over one or two pounds for a charity but it takes quite a commitment to hand over twenty pounds to a perfect stranger kitted out in a red and white polka dot shirt who had stopped for a pee with a haggis pie stuffed in his mouth in the middle of nowhere.

I thanked her for her extreme generosity and gave her one of my blog cards. She refused to give me her name but one of her friends did the honours. My wife mentioned her in my blog to thank her and she later emailed back to acknowledge.

Back on track I followed the minor road which runs parallel to the River Tay almost all the way to Pitlochry and with a strong wind behind me I flew. I was touching thirty miles an hour at times without trying. I'd probably cover the fifteen miles to Pitlochry in less than an hour at this rate. On a straight stretch cycling in the opposite direction to me but directly into the wind was a young woman. As we approached each other I could make out her facial features. She thrust her head forward as if she was straining to keep it attached to her shoulders and her cheeks were forced into her mouth making great hollows. Her eyes were just slits as she was attacked by the full fury of the wind. Her long fair hair flowed out horizontally behind her like a streamer on a wind machine. She was struggling to make any headway at all. As we passed she yelled, "I know who's picked the right direction today!" I had no time to answer as seconds later I was just a blur in the distance and a hundred yards down the road.

The road eventually swung round a hill and headed north. I was in Pitlochry, another seventy miles ticked off. The wind had surprisingly dropped after I checked into the campsite and pitched the tent.

It would appear that the further north I ventured the more luxurious the campsites became. The whole campsite was immaculate, individual bays set out for tents and caravans with water pipes close by. The water pressure was high and I engineered a high pressure jet wash by nipping the end of the hose attached to the tap. My bike needed a good clean after picking up all the grit and dirt through the earlier rain.

I was spoilt for choice in Pitlochry for a meal although being a popular tourist resort they were priced on the high side.

Tomorrow I will be tackling the Drumochter pass. It's going to be uphill for miles and miles, yet in some masochistic way I am looking forward to it........Goodnight!

171

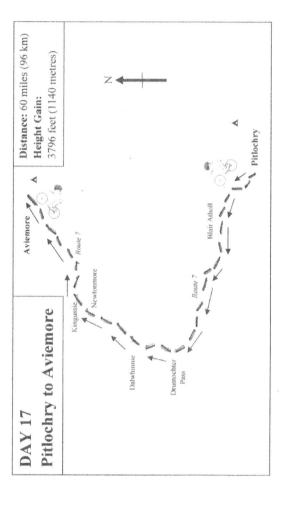

DAY 17
Pitlochry to Aviemore

Distance: 60 miles (96 km)
Height Gain: 3796 feet (1140 metres)

Day 17 – The High Route to Scotland's Ski Capital

The campsite was quiet with a blanket of dew everywhere when I left at about half seven. For some reason I'd overslept this morning but fortunately only by about half an hour. Perhaps it's my subconscious mind thinking there's only four days left and complacency has set in. The Route 7 signs were good, there being no scallywags around up here in the highlands to vandalise them and so I left my GPS switched off to conserve the battery life as much as possible. Anyway there's only one road north so I shouldn't get lost.

I knew that what lay ahead would be steadily up for miles then hopefully downhill into Strathspey and Aviemore. The route took me through Pitlochry then onto the old A9 towards Killiecrankie. It was difficult to imagine that in this narrow pass at Killiecrankie over six thousand men fought amongst each other in the Battle of Killiecrankie. Two and a half thousand fought for the Jocobites from the Highland Scottish Clans supporting King James VII of Scotland also known as King James II of England against three and a half thousand government troops. These were made up of mainly Lowland Scots, often incorrectly labelled as English, supporting William of Orange. The Jacobites had an overwhelming victory only to be defeated a month later further south at the Battle of Dunkeld.

For much of this part of the route I was sheltered by the gorge and by trees. Occasionally the route came into the open and I was reminded of the head wind that I would encounter once the tree line was exceeded. I shared the valley with the main A9 road to Inverness and the main rail line also to Inverness. The mountains seemed to grow taller and looked more remote. I spotted the first patch of snow ahead. There is a distinct sense of wildness up here. Although there was traffic on the main road nearby it felt far removed from my travelling environment. The drivers and passengers weren't sharing my experience. The windows of their vehicles were closed and most likely today, even though it is June, they had their car heaters turned on. I passed by Blair Atholl whose most famous feature is Blair Castle. The Duke of Athol is the only private person allowed to have his own private army in Britain but I didn't spot any soldiers on parade or manoeuvres today.

Clouds whipped across the mountain tops and the combination of the constant ascent and wind made my progress slow. I'd only managed eleven miles in over an hour without any stops. A family who had camped next to me in Pitlochry had travelled from John o'Groats on this route the previous day; (My wet experience day up through Killin). They had had hail in John o'Groats and also over the Drumochter Pass.

"Was today to be a reflection of yesterday?" I asked myself!

The old road became narrower and less used and Route 7 was now a rough track. A sign appropriately positioned at the start of this track warned about the severe weather changes and drifting snow between October and May. I wrapped up well to keep out any angry weather.

Route 7 was now squeezed between the main A9 to my right and the railway to my left. The ascent didn't look very steep and probably didn't seem like it for the traffic speeding by, but I was constantly changing down to the lower gears on my bike now and the climb was relentless. There was no respite just constant pedalling. No freewheeling just up and up. I was now in the lowest gear, forcing my way up this never ending hill. Since starting I'd been on lots of steeper hills but never one as long. I managed to achieve some small rests at the handful of kissing gates along the route. My thighs began to burn but the gradient was constant and as long as I didn't push too hard and continued to maintain a manageable rhythm the summit would soon arrive. A large white sign appeared in the distance with what looked like the shape of an osprey embossed on it. I was cycling through the gateway to the Cairngorm National Park. Another large sign further ahead read 'Drumochter Summit, 1516 feet above sea level. The relief was overwhelming, I knew now that I could look forward to a long descent down to Dalwhinnie where hopefully there might be a facility for a cup of tea. It had taken me three hours to cycle the twenty eight miles from Pitlochry to the Drumochter Summit. The top of this pass was as high as the highest hill over Exmoor, but here the mountains continued to soar above all around. I was standing on the highest point of my entire journey.

Unlike the majority of cycle routes I'd been on over the last seventeen days this one was quite overgrown. This was proof that there wasn't a lot of pedalling traffic up here. I didn't see another cyclist all day.

After a brief stop I was back on the bike still battling the head wind, although it was a little easier now that I'd conquered the ascent. The wind picked up and just to remind me that I was at the top of one of the most uninviting passes in Britain the rain started to throw itself at me, directly into my face. Even now as the track levelled and started to descend I had to get up out of the saddle to fight against this foe to keep moving. As I passed the highest mountains on either side of the pass the wind suddenly changed. It was as though it had been parted at the top of the pass. Half of it was blowing South and the other half to the North, although this split didn't render it half as strong.

With the wind and rain now behind me I felt a sudden surge of warmth and power. As the descent increased so did my speed. I began to cover double the distance in the same time as the ascent from the South. I could see buildings ahead, it was finally Dalwhinnie. I became eagle eyed looking for a sign which might direct me to a tea shop. I passed a filling station then a few houses dotted around but no tea shop. I cycled through a collection of buildings not even big enough to call a village when a large sign, big enough not to be missed, was conveniently displayed advertising the distillery ahead. Ah! Visitor attraction, they're bound to have a snack bar of some sort. I cycled through the car park looking for the entrance, parked the bike and made enquiries within. Disappointment was written all over my face brought on by a shake of the head from the lady at the enquiry desk. She did tell me that I could probably get a cup of tea and a sandwich from the filling station two miles back down the road. "Back down the road! – Not likely," was the thought that flashed through my head. However there was a cafe about ten miles up the road near Newtonmore called Ralia.

Having not eaten for several hours, I had to raid my larder. I still had a couple of sandwiches bought yesterday at Tesco Express in Callandar so I parked myself on a seat sheltered from the wind and rain near the door and restocked on energy.

The next ten miles to Ralia was almost level. I had left the mountains behind for a while. The Spey Valley is long and flat. The mighty Cairngorms rise to the east and the Monadhliath Mountains to the west. I felt as though I was in paradise having battled my way here over forbidding country and tempest. At Ralia I sat on the veranda enjoying my refreshments in warm sunshine. The rain and wind were left behind over Drumochter as a barrier to this peaceful valley.

The ride from Ralia, about a mile South of Newtonmore, to Kingusie was also level and quiet, most traffic choosing to travel on the main A9. Kingussie, meaning 'Head of the Forest' is also near the site of Ruthven Barracks, a fairly well preserved fort, built in the early eighteenth century by the British Government to help fight against the Jacobites. From Kingussie Route 7 crosses the valley and continues north along the edge of the forest and mountains.

As soon as I reached the main road that linked Aviemore with the Cairngorm Ski area there was a noticeable increase in human activity. Traffic, gift shops, restaurants, pavements and cycle routes were in abundance. With the valley being reasonably flat, cycle routes had been constructed throughout Rothiemurchus Forest and there was a superb off road route into Aviemore.

After a pleasant fourteen miles I cycled into the campsite at Coylumbridge about two miles east of Aviemore. The warden made me feel welcome, yet another friendly soul. There was a £10 deposit for the key to the toilets and showers, retrievable on departure when the office opened at 9am. I explained that I would be on my way by seven, so he trusted me to shove the key through the letterbox in the morning.

Camping was in the forest so things were a little different to all the other grass sites I'd been on. It was a case of finding a level spot between the trees big enough to take the tent. There was no grass, just dirt, pine needles, pine cones and twigs. Once a site had been found and cleared of lumps and sharp objects, the next challenge was to find a way of inserting the tent pegs far enough into the ground for them to function correctly. Up until now I'd managed to just press them home with a sturdy foot or even just the heel of my hand. However, this is the highlands and things are a little more challenging. I managed to find a mallet sized rock and by wangling each peg at the correct angle between the roots of the surrounding trees and bashing them gently to avoid bending, finally erected my tent. As long as there was no wind or torrential rain during the night then it would probably stay up till morning.

With my temporary home established and the bike fastened to a nearby tree I went off to try out the £10 key, which was in fact an upmarket swipe card. After circling the ablution building a couple of times and not spotting two different entrances for men and women I swiped the card through the lock of the only door and cautiously entered. They were unisex, but not so anyone could see what you were up to. There were separate cubicles and in each one was a shower, wash basin and loo. And they were very posh! These were the best loos and showers that I'd encountered since Land's End, seventeen days and seventeen campsites ago.

Freshened up once again and wearing my 'going out clothes' – that's the spare T-shirt – I cycled into Aviemore to stock up on a few things to get me to John o'Groats.

I'd been to Aviemore a few times but as I cycled past the Youth Hostel I remembered an incident from way back in 1982 when I was part of an MLC (Mountain Leadership Certificate) winter mountaineering introductory course organised by Howtown Outdoor Centre on Ullswater in the Lake District.

Throughout the 1970s and 80s, Howtown was Durham County's flagship outdoor centre and many teachers employed by Durham signed up to achieve outdoor qualifications which enabled them to take children into the British mountains. During the February half term of 1982 there were twelve of us, all men who signed up for the mountaineering course or a ski leaders' course.

We'd been out ice climbing on our third day and returned to Aviemore Youth Hostel along with the skiers to enjoy a hot shower and a meal, which we had to cook ourselves. The kitchen was packed with climbers and skiers using every pan and stove in site so we decided to nip up to the swimming pool and spend an hour or so in the pool until the novices in the kitchen had finished.

Unfortunately none of us had brought our swimming costumes with us but managed to hire some from the pool. It was cold outside with about a foot of lying snow but inside the pool building it was tropical. All twelve of us plunged into the empty pool, managed a couple of lengths then someone noticed the Jacuzzi. Not one of us had ever experienced the delights of one of these new fangled tubs. There was no-one else in the pool apart from the dirty dozen weary and hungry fellas. The Jacuzzi was like a magnet. There was no way that all twelve of us would fit around the Jacuzzi. There was a mad dash to grab a space on the circular submerged seat. It was a bit like squeezing the cork back into a wine bottle. It was difficult but we managed to fit in. Shoulder to shoulder and thigh to thigh we half sat and half lay in a gurgling and now giggling circle. Our weary muscles were soon relaxed and jokes flew around thick and fast.

There were newcomers standing by the pool side, they made their way over to the Jacuzzi looking for a gap. The newcomers were two shapely blondes probably in their early twenties. We all looked at them and from being squeezed together there were now gaps appearing everywhere.

"Plenty of room here!" everyone invited in unison.

One of the young ladies placed her foot between me and my fellow mountaineer on my right. She slithered into the Jacuzzi and neither of us could wipe the smile from our faces. One of our instructors was Scottish and was hoping that one of them might sit beside him. To his disappointment, neither of them did. He looked at each of us in turn and with envious retort coupled with a smirk said, "Behave yourself laddie!"

Now these hired swimming trunks were not up market designer kit but were made out of wonderful 1960s bri-nylon. The bubbles generated by the Jacuzzi managed in some way to find themselves congregating inside mine forming an inflated balloon which unavoidably made my groin rise to the surface displaying the trunks in a large mound through the foam. Once my body was horizontal the bubbles managed to escape making a loud 'Bloop' sound thus submerging my groin once again just for the trunks to re-inflate to repeat the embarrassing process. Thankfully the girls saw the funny side as well my mates who made all kinds of humiliating comments.

Unfortunately our time was up and we returned to the Youth Hostel kitchen to find it full of unwashed, burnt and filthy pans piled high in sinks blocked with all manner of waste food. The perpetrators were nowhere to be seen having probably gone to the pub leaving us to clean up if we wanted a meal. Complaints were filed with the warden.

I cycled past the Youth Hostel then a pub that looked inviting enough for a bar meal which unfortunately didn't open for meals until six o'clock. I had an hour to kill so mooched around a few shops next to the station. I managed to buy a small bottle of meths which should last me for the rest of the journey and a few items for the larder as I envisaged the final two stages to be very remote.

After a very relaxing bar meal and a couple of pints I cycled back to the campsite and was reliably tucked up in my sleeping bag by 9pm. This was definitely the hardest ground I'd slept on.

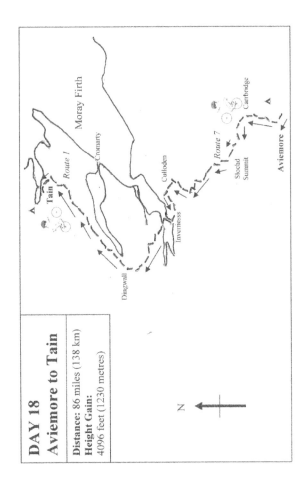

DAY 18
Aviemore to Tain

Distance: 86 miles (138 km)
Height Gain:
4096 feet (1230 metres)

Day 18 – Burial Chambers, Battles and Whisky

Was it rain I could hear on the tent or pine needles falling off the trees? The gentle tap tap on the tent had me confused until I ventured outside. It was a mixture of both but the rain that fell was insignificant. I lit my stove as normal and went about my usual routine. There were more tents here than all of the other campsites I'd camped at except for Staveley near Kendal. The date was now after mid June and I am in one of the most beautiful regions of Britain so I suppose there is a bit of an attraction here.

All was still quiet as I packed away and posted my toilet key card through the site office letterbox. Since planning my route from Aviemore to Inverness, there have been a few alternatives added to the route shown on my ten year old map. I could follow my planned route which would take me on several dog legs through the forest or follow the old A9 road which was more direct. Either way I would still have to tackle Slochd Summit which is about three hundred feet lower than Drumochter Pass. The decision had to be made at the campsite entrance. Turn right for the wibbly wobbly route through the forest or turn left for a more direct route. The decision wasn't difficult to make, I turned left and headed into Aviemore. At 7am up here in the Highlands there aren't any factories changing shifts or people breaking their necks and the speed limit to get to work in order to grab a parking place. Everywhere was very peaceful. What rain there was when I awoke over an hour ago had since moved away east and the sky was filled with blue wonder. The wind was light and it looked as though I was going to enjoy a friendly weather day. For mile after mile I encountered barely a handful of cars, even on the parallel main A9 the traffic was light.

This new route took me through Carrbridge, a place I'd heard about but had never visited. Apparently the bridge the town is named after is the most photographed bridge in Scotland. Having been built in 1717 it forms a steep thin and narrow arch over the river. There was a perfect photo opportunity from the present road bridge next to it. It's as though whoever designed the new bridge thought about the perfect position for photographs. It was not yet eight o'clock and the town was still quiet, yet another photographer joined me to make an addition to his photo memories.

From Carrbridge the alternative Route 7 was well signed and quickly started to rise towards Slochd Summit. The surface was good and where the old road had been absorbed by the new a fresh cycle track had been laid. Within half an hour of leaving Carrbridge I was resting on Slochd Summit. Just like on Drumochter Pass the cycle track was sandwiched between the A9 and the railway. This old road seemed to follow the contours of the hills and started to wind its way down towards Inverness now a mere three hours away.

Several years ago this old road would have been very busy being the main artery between Edinburgh and Inverness. It is narrow in places, especially as it winds its way around these hills. There aren't many houses up here but the few that there are provide accommodation for their fortunate owners in this beautiful place but are also unfortunately built by the edge of this once busy major trunk road. The owners had understandably been frustrated by many selfish and thoughtless people driving their cars almost out of control at speed past their home. One home owner who has attached a large sign in the shape of a coffin to a telegraph pole, about two hundred metres before their house, either had a very imaginative sense of humour or realised that he should probably be targeting mobile phone users and had written the sign in text language. It was displayed in large print – 'KILL UR SPEED NOT US'. When I first spotted this sign I imagined an 18th Century Clansman wearing a kilt and armed with sword and shield yelling this out with a deep course Highland accent at passing motorists. Perhaps the sign was put up to be humorous as well as serious to get the message over.

Having just dropped off, so to speak, the Summit top I expected the road to descend as rapidly as that from Drumochter Pass, but it didn't. It follows the contour of the hills for miles, dropping a little then rising again. The cycle route eventually rejoined the main A9 on a cycle track then continued on country roads towards the town of Culloden.

Just after turning off onto the more country style road my attention was drawn to a bus shelter. Totally intact with its glass panels and entirely graffiti free, it was furnished with a coffee table and chair. The buses on this route must be quite infrequent so some kind resident has made the shelter as comfortable a wait as possible. It was however missing a TV and a handful of magazines. I could only think that this must be one of the fewest places in Britain where furniture in a bus shelter remains intact.

I stopped at the remarkably preserved Clava prehistoric burial cairns on the outskirts of Culloden battle field. Only at Kilmartin, south of Oban had I seen anything as well preserved as these. The atmosphere surrounding the cairns shaded by mainly ancient looking oak and other deciduous trees seemed to demand respect from all visitors. As I looked around I felt as though a thousand spirits were watching me in case I trod on the stones. I could sense their invitation to venture around, to take photographs, to look and to learn but to alter or to disfigure the cairns in any way would certainly bring an ill fated future for the perpetrator.

Just before the end of the 20th Century a parcel arrived at the Inverness tourist information centre. On opening the parcel a stone was found with a letter from a Belgian gentleman. The letter pleaded with the information centre to replace the stone on the Clava Cairns, as he had taken it a couple of years ago as a memento of his holiday in the Highlands. However, since then, both he and his family had suffered continuous bad luck, so he wanted it returned. The information centre was happy to oblige - I wonder if the Belgian gentleman's luck has now changed?

The Culloden battle field where in 1746 the Jacobites were finally crushed in the last battle on British soil was a few miles off my route so I didn't get the chance to see it.

I approached the built up area along the edge of the Moray Firth and knew that for the next few miles I would have to take extra care looking out for Route 7 signs. The next sign I spotted read Route 1 which I now joined to take me all the way to John o'Groats. Within a few miles I was pleased to find myself almost in the centre of Inverness. A steep path led down towards a shopping precinct when a small gurgling in my stomach reminded me that I hadn't stopped, except to take a few photos, nor eaten since my usual Fruit and Fibre breakfast at 6.30 this morning. This was psychological cruelty and I must find a tea shop. It must have been the drifting aroma of coffee and hot pasties that attracted me to the little shop on my left. There were two tea shops next to each other, one was bulging at the seams and the other had plenty of spare tables. I locked the bike to a drainpipe and settled down in a window seat in the one with spare tables. The world passed by as my order for hot sausage sandwiches with salad, a chocolate slice and a pot of tea was being prepared. Unfortunately the other tea shop had the hot pasties and I would have preferred to have sat outside in the warm sun but neither café had the space for any outside tables. Today was Saturday and the shopping precinct was very busy. My journey for today wasn't yet half over so I needed to replenish my energy for the five hours and fifty miles that lay ahead. My plan was to cross the Moray Firth on the Kessock Bridge then turn east towards the Cromarty Ferry after which there would be about twenty miles heading north to Tain.

This must have been a Saturday job for the young female waitress as she didn't seem very experienced or chatty. In fact when I placed my order, I did all the talking. The cafe was empty apart from an elderly couple and myself. It was embarrassingly quiet. I had no-one to talk to so sat in silence and read through the menu about twenty times, the waitress wrote my order down on a scrappy piece of paper and took it into a back room before re-emerging in silence. The elderly couple who had probably talked themselves out over umpteen years of wedded bliss also sat in silence.

The only thing I had to read apart from reading the menu again was my GPS which I always removed from the bike whenever I left it. After a few minutes, which seemed like hours, the white bread sausage sandwiches arrived accompanied with half a lettuce leaf. Again I was the only one who spoke saying, "Thank you"!

It was now quite evident why the tea shop next door was bursting at the seams and this one was empty. This was something to bear in mind if ever I am in a dilemma about which of two adjacent tea shops to support with my custom.

It was time to pay the bill. Could the young waitress be tempted to speak? Would she just ring up the amount and point to the till screen, as they do when Brits are on holiday in Europe. Perhaps she's used to dealing with foreign tourists and consequently never talks to them.

"How much do I owe you please?"

"Four pounds eighty!"

I gave her £5 and told her to keep the change as a tip for her excellent service and left the shop. The elderly couple still hadn't uttered a word, eaten anything or poured anything from the tea pot that adorned their table like a dormant vase. Perhaps they were dummy customers as a ploy to attract custom!

I walked through the city centre pushing the bike as it was now bursting at the seams like the cafe I didn't use. I passed a stall promoting the Bird of Prey Rescue Centre, guarded by two magnificent Eagle Owls sitting on two perches perpendicular to each other. They sat there swivelling their heads through 360° and always keeping two eyes between them on the passing public. They could see what was happening behind as well as in front and at the sides at the same time. Their handler hid behind a screen puffing on a cigarette.

Perhaps not the best advert to promote wildlife. A large sign invited photographs but warned people against using the flash on their camera.

At the end of the traffic free shopping centre I came to a cross roads and traffic. The Route 1 sign pointed to the right so I was once again in the saddle heading out of town. The route followed the south bank of the River Ness which links up with the Caledonian Canal. I followed this past factories and wharfs until I could see the Kessock Bridge which takes the main A9 across the narrows of the Moray Firth ahead.

Two fully laden cyclists were stopped ahead studying their map. They were Belgian, a married couple who told me that they cycle every year in Britain. This year they were cycling from John o'Groats to Carlisle following Routes 1 & 7 then joining Route 6 to Southport and finally crossing the Pennines on Route 62 to Hull before catching a ferry back home. They were a little confused about the route through Inverness but I assured them that it was easy enough to follow.

Their bikes were intriguing. They were both of the sit up and beg variety which would have been extremely difficult to attack the hills. The handlebars on the man's bike had enough gadgets attached to fly a plane, many I didn't recognise. I think one of them made a cup of tea whilst on the move and another a sausage sandwich. I should have asked him where he bought them then I could continue cycling without ever stopping except for a pee. Maybe he had a gadget for that as well!

They asked me where I was headed and after much discussion convinced me that a new route via Dingwall, thus avoiding the Cromarty Ferry and shortening my route by about five miles would be the best option. They said that it was well sign posted and I would have no problems following it. I left them to negotiate their way through Inverness and I climbed the zigzag track onto the Kessock Bridge.

The view from the middle of the bridge was stunning. To the south I looked back over the roof tops of Inverness and to the west I could see mountains galore some still with snow on them shimmering in the warmth of the June sun. Below, there was a distinct line of white water, attached to a spur of land opposite and disappearing beneath the bridge I was standing on. As the tidal sea water forced itself through this narrow gap from the massive Moray Firth, it fought against the fresh water flowing down from the mountains out of the Beauly Firth. It appeared to be stale mate and the stationary turbulence would probably remain until the tide abated.

My general direction was north-west towards Dingwall but first descended from the bridge into the small quiet village of North Kessock which was the northern ferry terminal for the link between Inverness and the Black Isle until 1982 when it closed a few years after the bridge was completed. Until then it was a busy place. Once through Charleston, next to North Kessock I turned away from the coast and headed inland. The route was well sign posted and after about an hour I was heading high up along the north shore of the Cromarty Firth. The view down towards the water was stunning and could just make out traffic travelling along the pillared two mile long bridge that spanned the Cromarty Firth. I could also just make out the gap near the small village of Cromarty where the little ferry crosses which had been my intended route before I met the Belgian couple.

The route took me through a little village called Evanton when unexpectedly out of the blue there appeared a cafe. I didn't even have to make a few metres detour. The attraction was too great especially as my backside was not only suffering from the normal cyclists complaint but the constant rubbing had brought back the soreness that I experienced back in Cornwall and do from time to time even when on long walks. I would need to administer the Vaseline in generous proportions tonight!

This reminded me when several years ago on a four day school camp in the Lakes I'd been suffering from a bad bout of backside chafing and each night within the privacy of my own tent dipped a finger into the Vaseline jar to smear copious amounts of the wonderful stuff on the soreness. It always worked wonders and after a night's sleep the soreness had all but disappeared. On our third day after a good walk across the fells the chafing returned and earlier than normal I administered the potion in the usual way. A couple of hours later we were sitting around chatting when one of our younger female staff asked if anyone had any Vaseline. Without thinking I offered her my tub and went off to my tent to get it. I handed it to her; she removed the lid, scooped out a fair chunk with her index finger and smeared it well into her dry lips. It was too late to tell her that I'd just smeared the stuff on my backside. She handed me the jar with a smile and said, "Mmmmm....that's better! Thanks!" She still doesn't know the full story.

I locked my bike to the ever convenient drain pipe and found a table inside the cafe. Not just table and chairs in here but low level coffee tables with lounging chairs around them. For such a tiny village this was very comfortable and up market. I hope it's not a Greek Restaurant in disguise. The waitress brought me my order of a Devon cream tea and I wondered if they sold haggis pies in Devon! She then went over to the door and locked it. I'd just got there in time before they closed. The only other customers were a family also enjoying Devon cream teas. About five minutes later a young man tried the door to find it locked then started knocking loudly on it calling out what I assumed to be the waitresses name. She had long since disappeared into a back room along with the rest of the staff. The family and I looked at each other and shrugged. The man continued to shout and knock even louder. He didn't look aggressive so I let him in then re-locked the door. He found an empty table, sat down and read his newspaper.

"Who the hell let you in?" demanded the voice that reverberated around the room. There was no answer, no other sound and the waitress disappeared back into the back room.

I finished my cream tea, paid the bill and resumed my journey.

At the next village I turned left and headed into some low lying hills covered with forest. A well mowed council owned grass verge on the edge of the village had two three foot high red and white road cones on it which must have been standing there for months and even though the grass was short around them, tufts of grass poked up through the holes in the tops of the cones to a height of nearly four feet. Perhaps it was a sculpture, or perhaps moving the cones to cut the grass was not part of the grass cutter operator's job description.

Onward to Tain, another fifteen miles over fairly level country roads and I'd be there. On the last straight stretch, about a mile long there were two teenage boys about two hundred yards ahead of me, on BMX bikes weaving from side to side, doing wheelies and other such stunts that teenagers do on roads whether the roads are busy or not. They looked back and spotted me bearing down on them. They straightened their course as I sensed that their goal now was to beat me to the end of the road. I sensed a challenge, a Wembley Final or a Wimbledon Final, I had the bit between my teeth and all the pain oozing from my sore backside was forgotten with the rooftops of Tain now in sight. My goal was also to beat them to the end of the road. On this level road I had built up a good head of steam, I was in top gear and with head down forced my way along the road. They stood up on their pedals pushing them down as hard as they could with heads almost resting on the handlebars to minimise wind resistance. They were no match for my highly geared bike coupled with the momentum I had stored. I rapidly caught them up and within ten yards would have sped between them like a bullet train. At the last minute the one on the right turned into a field without warning. His mate looking petrified and now alone; felt the tension build around him with the increasing sound of me bearing down on him. He stuck out a rather shaky right arm as he just managed to cross my bows within a split second of impact. He also disappeared into the field. It was my victory as I considered them to have withdrawn from the competition before the finishing line. I triumphantly held up the imaginary trophy. Tain centre was but a few hundred yards down the hill. I stocked up with milk and a few odds and ends then found that the campsite was a further two miles north along the A9.

I'd never heard of Tain before planning this adventure but later learnt that this is the home of Glenmorangie meaning 'Glen of Tranquility' and is the most popular malt whisky sold in Scotland. Although I'd heard of Glenmorangie quite a few times! The whisky has been distilled here next to the Morangie farm since 1700 but only became legalised in 1843. There were sixteen men who set up the distillery and even today there are still only sixteen men who distil the whisky. Not the same ones though! They are famously known as 'The 16 Men of Tain'.

The wind had been behind me between Dingwall and Tain which was in a general easterly direction but now I was heading in a north westerly direction along the coast. The wind was now against me and even on the level I was nearly in bottom gear. This was as strong a head wind that I'd experienced throughout the whole journey. The 'CAMPSITE 300 YARDS' sign gave me a sense of relief that I will never forget. The stage from Aviemore had been one of the hardest.

I found the office and the owner took one look at me and said!

"You look relieved to be here!" To which I gave a large sigh accompanied with a huge silent smile.

He recommended the bar meals at the local pub just around the corner which suited me and I looked forward to waiting at the door for the 6pm opening time.

I asked if there was a public telephone to which he answered with an apology. However he offered me the use of his own phone but there was no-one in at home when I called.

The campsite was long and narrow, the office and toilet/shower block were near the entrance and the campsite was about two hundred metres further down the narrow strip which would make life a little awkward in the middle of the night.

I was given a pitch and cycled down the rough track to find it. After a hot shower and a well earned rest I wandered around to the pub. It was open and empty.

"Hi!" The landlord took one look at me, a stranger, and said in a pleasant way,

"You don't want a bar meal do you?"

"Yes please!"

"Could you come back in about an hour, I'm a bit pushed at the moment?"

"Have you got a big party coming in?"

"No! Just six."

There were some newspapers on the table next to two arm chairs and a roaring log fire. I opted to buy a pint, settle in one of the armchairs and read the newspaper. This was the first newspaper I'd read since the day I caught the train from Darlington to Plymouth almost three weeks ago. I hadn't missed much. It was all doom, gloom and criminal activities as well as hundreds of adverts trying to sell stuff that nobody really wants to buy. Anyway, it kept me occupied for a few minutes before the landlord showed me a menu and told me I might as well place my order and he would give me a shout when it was ready.

After about twenty minutes he shouted me through to the dining room where not a large, but enormous plate of cottage pie and vegetables awaited me. The cottage pie was in a round dish about ten inches in diameter and two inches deep. It was overflowing. Piled on a separate plate was a full selection of vegetables. Another pint was needed to help wash it all down. I'd already told him my story and he remarked:

"That should fill you up, you'll need the energy!"

He even let me use his personal phone to phone home. This time I got an answer.

Again the friendship shown to me wherever I've been has been overwhelming except for Miss Jobsworth and the drunken toff! I took my time with the meal. It had been freshly cooked and was delicious.

A family of six arrived for a birthday meal which I assumed was the reservation he expected.

Back at the campsite a couple of lads in their early twenties had camped next to my tent. They had bikes and we chatted. They had only just started JOGLE two days ago but had cycled down the A9 from Helmsdale today.

My route tomorrow, following Route 1 would take me across country to Lairg then north along one of the loneliest roads in Britain, the A836, to Tongue, then east to Bettyhill. This was about 75 miles and the roads were hilly, windy and single track. My reason for not cycling up the A9 directly to Wick was that I'd heard that it was narrow and very busy with fish lorries. However the lads had said that they had travelled down today, Saturday, and it was very quiet. Tomorrow being Sunday it would probably be quieter, plus the road doesn't have many hills except for around Helmsdale and the Berriehill Braes. I decided to follow their advice and cycle directly up the A9 to Wick where I would camp before cycling to John o'Groats the next day.

I'd spent the best part of nine months preparing for this venture whereas these lads seemed to have piled a few things into their pannier bags along with a laptop. They hadn't planned any route at all except that they were cycling from John o'Groats to Land's End; in other words... south! Their theory was that if they got the daily weather report over the internet they could plan their route for the day by always keeping the wind behind them thus making their journey much easier. The last I heard they were cycling through Belgium. Hadn't anybody told them that most of the time the prevailing winds in Britain blow from the south-west?

I'd been well satisfied with my £6 cottage pie as the two lads enjoyed a half cooked, half burnt chicken leg done on a throw away BBQ when I bade them goodnight and wished them a safe journey if I didn't see them in the morning.

I awoke with a start, desperate for the loo. It was light and heavy snoring reverberated from the lads' tent.

'I've slept in!' was my immediate thought and with half open bleary eyes reached for my glasses and watch. It was only 10.22pm and I'd only been asleep for less than an hour and a half. That couple of pints with the meal earlier on must be the culprit. I poked my head out of the tent. There was no-one about so I crawled over to the hedge and knelt down to relieve myself in the bushes.

I snuggled back into my sleeping bag with the pleasant thought that I still had nearly seven hours of sleep ahead of me.

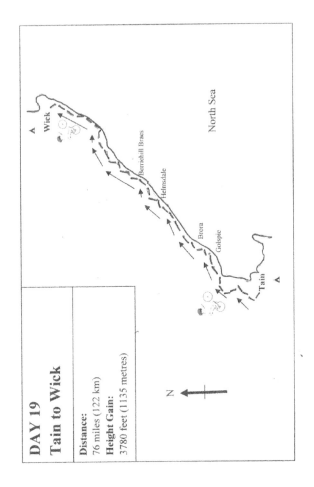

DAY 19
Tain to Wick

Distance:
76 miles (122 km)
Height Gain:
3780 feet (1135 metres)

N

Wick

Berriedale Braes

Helmsdale

Brora

Golspie

Tain

North Sea

Day 19 – The Great Norse Road

Excitement greeted me this morning as well as a perfect morning. Today would hopefully get me to Wick then with only 18 miles to John o'Groats tomorrow, my challenge would be complete. There was heavy harmonious snoring reverberating from the next tent. At half five in the morning, the two lads were very much still in the 'Land of Nod'. I emerged from my tent with determination, encouraged by the deep blue sky and clear still air. After an hour following my usual routine and ready to go, the lads emerged bleary eyed also showing a spark of determination. The difference being, that I only had about 85 miles ahead of me to get to my destination whereas they had probably a thousand miles or more before they realised their challenge. Hopefully the wind direction wouldn't take them too close to Dover nor too far away from Land's End. We wished each other luck before I made my way to the gate.

Even though there was only one road ahead of me I still planned it into my GPS to give me some idea of time and distance.

Back along the road to the 'CAMPSITE 300 YARDS' sign was the only major junction I'd see for miles. If I'd turned right out of the campsite I would have been following my initial planned route with 75 miles to Bettyhill then 58 miles to John o'Groats plus the 18 miles to Wick for the train. Thankfully with it being Sunday and less traffic I'd got about 68 miles ahead of me to Wick then 36 miles to John o'Groats and back tomorrow.

Looking along the new bridge across the Dornoch Firth the north shore was about a mile and a half away. I had the bridge all to myself. Not a vehicle in sight. Without any wind the sea was flat. The shoreline was the horizontal axis of symmetry there being little difference in the clarity between the object and the image. Only because the image was upside down could I determine which was which. I started off wearing my jacket but removed it when only half way across the bridge, it was so warm even before 7am.

The first vehicle passed going in the opposite direction fifteen minutes later. The first of only two lorries passed about half an hour later. I could have been on the loneliest road in Britain and not the main A9 to Thurso and Wick seeing only three vehicles in the first hour. This was pleasant. No significant hills and perfect weather with only a very slight breeze from behind.

I was soon cycling through Golspie, which still appeared to be asleep, and past the entrance to the enchanting Dunrobin Castle, home to the Duke of Sutherland. The first Duke of Sutherland was notorious in the initiation of the sweeping reforms to his enormous estates in the highlands; later referred to as the Highland Clearances. Even though he was probably responsible for the removal of hundreds of families from their homes and the burning of their buildings a huge memorial was built in his honour in 1837. It stands 100 feet high and dominates the skyline from the top of the bleak hill overlooking Dunrobin Castle and the town of Golspie.

Villages were now fewer and further apart and within six miles I was cycling through Brora. It always amazes me how towns stuck out in the middle of nowhere all become famous for something; probably because there's no competition for a neighbouring town or village to attract that fame. Tain for Glenmorangie and 'The 16 Men of Tain', Golspie for The Duke of Sutherland and now Brora known as 'The Electric City' as it was the first town in Northern Scotland to get electricity in 1911. The radio station here was also a top secret Ministry of Defence listening centre during the cold war between 1949 and 1986.

It was now just after half past eight and I'd covered almost 25 miles and needed my usual energy boost. The only shop open was the newsagents but no tea shops, not here on Sunday and certainly not at half eight in the morning. I found a seat and ate a couple of two day old sandwiches. A further two cars and the second lorry passed. The lads in the campsite back in Tain had told me that the busiest stretch was south of Brora. I was now at Brora and hadn't even encountered enough vehicles to count on two hands so further north the prospects looked promising, although as the weather is perfect today, things might get busier.

The surrounding landscape became a little more undulating the further north I travelled but nothing significant to hold me back. The lads had mentioned 'The Berriedale Braes' which are steep hills a little further north of my present position. The views all around were crystal clear. Steep cliffs swept down to a flat calm sea and I could even make out the headland near Tain about 25 miles behind me. A recently renovated stretch of road included long wide sweeps of velvet smooth tarmac. As soon as I hit the uphill section I was walking. A big Jag appeared on the horizon at the top of the hill and must have passed me doing well over a hundred miles an hour. It was frighteningly close and thankfully passed me without incident.

I'd made the same mistake as I made in Glentrool and forgot to make sure my water bottle was full. There was nothing here except for tiny streams about a hundred feet below the road. I would manage until the next town.

As the time crept past ten o'clock more traffic began to appear on this one and only road for miles. Vintage cars by the dozen passed me going south as part of a rally I'd seen advertised on my way to Tain. I was totally puzzled by the huge number of these wonderful old cars which have emerged from this scarcely populated area of Britain. To the north where this traffic had driven from were only two towns of notable size, Wick and Thurso. To the east was the sea and to the west only miles of wild country and mountains. In fact this is the region where some landowner, whose name I can't remember but watched a programme about it on the TV, perhaps the nth Duke of Sutherland, wants to introduce wolves and bears and possibly a few other species, long since extinct to Britain. He also wants to enclose the whole area, several hundred square miles, with a huge electrified fence to keep them in so they won't trouble the sheep or people for that matter. Sounds like hints of Jurassic Park!

The road now has long sweeping hills which make pleasant relaxing riding downhill but hot sweaty energy sapping struggles uphill. Even though I was just wearing shorts and my 'King of the Mountains' sleeveless shirt my water was rapidly running out. On one of my downhill stretches a young couple riding towards me were struggling uphill on their tandem fully laden with bags and a tent. The male of the duo was in the usual male position on a tandem, at the front and the female, on the rear seat. There is always a reason for this. The male takes the front because he would like to think that he is the strongest and ablest of the two so he has prime control over the bike or is it that the female takes the back seat because she is the more cunning to block the one at the front getting the full picture because they can't see what is happening behind.

The male, at the front, with bright red face and gritted teeth had sweat pumping out of him like a watering can in full flow even though he was only wearing a thin T shirt and shorts. The female, behind, was fully clad in waterproofs, full length leggings, woolly hat and gloves with not an ounce of sweat exuding from her face. Assuming that they were attempting JOGLE or some other long distance cycle ride I raised my right arm and shouted "Hi! Best of luck!"

He barely nodded, his knuckles grasping the handlebars firmly with his head as far down as possible to transfer as much power through the pedals as he could. She raised her right arm, smiled without any effort and shouted back, "Thanks, you too!" Perhaps it was her turn for a rest and further down the road they might change places!!!!!

For mile upon mile there were only odd houses by the road side until twenty seven miles after Brora I came to Helmsdale, an old fishing village built around a wide ravine. A sign pointed to the visitor centre. Perhaps here I might be able to find a tea shop and stock up on energy plus a longed for rest. I found the visitor centre which was open. Not another person could be seen anywhere and moving traffic was non-existent. I don't know why I locked the bike to a drainpipe but it was a useful precautionary habit that I'd got myself into. The visitor centre was deserted except for a lady behind a desk. It was obvious they didn't have a tea shop but I asked anyway. She pointed across the valley to a white building about a mile away on the opposite side.

"If you're going north that's the next place you'll get a cup of tea and if you're going south it's another twenty seven miles."

With relief I was going north. She filled my water bottle. I thanked her and rejoined the main road. The road swept down almost to the valley floor then across the side of the hill on the opposite side to the tea shop before disappearing out of sight. I picked up speed on the downhill section and because it was smooth, wide and new I didn't immediately get a true sensation of the speed I was accomplishing. A bit like being on a four lane motorway with no traffic around travelling in one of the middle lanes, glancing at the speedometer just to confirm to yourself that you are doing 70mph and find that you are in fact touching 100mph.

It wasn't until I must have been travelling with such speed that my helmet left my head and was only restrained by the loosely fastened chin strap which I'd loosened several days ago on my way to Paisley so that I could accommodate my jacket hood under my helmet without choking myself. The helmet must have been a full two inches above my head when I was in fear of it flying off into the ravine below. I released the grip on the handlebars with my right hand to push the helmet back into place but as soon as the pressure on the handlebars was relaxed the bike started to go into a wobble. I put up with the displaced helmet and regained control of the bike with both hands. I was now in survival mode with my helmet acting like a mini parachute trying to tear my head away from my shoulders - at least that's what it felt like – and focused my concentration in a desperate attempt to keep the bike in a straight line. Visions of my helmet flying off like a Frisbee into the valley below seemed too real.

'I must not brake, or swerve, or wobble, or look around, or glance to the side, or get an itch, or pedal or do anything to alter my course down this underestimated hill', were the thoughts racing through my mind. I was actually looking forward to the hill rising again. I must have been doing in excess of what felt like 1000mph (probably about 40mph) when my helmet decided to levitate. Finally the road levelled out and as I slowed down I managed to raise a hand and squeeze the helmet back onto my head.

In what seemed like a split second since joining the road from the visitor centre I cycled into the tea shop car park. It was a hotel and had only just opened for the day; guests being a rare breed in this part of the world. The usual toasted cheese sandwiches and pot of tea followed by a warm scone and jam were ordered then I settled myself at a picnic bench in the garden overlooking the bay, the little village of Helmsdale and the big dipper hill I'd just survived. My heart was still pumping with fear with my first task being to tighten the chin strap on my helmet. Only about 17 miles lay ahead of me to Wick and even at a leisurely pace I should be there by mid afternoon.

This north-east coast of Northern Scotland was a magnet for the Norsemen over a thousand years ago being only a short sail from Scandinavia. The names of many towns and villages on this coast originate from Norse. Helmsdale, where I was now, possibly got its name from the battles fought here - 'Dale of the Helmet', but there is even evidence that the Romans visited this village. The Romans described the men from this region as being tall and red headed which reminded me of those comical tartan caps you can buy with straggly red hair sticking out of the back. Perhaps they are modelled on the men of Helmsdale from Roman times!

The town of Tain was possibly called *Thin* by the Norsemen meaning 'Place of Assembly'. Wick was called *Vik* meaning 'Bay', but Brora seemed to originate much later as 'River of the Bridge' meaning that Brora had the only bridge in Sutherland at the time.

After another pot of tea and second scone I was back on the bike heading for Wick. About 400 yards up the road there was another tea shop which was in fact the one pointed out by the lady at the visitor centre. Two cyclists in the doorway shouted,

"Only 35 miles to go!"

"Cheers!" was my reply knowing that I only had half that distance to travel today.

My curiosity had been moved to the front of my mind due to the next notable place being the Berriedale Braes which I had never heard of. Even if I had heard of them I wouldn't have known what they were until the two lads had described them. About half an hour later the road decided to sweep down incorporating a few hairpin bends to the bottom of a deep gorge. The two lads had compared the Braes to the most severe switchbacks in The Rockies or The Alps. They were ecstatic about having cycled down the northern side but had walked up the southern side. Knowing that two fit young cyclists also walk up steep hills gave my ego a substantial boost. It looked as though I would be matching their attempt but in reverse. I was soon winding my way down to the bottom of the Braes. Visions of careering down the hairpins brought back memories of my fiasco about an hour ago. There would be no escape to be out of control on such a hill. The lads were right in thinking that these were steep hairpins but really couldn't be compared to anything in the Rockies or Alps. I was at the bottom but my view of the climb out was impaired by trees and the hill side. I ensured that bottom gear was selected before I attempted to go up. This north side was far steeper than the south side that I'd descended. Within ten yards I hit an invisible force. I could see the road and the surrounding foliage but the incredible gradient forbade me to turn the pedals. I was now walking. It felt almost vertical pushing the bike around the steepest part of the hairpin. Fortunately there was enough room by the side of the road for me to keep out of the way of a coach full of tourists as it struggled up the hill. I kept my fingers poised over the brakes to squeeze in case I needed to stop. Finally at the top I parked my bike in a lay-by, gulped a few mouthfuls of water, enjoyed a chocolate bar then proceeded towards Wick.

About 7 miles further on, I came to only the second major junction within 60 miles since I left the campsite at Tain. At the first I continued straight ahead but at this one I needed to turn right off the A9 which continues to Thurso and onto the A99 to Wick then John o'Groats.

There was mile after mile of bleak landscape without a tree or bush, except within hidden creases in the landscape where the onslaught of fierce weather could not get at them. The closer I got to Wick the more houses appeared although they all appeared to be bungalows. Perhaps because they are closer to the ground, bungalows are less vulnerable to bad weather and consequently need less repair work. There is a lot of land up here, a lot of open space, but not many people.

There wasn't much traffic on the A9 but what there was seemed to have disappeared off to Thurso. Hardly a car passed and for the last ten miles the traditional sore backside had returned. Even though I was now well into single miles before Wick I was doing a lot of shuffling on the seat to relieve the soreness.

In the distance I spotted a large collection of rooftops but probably due to the sore backside, aching muscles and the thought of just getting there, I couldn't be sure if it was Wick. My mind seemed to be mixed up and I was convinced that there was another town before Wick. Tromso – that's what it was! I felt dejected and defeated. Another town to cycle through before I got to Wick. I stopped beside a grassy patch next to an open farm gate, laid the bike down, sat on the grass and then un-wrapped another chocolate bar.

I was still confused about this town. One half of me told me that it must be Wick and the other half was convincing me that there was a town just before Wick called Tromso. I switched on my GPS to confirm which of my thoughts was correct when my brain came to its senses and the information unscrambled – 'Tromso's in Northern Norway you fool, not Northern Britain'. Those were the rooftops of Wick that I could see about a mile ahead of me. There was a sudden metamorphosis from feeling dejected to one of victory. My position about a mile south of Wick was confirmed as the GPS warmed up and latched on to a few satellites. All of these Viking settlements must have sparked my subconscious into thinking I was actually in Norse country. Being in a part of Britain that looks entirely different to anywhere else in Britain often makes you think you're abroad. At least that was my excuse!

Back on the bike the sore backside appeared to have mysteriously vanished and there was a new injection of life in my legs. I was heading directly into Wick. There was a large sign board ahead which I couldn't quite make out until I was about 30 yards from it:

'THE ROYAL BURGH OF WICK'

My right arm instinctively punched the air and I shouted a huge 'YES!!!!!' followed by a whoop of joy which must have reverberated around the nearby houses. I didn't care, I was here and over 1300 miles were now behind me. I could now spend a leisurely evening before tackling a mere 18 miles to John o'Groats tomorrow and needn't get up so early.

I rode towards the centre of town until a very prominent brown sign pointed towards the campsite about half a mile away. I passed a Coop and replenished my stores. I even bought a few extras and luxuries because tomorrow I could leave the tent up and travel light up to John o'Groats.

The campsite was only about a hundred yards from the station so I wouldn't have far to ride in a couple of days to catch my train just after eight in the morning. I booked in for three nights and found a quiet spot in the sun away from about half a dozen tents already pitched. Ah! The peace, the quiet, the relaxation, and the contentment, knowing that tomorrow I would only have eighteen short miles to the top of the British mainland and that a non-stop three weeks ago, I was standing at the bottom of the same island.

I pitched the tent and was just in the process of moving a vacant picnic table next to my tent door when a motor cyclist rode onto the site. The black motorbike with the rider fully kitted out in black leathers wearing a black helmet and darkened visor purred around the site looking for a suitable pitch. There was a lot of empty space. The bike passed me and continued to the bottom of the site, turned around and returned up the other side before crossing over the field and stopping about ten feet from my tent.

'I don't believe it! Acres of empty space and a biker parks almost on top of my tent!' The rider pulled the bike back onto its stand and turned off the engine. I continued to move the picnic table and glanced curiously up to see who had invaded my space. The biker dismounted and with two hands removed the helmet then shook her head to unfold her long black hair waving about in slow motion as if in one of those shampoo adverts. It had probably been compressed into the helmet for most of the day. She was probably about 40 but looked a trifle younger in black leathers. I was no longer bothered about the invasion of my space and welcomed her.

She said "Hi! That's a good idea, now we can both share the table!"

"Yeah! No problem. Have you travelled far?"

Embarrassing thoughts filled my head.

'What happens if I snore too loudly or fart in the night? – I might wake her up and then we'd both be embarrassed in the morning. Even more embarrassing – 'What happens if she snores and farts in the night and wakes me up?' I decided the only way out was to get up early as usual. In this way I would hopefully be away before she got up and also the roads would be totally empty. She might be gone before I returned.

I put my pan on to make a brew but she declined my offer of a cuppa as mine was the only cup then went over to the office and returned with a free coffee given to her by the warden.

We chatted for a while over our drinks albeit from different sources and she revealed her task. She was from Prestwick near the airport and had ridden to Aviemore, camped then travelled here. A journey I'd taken two days over. She was on a sponsored ride and her task was to find various landmarks and get herself photographed with her bike as evidence that she'd been there. She was raising money for some medical charity attached to the hospital where she was a nurse near Prestwick. Ayr I think. I didn't quite catch what her first task was but between Aviemore and Wick she had to cross the Cromarty Ferry and get a photo to prove it. That was my intended route before I met the Belgians near Inverness. From Wick she was intending to travel to somewhere off the beaten track near Altnaharra right in the middle of Northern Scotland to find a brock, then to Cape Wrath where she would have to get a Landrover from the main road as Cape Wrath is owned by the Ministry of Defence and can only be visited using their transport. She would have to photograph her motorbike in the car park.

She was then off to *Rubha Reidh* which is a lighthouse stuck right out on the peninsular west of Gairloch. I remember cycling along to *Rubha Reidh* lighthouse from the campsite at Bigsand near Gairloch many years ago and have always remembered its name because it sounds like *Rub yar head* which I've found is a neat way of remembering Gaelic names. I think she was returning home after a further visit.

The warden had recommended three pubs in the town. The first being Mackay's Hotel which has its entrance opening onto the smallest street in the world; Ebenezer Place which measures only 6 feet 9 inches long which is just wide enough for a door, The Crown Hotel and the Alexander Bain owned by Weatherspoons. I couldn't find Mackay's Hotel because the street was too short and didn't fancy The Crown so ended up in The Alexander Bain. For £6 I got a huge plate of pie, veg. and chips and a pint which isn't bad value.

My neighbour and I chatted over the picnic table till 9 o'clock when I apologised for my eyelids having a mind of their own and showing signs of weakness. We wished each other luck on our travels and turned in for the night.

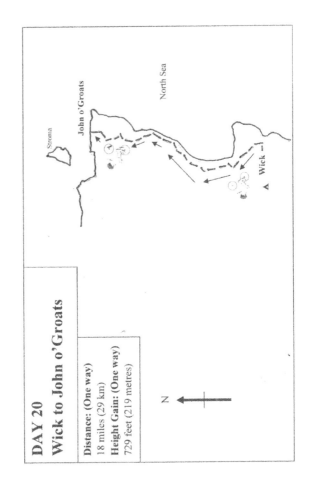

DAY 20
Wick to John o'Groats

Distance: (One way)
18 miles (29 km)
Height Gain: (One way)
729 feet (219 metres)

N

Stroma

John o'Groats

North Sea

Wick

Day 20 – The Final Assault

A quietly opened tent zip revealed an overcast and damp looking sky. The only sound came from the adjacent tent. A quiet purring, a little bit like the motorbike she arrived on but not quite as harsh. I gathered a few essentials together and was on the road taking half an hour less than usual. I left behind a huge bag of satsumas and all of the other goodies I'd bought yesterday on arriving in Wick. I took only a snack to eat.

More than nine months of preparation would finally be fulfilled in about two hours of cycling. Would countless hours spent planning the route following little green dots that represent cycle routes on the 1:50000 maps that cover the UK have been worth the effort? Trawling through countless websites and Local Authority cycling leaflets to confirm the correct route would culminate in fruition of my task this morning. I now know that the time spent researching campsites and equipment suitable for my task had proved to have been worth the effort. The numerous days out cycling over different grades of terrain, slowly building up my fitness to be able to cycle between fifty and a hundred miles every day for twenty consecutive days had proved to be essential. With only eighteen miles to my destination I could put my hand on my heart and say with conviction, 'I've cycled LEJOG without support!' But had I accepted that lift from Troon to Paisley then continued from Paisley I would have felt like a fraud and totally unfulfilled. Thankfully I resisted.

I always remember that famous quotation by Benjamin Franklin:

'Failing to Prepare is Preparing to Fail'

This simple statement can be applied to all aspects of life in everything we do and in my case I spent over nine months of preparation for a three week challenge. However this does not account for years of experience in camping and navigating using a map and compass even though there were occasions when I became a little complacent with these skills.

I've had a brief glimpse at the time and effort an Olympic Athlete adopts just to compete in the Olympic Games over years for it all to focus on a brief moment of victory or failure. My Olympic Final was approaching.

I managed to see the weather forecast in Weatherspoons last night. The weather map showed a completely cloud free Britain apart from the tiny north east corner of Scotland cut off by an imaginary line drawn from Wick to Thurso. This triangle of land would be overcast with drizzly rain getting heavier towards the coast then drifting out to sea as the sun became warmer. However, fog might drift onto the shore from time to time during the day.

It was fairly cold, unlike the warmth of yesterday, when I made my way through the centre of Wick. I counted only a handful of cars and a dozen people at 7am. The first distance sign I passed read '**JOHN O'GROATS 17 MILES**', I felt as though I'd been injected with energy knowing this was my victory stage. The buildings of Wick were soon behind me. I'd never felt stronger during the whole Challenge, most likely because the bike was minus a soggy tent and the equivalent of one and a half full pannier bags. The landscape comprised of low rolling hills with a slight head wind holding me back a little on the meagre ascents.

Only about three miles north of Wick the A99 turned right towards John o'Groats. There were only fifteen miles now which would take me about an hour and a half. At this rate I'd be standing next to the famous sign post that points to various places around the world, by half past eight. This part of Caithness was as different again to the long A9 south of Wick. This was bleak; the inhospitable landscape bred only tough, hard individuals. There was no corner shop here when you run out of bread nor Indian takeaway when you can't be bothered to cook. Not even a local pub to share the day's troubles with friendly neighbours on an evening. The odd bungalow appeared out of the drizzle neighbouring the odd derelict croft. The bungalows were mainly white with tiled roofs covered in an orangey yellow moss. The crofts comprised of stone walls without any tiles and just a few rotting beams for roofs. Further south there were gardens full of vegetables and colour. Not here. In fact there weren't any trees, not even in the creases formed by streams as there had been further south.

Within the first few miles after turning off the main road to Thurso I only saw two cars, one behind the other. Then there would be a gap lasting about 15 minutes when another two or three would pass. This regular occurrence was repeated over the next hour or so. I spotted a collection of roof tops ahead on the crest of a long hill. Could this be John o'Groats? The wind had strengthened and I needed to push down on the pedals with every ounce of strength I could muster to get up the hill. I was tempted to walk to the top but managed to resist the urge. Once over the hill and past the rooftops a sign informed me that they didn't belong to John o'Groats which was a further 4 miles.

I turned into a lay-by next to a derelict cottage. There must have been a terrific panoramic view from the evidence being provided by a viewpoint board pointing out which of the Orkney Islands could be seen. I could only see drizzly mist all around. John o'Groats could only be a mile or so down the hill.

JOHN O'GROATS 1 MILE was the inspiration I needed to get there in one go. The only stop having been at the viewpoint back up the hill. The wind was a little stronger, wetter and colder. The first building I saw was called 'The John o'Groats Guest House' which was nothing like any of the other buildings I'd seen since Wick. It was characterless being just a box with a flat roof and painted white. There was also the most northerly Post Office attached to it which doubles as the general store. I continued along the road into the mist.

Finally I rode into a small complex of buildings which surrounded a large car park. It was exactly 8.30am. There was no welcome party. Not even a soul. The ground was wet, the air damp and a cold wind blew in off the sea. I was alone and felt alone. I'd cycled for three weeks alone quite happily but for some reason I now felt lonely. My Challenge was over and I felt empty. The tea shop with the sign '**John o'Groats - Cafe Bar - Journey's End**', where the compulsory book signing brought satisfaction for End to Enders was closed. It didn't open till 10am. What about me I thought, can't someone just turn up, open it up so that I can sign the book then go home again. They could come back at ten o'clock! I tried the door and knocked just in case someone was hiding in a back room but it was deserted.

As the whole place was also deserted I positioned my camera on a picnic table to take a photograph of me standing in front of the Cafe Bar sign. I pressed the timer button, dashed back to stand next to my bike and waited for the red light to stop flashing. More importantly I wanted a photograph of me and my bike standing in front of 'The Sign', so I walked about dragging my bike with me to look for 'The Sign'. I remembered from photographs I'd seen that 'The Sign' was near the entrance to the John o'Groats Hotel which was right in front of me but also wearing an eight foot high steel fence around it because it was closed and in a sorry state of disrepair. None of the windows were boarded up unlike in populated areas where the windows of unused buildings are smashed within the first few hours of being deserted. Weeds grew all around the base of the building showing that it had been neglected for months if not years.

I wandered down to the gift shop that overlooks the small harbour. There was a passenger ferry tied up at the end of a short pier which looked as though it was clutching the walls to protect itself from the thick mist a few hundred yards behind it. The gift shop was open. It was full of Scottish tat. Pens, pencils, trinkets, ornaments, key rings and anything you could think of that took up a space less than a few square inches. From outside, the shop looked like a small cabin but inside it was huge, like the Tardis. It even had a cellar full of more Scottish tat! I wanted to buy something as a souvenir to remind me of the mammoth task behind me but could only find a white T shirt over printed with a huge map of Britain, Land's End, John o'Groats and a wavy line connecting the two places. Why did I buy it? It's the most hideous T-shirt I've ever bought. I was looking for something a little classier. Perhaps the suppliers of such tat don't think that classy people travel from Land's End to John o'Groats as a challenge.

There was a small museum attached to 'The Last House in Scotland' in which I spent about 30 minutes trying to soak up the information attached to the walls and in small cases. The only thing I could remember was that John o'Groats gets its name from a Dutchman called Jan de Groot who in 1496 was given permission to sail a ferry between the Scottish mainland and the Orkneys which had then recently been obtained from Norway. Did Jan charge a groat for the journey? That is one theory.

The time was still only 9.15am. I hadn't found the famous sign yet and the Cafe Bar wouldn't be open for another 45 minutes. There was a Costa coffee shop on the other side of the car park so I popped in for a coffee and a bacon sandwich. There were people in here. All were having a hot drink and a warm sandwich. The cold damp weather still persisted. It reminded me of a cold damp morning in November waiting at a railway station in the middle of nowhere for a train that never seems to arrive.

After about 20 minutes I returned to the dank atmosphere surrounding this cluster of buildings. Strangely it was now bustling with people of all nationalities except British. Within ten minutes they had all made their way onto the ferry and once again the place was deserted.

Just before 10 o'clock I noticed a light on in the Cafe Bar. I tried the door which I found to be open. I asked if I could sign the book having just completed LEJOG which they kindly allowed me to do. I was also given a complementary cup of tea for my efforts.

I read through a few of the most recent entries in the book and End to Enders ranged from groups running it in relay to cyclists, to walkers and drivers in all kinds of prehistoric vehicles. There is no prize for doing End to End or for signing the book. By signing the book there is no proof that you have actually done it. LEJOG is purely a personal challenge getting from the two most extreme points in mainland Britain by whatever means the challenger thinks fit. In lots of cases the weirder the better. I signed the book, finished my tea and returned once again to the busy outside.

Two men arrived on bikes. They were cycling from Ullapool to Aberdeen travelling around the coast. A couple in an old MG Midget arrived leaving a trail of thick blue smoke behind them. Their task had been to cover 900 miles in 24 hours from Land's End to John o'Groats. Hopefully they have a break down truck booked to get them home.

Then a van arrived. The driver got out, opened the back doors and withdrew a long white post with direction signs on it. He walked over to a flat concreted area above the harbour and slotted the post into a hole, much like a rotary washing line post. This was 'The Sign' that I'd been searching for – it's private! He erected a sandwich board which advertised for £10 that I could get my photograph taken, professionally, by him. This would buy me the economy print and for extra cash I could get the enlarged version(s). It was forbidden to ask someone to take my photograph with my camera standing next to his post without his specific permission. I've since found out that the same photographic company also owns 'The Sign' at Land's End. Let's hope they don't get them mixed up!

The couple in the MG looked as though they were toying with the idea of having a photo taken but were having problems getting the MG in the shot. My previous thoughts were thinking that one day someone might charge challengers for doing End to End. If you want photographic evidence then someone has already done it. A photograph at Land's End for £10 then one at John o'Groats for another £10 plus a certificate thrown in makes an easy £20 for the LEJOG photographic company!

It's after half past ten now and I've been here for over two hours. The mist has lifted a little and the nearby island of Stroma is just visible. Inhabited until 1962 it is now a conservation area but can be visited.

My journey back to Wick was easy with a brisk tail wind all of the way. Within a couple of miles the mist had gone and I could see for miles down the coast. I was welcomed back into Wick by unbroken warm sunshine and looked forward to a lazy afternoon.

My neighbour had gone, probably photographing her bike next to some ancient brock by now. There were still a few tents on the site, some touring caravans and a motor home complete with trailer carrying a huge motorbike. The owners had been retired several years and were now over 70. They enjoyed their near permanent holiday in their newly acquired motor home upon retirement but found parking was restrictive when visiting various attractions around Britain and Europe. Their answer was to buy a motorbike to travel around and leave the motor home securely parked on a camp site. Since neither of them had ever sat on a motorbike before the husband took his motorbike driving test at the age of 73 and passed first time, this has opened up a whole new world for them to prove 'You're never too old!'

I had a whole one and a half days to kill before my train at twelve minutes past eight on Wednesday morning. The weather was superb; I couldn't just sit around all day waiting or ride the bike to Thurso or Dunnet Head, the true most northerly point on the mainland. I'd had enough cycling for a while. I opted to visit the sights of Wick.

It was only a short ten minute walk into the town so armed with a street map and guide I headed for the harbour. Thick fog kept rolling in smothering the harbour then the adjoining streets then retreating upon reaching the town centre. Its advance was slow but determined with nothing to stop it except for closed doors and windows. The tops of masts and the ends of the piers disappeared behind the gloom. Its presence caused a drop in temperature from 22ºC to 12ºC in a few minutes then back up again when it retreated. The shore and harbour were now regularly under a cold white veil whereas the campsite which was only a ten minutes walk inland was basking in warm sunshine.

I followed my guide and made my way to the Wick Heritage Centre, housed in a few terraced cottages linked indoors. Until my visit here I was unaware of the huge herring industry that had been built up in Wick. Between 1860 and 1890 this was the World's premier exporter of herring. Old photographs showing hundreds of fishing boats tied up in rows between the piers and thousands of barrels containing salted herring for export were piled high on the quay sides. In its heyday, Wick was home to over a thousand fishing boats employing over six thousand men with an extra six thousand being employed in land based industries to support them. The port would be visited by a further one thousand boats a year bringing supplies and taking away the thousands of barrels of salted herring to all corners of Europe. The town was probably home to about 20,000 people compared to only 8,000 today. There were forty five pubs which no doubt helped to take the wages off the fishermen after a few days or weeks at sea. Around 1890 the herring stocks in the North Sea became fished out and the bustling life in Wick rapidly declined. Although there is still a small fishing industry based at Wick its main life line today is as a stepping stone for the North Sea oil rigs.

Having absorbed the sights of Wick I wandered back to the campsite for an hour or so before sauntering back into the town for my evening meal. Today has felt like the longest day for over three weeks. My thoughts are focussed on making sure I am waiting at the station on time for the 0812 tomorrow.

Day 21 – The Journey Home and Beyond

My greatest fear was to sleep in and miss my train. A later train wouldn't do as I only had minutes to wait for the connecting trains at Inverness and Edinburgh. I had no need to worry. My eyes leapt into action at quarter to six and after my usual routine I left the campsite at half seven before anyone else had stirred. The station was deserted although there was a train waiting, silent and cold where it had probably been parked overnight. Being a novice at rail travel I sat down and waited for instructions. An American couple arrived to catch the same train. I'd chatted with them the previous evening in the pub. They were as confused about the rail system as me. Eight o'clock arrived and passed. We were the only occupants of the station. No external sounds, no taxis arriving outside, slamming doors then driving off. No sound of whistles or voices echoing around the station. Ten past eight approached when the station door burst open and two frantic cyclists hurried in pushing their fully laden bikes. They were obviously clued up rail veterans who had most likely slept in, as they confidently walked through the gate onto the platform and lifted their heavy bikes onto the train.

The American couple and I looked at each other with mutual shock. This must be the train for Inverness. Come to think about it, to even ponder over whether this train went anywhere else except Inverness was very foolish as there is only one railway line between Wick and Inverness. The train couldn't go anywhere else. I grabbed my bike and they their bags, all of us making a hasty almost panic like dash for the train. The two cyclists had parked their bikes in the only two designated bike storage places. If I needed proof that my bike has been booked onto this train for weeks then I have the printed document with me. The guard appeared from nowhere and the diesel engines roared into action.

"Where can I put my bike?" I asked with an almost pitiful voice as though I'd been rejected from my rightful place on a train with only five passengers and three bikes.

The guard gave me a puzzled look and replied to my trivial question.

"Anywhere where there's a suitable gap, here'll do!" and showed me to a suitable parking place which was in fact better than the places commandeered by the other cyclists.

The train moved off and headed towards Thurso. The next station along the track was Georgemas Junction named after the historic St George's Day Agricultural Fair. Only a tiny cluster of buildings, an unmanned station and a car park to take no more than half a dozen cars with only one branch line was not complex enough to be called a junction. Two people got on at Georgemas Junction but anyone who had slept in and missed the train needn't worry because they could meet it again on its return from Thurso. After its trip to Thurso and second stop at Georgemas Junction the two-carriage train was about three quarters full.

The surrounding countryside became more remote as the train headed inland away from the north and east coasts. Tiny stations are stuck in the middle of nowhere, where a road crosses the tracks. One such station, Forsinard was where a very loud, talkative, disabled, very overweight gent got on. His motorised wheelchair was the oddest contraption I'd ever seen to transport a disabled person. Unlike most wheelchairs which are the size of a chair but with wheels, this one had the usual two large wheels at the side of the seat and a third wheel to steer, which he operated by means of a joy stick, at the far end of a long metal frame. It was a similar version to the sort used by paraplegic athletes doing marathons but was longer and reminded me of a dragster.

This added length made manoeuvring the chair almost impossible as its turning circle only rivalled that of the QE2. The guard laid down a ramp but the electric motor didn't have enough power to propel the chair and its probably twenty stone occupant onto the train; his companion waiting behind helped by pushing. When the chair was finally in the passage before entering the seated area of the carriage, it became firmly stuck. The companion swung the whole chair by pressing down on the chair handles to lift the single wheel off the ground. This looked so easy that if the disabled occupant had leaned back in this concoction of a wheelchair he would have fallen flat on his back.

Finally parked in a widened part of the carriage designed for bikes and wheelchairs, facing the way he'd entered and next to my bike, the occupant endeavoured to let everyone know about his business. Passengers buried their heads in newspapers, books and laptops while others pretended to sleep or just gaze out of the windows. Fortunately he was facing the wrong way to catch anybody's eye as to do so would have condemned them to several hours of sheer misery all the way to Inverness. I alternated my attention between my book and the fantastic wild views. A house in the distance looked strangely out of place with the only tree anywhere in view in its back garden. Both were dwarfed by the remote whaleback mountains all around.

Thirty miles after Georgemas Junction, the railway turns and heads east towards Helmsdale where it joins the coast. I had previously thought about trying to identify the landmarks I'd cycled past on my way north but my mind drifted and I began to think about all the people I'd met from different parts of England and Scotland, the warmth shown by everyone, (except two); the generosity of many and how accents alter from region to region as though each has its own dialect wrapped up in its own bag. The difference in older architecture reflected how the climate changes from the generally warmer and dryer south to the colder and wetter north. I began to wonder if nine months of preparation and three weeks of spasmodic physical torture had been worth it but then thought about the teacher in Nepal and his family whose only possessions were a picture of his dead brother and a wind up radio. My effort along with the generosity of my family and friends would keep that teacher employed for another two years resulting in possibly a hundred teenagers being educated up to the age of sixteen who otherwise would have been left without any prospects or hope at only fourteen. Who knows what branches would grow to benefit their deprived region from this single event? I had a great sense of euphoria now feeling totally relaxed and fulfilled and woke up just as the train pulled into Inverness Station.

The aisle in the now very full carriage was choked. I wouldn't be able to retrieve my bike until the wheelchair man had moved and he couldn't move until the aisle was empty. My train for Edinburgh leaves in ten minutes. The wheelchair occupant pressed a few buttons and his contraption moved towards the inner door. He moved the joystick to the right which turned the front wheel to the right at which point the whole thing became firmly wedged. The only answer was to put more weight on the back of the chair to raise the front and turn it. I waited along with a few other stragglers for his companion to come to the rescue but he never showed up. His companion wasn't his companion after all but just another helpful commuter who had long since disappeared, probably realising that it would be just as difficult to get the contraption off the train as it was to it get on.

He struggled to do a three point turn which was rapidly approaching a ninety three point turn when I felt the Good Samaritan blood in me kick into action. Desperation was setting in as I needed to get off this train which might have had something to do with it. I left my bike parked and pressed on the rear handles of the contraption with all my strength to swivel it round. The front end, two metres to the front, shot into the air tilting its occupant backwards. The guard couldn't get anywhere near as he had got off ahead to lay down the ramp. Fortunately I managed to balance the weight, turn the chair and lower the front end now pointing out of the door. It catapulted away and almost lost control on the ramp as it and its occupant disappeared off down the platform with not so much as a wave or a thank you.

I retrieved my bike and asked the first person who looked as though they worked in the station to point me towards the Edinburgh train. It was only on the next platform. A helpful guard pointed towards the correct door for bikes and followed me through. This was the designated area for bikes and wheelchairs. My heart sank when I saw that it was occupied by the loud, talkative, disabled and very overweight gent in the odd contraption of a wheelchair plus an enormous bloke taking up three seats and two square metres of space in front him to accommodate his enormous gut and legs. They were having an argument. The man in the wheelchair contraption was unable to fit it into the gap left available and the enormous bloke refused to move to allow him to do so. He would only have needed to stand up, move to allow the wheelchair contraption past then sit down again. The arguing began.

"I'm in a wheelchair!"

"So what, I was here first!"

"I'm booked in for a wheelchair space!"

"Well I'm booked in for extra space!"

"But I'm in a wheelchair and I'm disabled!"

"So what, I'm disabled as well!" this last argumentative comment being made by the enormous bloke.

To which the guard, who was getting a little impatient with them, looked at the enormous bloke taking up three seats, and commented with disgust.

"I can see that!" Paused for a moment then turned to me and said "Come with me!" before exiting the compartment quickly and taking me to a different carriage.

I felt so relieved to be free of the bitterness they imposed on each other and the forthcoming four hour journey to Edinburgh. What happened to them I shall never know. The train was full with me and my bike comfortably accommodated for the long ride to Edinburgh.

Once out of Inverness the railway runs almost parallel with my route all the way to Pitlochry where I joined from the west. The packed train laboured up the steep Slochd incline before almost freewheeling to Aviemore then repeated the process over the Drumochter pass and down to Pitlochry.

A few hours later the sight of the Forth Rail Bridge in the distance brought Edinburgh a little closer. I was yet again confused, this time by my rail ticket from Edinburgh. The departure station on my ticket was Haymarket, Edinburgh but the guards and cashiers in the ticket offices had told me that it was Waverley.

One guard had even said, "Why do they confuse people?"

Could I be left stranded at the last hurdle? I decided to trust the guards and not the ticket.

Waverley Station is a totally different animal to the stations at Wick and even Inverness. There were electronic destination boards up all over but none were showing my train to Darlington. I asked at enquiries – he was as confused as me and told me to look at the destination board. He did however tell me which platform it would leave from if there was such a train and that all the employees of National Express would be wearing a distinctive uniform.

I made my way over to the designated platform and was lucky enough to find a growing band of National Express employees. They confirmed that I was in the right place for the next train for Kings Cross calling at Darlington.

Passengers packed the platform waiting for the train to arrive. Fortunately my seat was booked as was a place for the bike. I had visions of having to hang my bike on a meat hook as I had done on Cross country Trains when I left Darlington three weeks ago. Perhaps things have progressed since then!

The train arrived at speed. This was a real train; none of this calling at every stop on the line. This was an Intercity 125 and was a first for me. It stopped and six of us with bikes were ushered into the carriage at the front of the train. This time there were special parking bays for the bikes and bags could be left on the bike, although I was only told after I'd taken mine off.

The guard became impatient; two of us were taking too long to park our bikes. We fumbled with the security straps which were impossible to work out so we just tied them in a knot and hoped for the best.

"Hurry up! We should have been away two minutes ago!"

There seemed to be panic as he shouted again.

"Come on, come on!"

The bike store is not accessible from the rest of the train so we had to jump out then get back on further down the train. Our carriage was about half a mile down the platform at the back of the train. We jumped on the next carriage which was first class. The train pulled away seconds after getting back on.

Ten minutes later I found my seat in the packed train which was almost bursting at the seams. The carriage was a bit hot and steamy and probably due to this I became aware of a sweaty odour floating around the vicinity of the double seat I was sharing with a fellow traveller. He probably thought the same as me – 'Is it me or is it him?' He got up probably to go to the loo or spray under his armpits. Unfortunately the uncomfortable pong didn't leave with him so I must be the culprit of this unwelcome odour. While I had been sure to wash my shirt, socks and shorts regularly, what I had not been able to wash was my jacket. It had developed its own whiff of rancid cheese in this humid atmosphere. I leant away from my seat mate when he returned to keep the smelly atmosphere as close to myself as possible.

This was a fast train only stopping at Berwick and Newcastle before my stop at Darlington and took less than half the time it took the Inverness to Edinburgh train to cover roughly the same distance. As the train passed through Durham, about 25 miles north of Darlington I made my way down to the front of the train passing through every carriage. I made sure that I was well prepared to retrieve my bike from the bike compartment.

At Darlington station the train staff showed how well organised they were and knew at which station each cyclist was leaving the train. My bike was standing on the platform within minutes of the train arriving and seconds of it leaving. My good friend Julian whose hand was now functional enough to drive was waiting to give me a lift home. Unfortunately his small car wasn't big enough to take the complete bike and we had to remove all the usual rubbish that most people carry around with them out of the back of his car and detach the front wheel from the bike to get it in. The clobber was put back on top of the bike where space would permit.

Knowing that I'd raised over £2000 for the school in Nepal, a home cooked meal and a hot bath was welcome but my body refused to lie in the following morning. The soft bed felt strange and the hernia started to play up once I started walking a lot rather than riding a lot. In a bent forward position when riding a bike, the hernia seemed to be protected but when walking upright it just popped out and became painful. The only remedy was to walk around with my left hand in my pocket to mask the fact that I permanently had to have my hand on my groin to push the lump in. Pushing it in produced a squirmy squelchy sound and feeling which also produced copious amounts of wind.

It was time to pay a visit to the Doc's to get this hernia sorted then I could safely let friends and family know about it. I eventually got an appointment to have the hernia fixed three months after the initial visit and a good friend offered to take me to hospital as my wife is still working.

In the area where I live there are two hospitals, fifteen miles apart, but both belong to the same Hospital Trust and consequently have very similar letter heads. My appointment with the specialist was at North Tees Hospital and the operation appointment was at the same hospital. Unfortunately the operation had been cancelled and I was given a new date.

My good friend picked me up and we had a leisurely drive to the hospital in good time for the eight o'clock start. He dropped me off and left. The instructions informed me not to be too early or late so following the rules I sat outside the reception area until five to eight before deciding to introduce myself. The rules also stated patients should not bring in vast sums of money or valuables and avoid driving for two weeks after the operation, hence the lift in.

I handed the all important letter to the receptionist. She took one look at it and said.

"You're at the wrong hospital. You should be at Hartlepool!"

With no transport, only a couple of pounds and no phone I was well and truly stuck.

The receptionist let me use her phone to phone my friend. Ten minutes later he met me at the same place he'd dropped me off and we rushed over to Hartlepool. We arrived at twenty past eight. He left me again but suggested waiting for ten minutes in the car park. The instructions on the letter didn't seem to fit any sign I passed and could have reflected any route in any hospital anywhere. Unfortunately I was unable to refer to my GPS this time so I asked the first nurse to pass.

"Down to the double doors, turn left and it's on your right."

Following these instructions I must have turned left at the wrong double doors. There was no sign of my designated room. I asked a passing porter with a trolley. He was totally unaware that any such place existed. I saw a desk with a nurse. She gave me extra instructions.

"Go to the end, turn left, go down to the double doors then turn left and it's on your right."

These were the same instructions as before; I mustn't have gone far enough. Eventually I arrived at the pre-op room, half an hour late. I noticed a board full of names with ticks next to them except for mine. Fortunately the receptionist at North Tees must have telephoned ahead to inform them that I was on my way. I was shown to a small room and told to strip then wear the gown that fastens at the back. The first time I wore one of these I put it on the wrong way round and unwittingly displayed everything I had at the front when it came loose.

There was a stream of nurses and doctors, all of whom checked my name, address and ailment every time. The surgeon drew a thick black arrow on the left hand side of my groin and gave me an option.

"You can have the operation done with a slash which will need stitching but you'll be unable to do any hard physical activity for at least six weeks (like cycling), or you can have the keyhole surgery which involves making three tiny holes and will only take about a fortnight for complete recovery. Unfortunately I'm the only one here and there's no-one to hold the camera for me because they're all off ill with swine flu so I'm afraid it's going to have to be the slash or you can come back at a later date!"

"I'll have the slash!"

He made a note and left.

My designated nurse returned, checked my name again, took a few readings then fitted me with tight leggings which irritate and itch constantly then left.

Two heating engineers arrived and asked if it would be okay to check the two vents in the ceiling. They didn't check my name. One of them held a rod about a metre long with an electronic meter at the handle end and a small fan at the other. He held it up to each corner of each vent, the small fan rotated slowly and then he read out the volume of air being either sucked out or blown into the room. The other engineer wrote down the readings on a clip board; yet more Health and Safety Regulation rigmarole.

A porter arrived, checked my name then walked me round to the operating theatre waiting room. The time had arrived. I was laid down on a trolley, half propped up. A different nurse checked my name then left. A more official looking nurse, younger and very smart appeared in the doorway from the operating theatre, washed her hands and glanced over to me with an inviting smile then walked over to me. She checked my name, gave me hers then wheeled me into the operating theatre chatting on the way. I was lifted onto the operating table; my gown was unfastened and whipped away being replaced with a pristine white sheet.

She kept me informed about the procedure as the anaesthetic mask drew closer.

"Just think about going on holiday to a tropical island and taking me with you!"

I drifted off and got as far as the front door.

"Wake up David. It's all over; you're in the recovery ward now!"

Table 1 – Equipment List

Item	Wt(gms)	Tools	
Batteries 15AA, 3AAA	460	Allen Keys	
Battery Charger	409	Chain Rivet extractor	
Bike oil	73	Gaffa Tape	
Binoculars	202	Hand Cleaner	
Book	153	Multitool	
Buff	38	Pliers	
Camera	305	Split Links	
Cap	101	Tyre Leavers	
Cycle Helmet	293	Spare Inner Tube (2)	
Diary/Envelopes	302	Rubber Gloves	
Fleece jumper	192	Rag in a Bag	
High visibility Waistcoat	145	Tyre Pump	
Fuel/bottle	619	Bike Lock	**1173**
Gloves	59		
GPS	273	**First Aid**	
Handkerchief	9	Crepe Bandage	
Handlebar bag	585	Elastoplasts	
Handlebar mirror	100	Lipsalve	
Head torch	106	Paracetamol	
Jacket	443	Rennies	
Karimat	363	Safety Pins	
Knife	47	Scissors	
Knife/fork/spoon	21	Suncream	**203**
Maps/Blog cards	408		
Matches or lighter	24	**Washing Gear**	
Mobile Phone	121	Clothes Pegs(4)	
Mug	61	Shampoo	
Panier (Part of bike)	0	Toenail Clippers	
Panier bags	2822	Toilet Paper	
Pen/pencil	8	Toothbrush & paste	
Ron Hills	195	Towel	
Flip Flops	159	Tweezers	
Shoes (Cycling)	750	Vaseline	**434**

Shorts with padded inner	416		
Shorts	182	**Food and Drink**	
Silk Sleeping Bag Liner	126	Coffee	70
Sleeping Bag	700	Snacks	474
Socks (2 pairs)	46	T Bags	69
Stove	352	Food for two meals	255
Sun glasses/glasses in case	211	Breakfast	500
Sweat band for wrist	20		
T Shirts (2)	149	Rail Tickets	
Tent	2700		
Underpants (1 pair)	29	Handlebar bag	
Wallet	300	Black bin liners(2)	
Watch	125	Rear light	**750**
Water bottle and water	886		
Waterproof Jacket	394		
Waterproof Overtrousers	215		
Wooly Hat	73	**Total Weight**	**18133 gms**

Table 2 – Planned Stages

Date	Day	To Place/Town	Campsite Name	Distance to km	Distance to (m)	Height Gained(m)	Estimated time	Est time of arrival
Tues 2nd June	0	Lands End	Seaview Holiday Park	0	0	0	0	0
Wed 3rd June	1	Newquay	Hendra Holiday Park	114	71	1174	06:55	15:00
Thur 4th June	2	Bude	Upper Lynstone C&C Park	101	63	1270	06:44	14:45
Fri 5th June	3	Bratton Fleming	Greenacres Farm	99	62	918	06:37	14:45
Sat 6th June	4	Taunton	Tanpits Cider Farm	80	50	1220	05:19	13:15
Sun 7th June	5	Congresbury	Oak Farm Touring Park	75	47	326	05:00	13:00
Mon 8th June	6	Norton (Gt)	Red Lion Inn, Wanslode Hill	102	64	510	06:48	14:45
Tue 9th June	7	Bridgenorth	Unicorn Inn, Hampton Lode	84	53	903	06:18	14:15
Wed 10th June	8	Whitchurch	Mile Bank Farm	97	61	994	06:26	14:30
Thur 11th June	9	Southport	Riverside Holiday Park	141	88	457	09:27	17:30
Fri 12th June	10	Kendal	C&C Club Site, Staveley	126	79	982	08:25	16:30
Sat 13th June	11	Carlisle	Dalston Hall Caravan Park	90	56	1250	06:00	14:00
Sun 14th June	12	Castle Douglas	Lochside C&C Site	118	74	643	07:53	16:00
Mon 15th June	13	Glen Trool	Glen Trool Campsite	90	56	1040	06:00	14:00
Tue 16th June	14	Troon	St Medden Caravan Site	78	49	643	05:09	13:15
Wed 17th June	15	Aberfoyle	Cobeland	126	79	996	08:27	16:30
Thur 18th June	16	Pitlochry	Milton & Fonab Caravan Park	122	76	2210	08:08	16:15
Fri 19th June	17	Aviemore	Coylumbridge C&C Park	96	60	1140	06:24	14:30
Sat 20th June	18	Tain	Dornoch Firth Caravan Park	138	86	1230	09:14	17:15
Sun 21st June	19	Bettyhill	Craigdhu Campsite	119	74	1370	07:56	16:00
Mon 22nd June	20	John O'Groats	JoG C&C Site	82	51	780	05:27	13:30
Tues 23rd June	21	Wick	C&C Site, Riverside Drive	29	18	250	02:00	10:00

Made in United States
North Haven, CT
25 March 2022

17539166R00124